LES PRIX NOBEL

EN 1974

STOCKHOLM 1975
IMPRIMERIE ROYALE P. A. NORSTEDT & SÖNER

La présente série de publications est éditée par ordre des corporations chargées de décerner les Prix Nobel.

COMITÉ DE RÉDACTION :
MM. les professeurs K. Siegbahn, G. Hägg et B. Uvnäs, M. A. Österling, docteur ès lettres, et M. le directeur T. Greve ainsi que M. le baron S. Ramel, directeur général de la Fondation Nobel.

RÉDACTEUR :
Dr W. Odelberg, conservateur en chef de la Bibliothèque de l'Académie Royale des Sciences.

Conformément à une décision du Comité de rédaction des Prix Nobel, les discours introductifs ne sont présentés qu'en une seule langue depuis l'année 1972. On a également procédé à certaines simplifications rédactionnelles. Ainsi, les reproductions des médailles, qui ne doivent jamais changer, ont figuré pour la dernière fois dans la publication de 1971 à l'exception de celle de la médaille attribuée par l'Académie Royale des Sciences qui porte l'effigie d'Alfred Nobel et qui orne la feuille du titre. Enfin, on a joint les biographies aux conférences des lauréats.

ISBN 91-970072-2-6

Copyright © by the Nobel Foundation 1975
This book or any part thereof must not be reproduced in any form without the written permission of the Nobel Foundation.

Kungl. Boktryckeriet P. A. Norstedt & Söner
Stockholm 1975
753278

TABLE DES MATIÈRES

INSTITUTIONS NOBEL

LA FONDATION NOBEL est l'organisation à laquelle a été confiée la fortune léguée par Alfred Nobel dans l'intention de faire décerner un prix au plus méritant dans chacun des cinq domaines suivants : la physique, la chimie, la physiologie ou la médecine, la littérature et la paix. La Fondation constitue l'organe administratif du grand ensemble Nobel. La tâche essentielle qui incombe à son Conseil d'Administration est de gérer les fonds et d'autres biens de la Fondation. Les institutions chargées de l'attribution des prix et mentionnées ci-dessous élisent des mandataires qui, à leur tour, élisent les membres du Conseil d'Administration à l'exception du président et du vice-président. Malgré le caractère privé de la Fondation, ces derniers sont désignés par le Roi en Conseil.

Les institutions chargées de décerner les prix selon les stipulations testamentaires de Nobel sont les suivantes :

en Suède :
L'ACADÉMIE ROYALE DES SCIENCES — pour les prix de physique et de chimie;

L'INSTITUT ROYAL CAROLIN (les professeurs en titre de sa Faculté de Médecine) — pour le prix de physiologie ou de médecine; et

L'ACADÉMIE SUÉDOISE — pour le prix de littérature.
(Les noms des membres de ces institutions figurent à l'annuaire officiel de l'Etat suédois *Sveriges Statskalender*).

en Norvège :
LE COMITÉ NOBEL DU STORTING (PARLEMENT) NORVÉGIEN se composait en 1974 des membres suivants :
Mme Aase Lionæs, présidente du Odelsting, présidente du Comité, M. Bernt Ingvaldsen, directeur, vice-président, M. John Sanness, professeur d'université, M. Egil Aarvik, président du Lagting et M. Trygve Haugeland, directeur.
Suppléants : M. Sjur Lindebrække, directeur, M. Egil Toreng, éditeur.

Les institutions suédoises constituent des *Comités Nobel* spéciaux chargés de préparer des rapports et de formuler des propositions en vue de la désignation des lauréats.

En Norvège, les travaux préparatoires correspondants sont confiés par l'institution qui décerne le prix de la paix, le Comité Nobel du Storting Norvégien, à son président secondé du secrétaire du Comité et de trois experts dans les domaines du droit international, de l'histoire politique et des sciences économiques.

Les candidatures transmises par les personnes habilitées par règlements spéciaux à présenter des propositions sont étudiées par les organes préparatoires compétents, et des rapports motivés soumis aux institutions chargées de décerner les prix. Ces institutions prennent ensuite leurs décisions qui sont irrévocables. De tradition, toutes les délibérations et recommandations des comités sont secrètes.

En 1974 les Comités Nobel suédois chargés de préparer les affaires étaient composés des membres suivants :

pour la physique :

MM K. SIEGBAHN, professeur de physique à l'Université d'Upsal, *président du Comité;* B. EDLÉN, professeur de physique à l'Université de Lund; L. HULTHÉN, professeur de physique mathématique à l'Ecole Polytechnique Supérieure de Stockholm; P. O. LÖWDIN, professeur de chimie quantique à l'Université d'Upsal; S. LUNDQVIST, professeur de physique mathématique à l'Ecole Polytechnique Supérieure Chalmers de Gothembourg; *secrétaire du Comité :* M. B. Nagel, professeur de physique mathématique à l'Ecole Polytechnique Supérieure de Stockholm.

pour la chimie :

MM. A. FREDGA, anc. professeur de chimie organique à l'Université d'Upsal, *président du Comité;* G. HÄGG, anc. professeur de chimie inorganique à l'Université d'Upsal; A. ÖLANDER, anc. professeur de chimie physique à l'Université de Stockholm; B. MALMSTRÖM, professeur de biochimie à l'Université de Gothembourg; G. BERGSON, professeur de chimie organique à l'Université d'Upsal; *secrétaire du Comité :*M. A. MAGNÉLI, professeur de chimie minérale à l'Université de Stockholm.

pour la physiologie ou la médecine :

MM. B. UVNÄS, professeur de pharmacologie, *président du Comité;* U. BORELL, professeur d'obstétrique et de gynécologie, *vice-président du Comité;* S. BERGSTRÖM, professeur de chimie médicale, recteur de l'Institut Royal Carolin de Stockholm; A. ENGSTRÖM, professeur de biophysique; R. LUFT, professeur de médecine; membres adjoints : B. ANDERSSON, professeur de physiologie; J.-E. EDSTRÖM, professeur d'histologie; C.-A. HAMBERGER, professeur d'oto-rhino-laryngologie; G. KLEIN, professeur de biologie tumorale; J. LINDSTEN, professeur adjoint de génétique médicale; E. NORRBY, professeur de virologie; B. PERNOW, professeur de chimie clinique; P. REICHARD, professeur de chimie médicale; B. THORELL, professeur de pathologie; R. ZETTERSTRÖM, professeur de pédiatrie; *secrétaire du Comité :* M. le professeur B. E. GUSTAFSSON; (tous de l'Institut Royal Carolin de Stockholm).

pour la littérature :

MM. K. R. GIEROW, docteur ès lettres, sécretaire perpétuel de l'Académie suédoise, *président du Comité ;* A. J. ÖSTERLING, docteur ès lettres; L. GYL-LENSTEN, professeur adjoint; A. LUNDKVIST, docteur ès lettres; J. EDFELT, docteur ès lettres; *secrétaire du comité :* M. A. RYBERG, licencié ès lettres, conservateur en chef de la Bibliothèque Nobel de l'Académie suédoise.

Prix Nobel de la Paix :

En 1974 le groupe norvégien chargé d'assister la présidente du Comité Nobel dans la même tâche préparatoire se composait des membres suivants :

MM. Tim GREVE, directeur de l'Institut Nobel Norvégien, *secrétaire du Comité ;* P. MUNTHE, professeur de sciences économiques à l'Université d'Oslo; T. OPSAHL, professeur de droit à l'Université d'Oslo; A. SCHOU, ancien di-recteur de l'Institut Nobel Norvégien; J. SVERDRUP, professeur d'histoire à l'Université d'Oslo.

ATTRIBUTION DES PRIX

L'ACADÉMIE ROYALE DES SCIENCES
a décidé, le 15 octobre 1974, d'attribuer la moitié le Prix Nobel de Physique à

MARTIN RYLE
de l'Université de Cambridge, Angleterre,
et l'autre moitié à

ANTONY HEWISH
de l'Université de Cambridge, Angleterre,

pour leurs recherches de pionniers en radioastrophysique : Ryle pour ses observations et inventions, en particulier dans la technique de la synthèse d'ouverture, et Hewish pour le rôle décisif qu'il a joué dans la découverte des pulsars.

A cette même date, l'Académie a décidé d'attribuer le Prix Nobel de Chimie à

PAUL J. FLORY
de l'Université de Stanford, Californie, États-Unis,

pour ses contributions fondamentales, tant théoriques qu'expérimentales, à la chimie physique des macromolécules.

LA FACULTÉ DE MÉDECINE DE L'INSTITUT ROYAL CAROLIN
a décidé, le 10 octobre 1974, d'attribuer le Prix Nobel de Physiologie ou de Médecine en commun à

ALBERT CLAUDE
de l'Université Catholique de Louvain, Belgique et de l'Université Rockefeller, New York, N. Y., États-Unis,

CHRISTIAN DE DUVE
de l'Université Rockefeller, New York, N.Y., États-Unis,
et à

GEORGE EMIL PALADE
de l'Université de Yale, New Haven, Connecticut, États-Unis,

pour leurs découvertes sur l'organisation structurale et fonctionelle de la cellule.

9

L'ACADÉMIE SUÉDOISE
a décidé, le 3 octobre 1974, d'attribuer la moitié du Prix Nobel de Littérature à

EYVIND JOHNSON
de Suède

pour un art narratif aux larges vues historiques et contemporaines au service de la liberté.

et l'autre moitié à
HARRY MARTINSON
de Suède

pour un œuvre littéraire qui saisit la goutte de rosée et reflète le cosmos.

LE COMITÉ NOBEL DU STORTING NORVÉGIEN
a décidé, le 8 octobre 1974, d'attribuer le Prix de la Paix à

EISAKU SATO
du Japon
et à
SEÁN MAC BRIDE
d'Irlande.

Le nombre de propositions statutaires de candidatures aux différents prix Nobel en 1974 s'est monté :
en physique, à 97
en chimie, à 158
en physiologie ou médecine, à 162
en littérature, à 102
pour la paix, à 105.

CÉRÉMONIES NOBEL

REMISE DES PRIX A STOCKHOLM

Les prix de physique, de chimie, de physiologie ou de médecine, de littérature et le prix de sciences économiques institué en mémoire d'Alfred Nobel furent remis aux lauréats au cours d'un programme traditionnel établi par les institutions qui décernent ces prix et par le Conseil d'Administration de la Fondation Nobel. L'organisation de la fête avait été confiée au directeur général de la Fondation, M. le baron Stig Ramel. La cérémonie solennelle se déroula dans la grande salle du Palais des Concerts.

Parmi les invités on remarquait les lauréats de l'année MM. Hewish, Flory, Claude, de Duve, Palade, Johnson, Martinson, von Hayek et Myrdal (*prix de sciences économiques en mémoire d'Alfred Nobel*) et les membres de leurs familles, ainsi que certains lauréats des années précédentes : MM. Siegbahn (1924), Theorell (1955), Granit (1967), von Euler (1970), et Soljenitsyne (1970).

De nombreux représentants du Gouvernement, dont Son Excellence M. Palme, Premier Ministre, les Chefs de Mission et d'autres membres du corps diplomatique honoraient la cérémonie de leur présence. En dehors des organisations Nobel en Suède, différentes académies, diverses sociétés savantes et littéraires, l'université, la famille Nobel, le monde des arts, de l'industrie et de la presse s'étaient aussi fait représenter. L'assemblée comptait en outre de hauts fonctionnaires civils et militaires.

A 16 heures et demie S. M. le ROI, Leurs Altesses Royales, le Prince Bertil, duc de Halland et la Princesse Margaretha de Danemark entrèrent dans la salle, salués par l'hymne royal. Puis la cérémonie se déroula conformément au programme reproduit à la page suivante.

A la fin de chaque discours, prononcé par l'orateur chargé de présenter l'œuvre récompensée, S. M. le Roi remit au lauréat le *diplôme*, la *médaille* et un *document* indiquant le montant du prix. M. le professeur A. Hewish reçut le prix au nom de Sir Martin Ryle. Après un discours en l'honneur de M. Solsjenitsyne, lauréat en littérature de 1970, par le Docteur K. R. Gierow, S. M. le Roi remit au lauréat le diplôme et la médaille.

PROGRAMME

The Prince of Denmark's march .... *Jeremiah Clarke*

Les Lauréats prennent leurs places sur l'estrade

Discours du *Professeur Ulf von Euler*, Président du Conseil d'Administration de la Fondation Nobel

Greensleeves .... *Ralph Vaughan Williams*

Remise du Prix Nobel de Physique 1974 à MM. Martin Ryle et Antony Hewish, après une allocution du *Professeur Hans Wilhelmsson*

Remise du Prix Nobel de Chimie 1974 à M. Paul J. Flory, après une allocution du *Professeur Stig Claesson*

Marche des Janissaires .... *André Grétry*

Remise du Prix Nobel de Physiologie ou de Médecine 1974 à MM. Albert Claude, Christian de Duve et George E. Palade, après une allocution du *Professeur Jan-Erik Edström*

Épilogue du Conte d'hiver .... *Lars-Erik Larsson*

Remise du Prix Nobel du Littérature 1974 à MM. Eyvind Johnson et Harry Martinson, après une allocution du *Docteur Karl Ragnar Gierow*

Remise des insignes du Prix Nobel de Littérature 1970 à M. Alexandre Soljenitsyne

Ouverture de l'opéra Ruslan et Ludmila .... *Michail Glinka*

Remise du Prix de Sciences Économiques 1974, institué par la Banque de Suède à la mémoire d'Alfred Nobel, à MM. Gunnar Myrdal et Friedrich von Hayek, après une allocution du *Professeur Erik Lundberg*

L'Hymne National suédois : « Du gamla, du fria »

Musique exécutée par des membres de l'Orchestre
Philharmonique de Stockholm
sous la direction de *M. Sten Frykberg*

HÄLSNINGSTAL

Av ordföranden i Nobelstiftelsens styrelse professor U. S. von EULER
(Traduction en français page 15, en anglais page 17)

Eders Majestät, Eders Kungliga Högheter, Mina Damer och Herrar,
Å Nobelstiftelsens vägnar hälsar jag de närvarande välkomna till årets pris-
utdelningsceremoni. Jag vänder mig särskilt till pristagarna som genom lysan-
de insatser på olika fält bidragit till att stärka det anseende Nobelpriset kunnat
glädja sig åt även internationellt.

Valet av pristagare tillkommer ju de prisutdelande organen där ansvaret i
särskild grad vilar på de arbetande priskommitteerna. Nobelstiftelsen tar som
sådan icke del i denna uppgift. Däremot har Nobelstiftelsen i allt högre grad
kommit att bli en central instans till vilken man framställer förslag, riktar
vädjanden och — det skall icke fördöljas — framför kritik. Styrelsen har inte
kunnat undgå att uppfatta detta som någonting positivt: man har tilltrott
Stiftelsen ett inflytande och möjligheter att ingripa i ofta vittfamnande pro-
jekt av humanitär och vetenskaplig art. Sådana framställningar har inkom-
mit bokstavligen från alla världens hörn. Nobelprisens internationella karaktär
har i mångas ögon varit liktydigt med eller åtminstone förenligt med en inter-
nationell intressesfär med vidare gränser än det statutenliga prisbedömnings-
arbetet. Om detta å ena sidan uppskattas av Stiftelsen så är det å andra sidan
uppenbart att det medför ett ansvar eller i varje fall förväntningar som icke
kan negligeras. Stiftelsens handlingsfrihet är begränsad och det har därför
gällt att finna vägar för aktioner som står i överensstämmelse med det som
kan uppfattas som Nobelverksamhetens syften. Här kan en ny aktivitetslinje
sägas ha växt fram, grundad till stor del på vad man trott sig veta om Alfred
Nobels egna intentioner och livsåskådning, som de framgått av hans egna
uttalanden. Lyckligtvis finns här ett gott material att bygga på. Kort ut-
tryckt kan man säga att Alfred Nobels mål var att göra insatser för mänsklighetens välfärd i den vidaste bemärkelse.

En väg som stått Nobelstiftelsen öppen har varit att med medel som Riks-
bankens Jubileumsfond generöst ställt till förfogande stödja och stimulera
symposier som behandlar ämnen av grundläggande betydelse för mänskligheten. För dem som känner sig delaktiga av ansvaret för den kommande utvecklingen i världen har det här känts som en nödvändighet att på något sätt
bidra till ökat intresse för åtgärder som förhoppningsvis leder till en lycklig
framtid eller åtminstone reducerar de faror som syns hota.

I den andan har Nobelstiftelsen initierat ett under året genomfört symposium, som under titeln *"Man, Environment and Resources"* behandlat några
av de brännande frågor som ligger som hotande moln vid horisonten. Det
har varit Stiftelsens förhoppning att genom stöd till denna diskussion ytterligare betona nödvändigheten av att nu och icke senare slå in på vägar som

13

kan skänka våra efterlevande större trygghet, även om det skulle ske till priset av försakelser. En sådan tanke skulle icke varit Alfred Nobel främmande.

Om man betänker Nobels egna ord för motivering av pris — åt dem, som under det förlupna året gjort mänskligheten den största nytta — så ger den i själva verket även inom den nuvarande ramen för prisen en vidare marginal för belöning av insatser på olika områden än man kanske tidigare ansett. Sådana insatser kan t. ex. beröra handhavande av jordens resurser och skyddande av den miljö människan lever i och skall leva i, låt vara att en av årets pristagare låtit sin fantasi föra människan utanför denna sfär.

För att ytterligare fullfölja denna filosofi överväger Nobelstiftelsen att i vidgad grad i symposieform eller föreläsningsform ta upp frågor om vården och utnyttjandet av jordens tillgångar och dess relationer till en som det synes ständigt växande världspopulation. För Stiftelsen har denna inställning betraktats som en logisk följd av utvecklingen och kan ses som en naturlig komplettering till Nobelorganens övriga uppgifter, såsom de utformats i Alfred Nobels testamente och i Nobelstiftelsens statuter.

Det är Stiftelsens förhoppning att i fortsättningen på en vidare bas än hittills varit fallet kunna bidra till åtgärder som syftar till att — över de nationella gränserna och med testamentets ord — vara mänskligheten till nytta och sålunda verka i Alfred Nobels anda.

DISCOURS INTRODUCTIF

Par le président de la Fondation Nobel M. le professeur U. S. von EULER
Traduction

Sire, Altesses Royales, Mesdames, Messieurs,

Au nom de la Fondation Nobel je souhaite la bienvenue à tous ceux qui assistent aujourd'hui à la cérémonie de la remise des prix de cette année. Je m'adresse tout particulièrement aux lauréats dont les brillantes réalisations dans différents domaines ont contribué à affermir le renom dont le prix Nobel peut se féliciter de jouir même au plan international.

C'est en fait aux organes qui décernent les prix, où les Comités Nobel assument une responsabilité toute particulière, qu'il appartient de choisir les lauréats. La Fondation Nobel ne participe pas, comme telle, à cette mission. En revanche, la Fondation est de plus en plus fréquemment l'instance centrale à laquelle on présente des propositions, à laquelle on adresse des suppliques et — ne le cachons pas — des critiques. La Fondation n'a pu éviter d'y voir un élément positif: On l'a donc jugée capable d'exercer une influence et d'intervenir dans des projets souvent très vastes d'ordre humanitaire et scientifique. On l'a sollicitée, littéralement, de tous les coins du monde. Le caractère international des prix Nobel a signifié pour bien des esprits identité, ou du moins compatibilité, avec une sphère d'intérêt internationale dont les limites s'étendent bien au delà du jaugeage des œuvres présentées que stipulent les statuts. Si d'un côté la Fondation apprécie qu'il en soit ainsi, il est d'autre part évident que cela comporte une responsabilité, ou en tout cas une attente à satisfaire, qu'on ne saurait négliger. La liberté d'action de la Fondation étant limitée, il s'agissait de trouver des voies où elle pût œuvrer en concordance avec ce qu'il est permis de considérer comme les visées des activités Nobel. On peut dire qu'il s'est créé à cet égard un nouvel axe d'activités issu en grande partie de ce que l'on croit savoir des intentions d'Alfred Nobel et de la conception de la vie qu'il avait, telles qu'elles se dégagent de ses propres paroles. Heureusement, le matériau de base est solide. On peut dire en somme que le but d'Alfred Nobel était de contribuer au bonheur de l'humanité, au sens le plus large du terme.

Une des voies qui s'est ouverte à la Fondation Nobel a consisté à soutenir et à stimuler, grâce au Fonds du Jubilée que la Banque de Suède a si généreusement offert, des symposiums qui traitent des matières d'une importance fondamentale pour l'humanité. Pour ceux qui se sentent co-responsables de l'évolution future du monde, il est apparu nécessaire de contribuer de quelque manière à polariser l'intérêt sur des mesures qui, espérons-le, déboucheront sur un heureux avenir, ou tout au moins réduiront les dangers qui semblent menacer notre monde.

C'est dans cet esprit que la Fondation Nobel a pris l'initiative d'un symposium qui s'est déroulé cette année et qui, sous la rubrique « *Man, Environment and Resources* » a traité quelques-unes des questions les plus brûlantes dont l'ombre menaçante se dresse à l'horizon. La Fondation a espéré qu'en soutenant la réalisation de ces entretiens, elle soulignerait encore la nécessité de s'engager dès aujourd'hui, et non demain, dans des voies qui peuvent offrir à ceux qui viendront après nous une plus grande sécurité, même si cela ne peut se faire qu'au prix de sacrifices. Cette pensée n'aurait pas été étrangère à l'esprit d'Alfred Nobel.

Si l'on réfléchit aux propres paroles de Nobel, au motif qu'il donne en spécifiant que les prix seront décernés à ceux qui au cours de l'année passée ont rendu à l'humanité les plus grands services, on dispose en réalité, même dans le cadre actuel des prix, d'une marge d'option entre les apports de différents domaines plus large qu'on ne l'avait d'abord pensé. Il peut s'agir par exemple de l'utilisation des ressource terretres et de la protection de l'environnement dans lequel l'homme vit et vivra — bien que l'un des lauréats de cette année, convenons-en, ait laissé son imagination transporter l'homme hors de cette sphère.

Pour donner suite à cette philosophie, la Fondation Nobel pense actualiser plus largement sous forme de symposiums ou de conférences les questions de la sauvegarde et de l'exploitation des ressources terrestres et des rapports qu' elles ont avec une population mondiale qui semble être en constance croissance. La Fondation estime que cette façon de voir est la suite logique de l'évolution, et qu'elle peut être considérée comme un complément naturel aux autres missions des organes Nobel, telles qu'elles ont été formulées dans le testament d'Alfred Nobel et dans les statuts de la Fondation Nobel.

La Fondation espère pouvoir contribuer à l'avenir, sur une plus large base que jusqu'ici, à des mesures qui visent — par-delà les frontières et conformément aux termes du testament — à rendre à l'humanité les plus grands services, œuvrant ainsi dans l'esprit d'Alfred Nobel.

OPENING ADDRESS

By the President of the Nobel Foundation, Professor U. S. von EULER
Translation

Your Majesty, Your Royal Highnesses, Ladies and Gentlemen,
On behalf of the Nobel Foundation I should like to bid all of you here today welcome to this year's prize presentation ceremony. I extend a special welcome to the prize-winners, who through their brilliant work in different fields have helped to enhance the respect which the Nobel Prize also enjoys internationally.

The choice of prize-winners is of course the concern of the prize-awarding bodies where the responsibility rests particularly on the working prize committees. The Nobel Foundation as such is not involved in this task. On the other hand the Nobel Foundation has increasingly become a central body to which suggestions are presented, appeals made and—this is no secret—criticism expressed. The Foundation cannot avoid interpreting this as something positive; the Foundation has been credited with an influence and possibilities of intervening of often wide-embracing projects of a humanitarian and scientific nature. Appeals of this kind have been received from literally all the corners of the globe. The international character of the Nobel Prize has in the eyes of many been synonymous with or at least compatible with an international sphere of interest with wider boundaries than the statutory prize awarding work. If this on the one hand is appreciated by the Foundation it is on the other hand clear that it brings in its train a responsibility or at any rate expectations which cannot be ignored. The Foundation's freedom of action is limited and ways have had to be sought for measures which are in agreement with what may be regarded as the aims of Nobel activities. Here a new line of activity may be said to have developed, based for the most part on what was believed to be in agreement with Alfred Nobel's own intentions and outlook on life, as apparent from his own remarks. Fortunately, there is in this respect excellent material to serve as foundation. To put it briefly, it may be said that Alfred Nobel's aim was to contribute to the welfare of mankind in the widest sense.

One avenue open to the Nobel Foundation has been to use money, generously made available by the Bank of Sweden Tercentenary Fund, to support and stimulate symposia dealing with subjects of fundamental importance for mankind. For those who feel that they have a share in the responsibility for future developments in the world it has seemed necessary to contribute in some way to an increased interest in measures which hopefully will lead to a happy future or at least reduce the dangers that appear to constitute a threat.

In this spirit the Nobel Foudation took the initiative for a symposium held this year, which under the title of *"Man, Environment and Resources"* dealt with some of the burning issues that are gathered like threatening clouds on the horizon. It has been the hope of the Foundation, by supporting this discussion, to underline still further the necessity of now and not later following a course that may accord greater security to coming generations, even if it were to take place at the price of sacrifices. This kind of reasoning would not have been unfamiliar to Alfred Nobel.

If one considers Nobel's own words in respect of the qualifications for the awards—to those who during the course of the past year have rendered the greatest service to mankind—they give in actual fact, even within the present framework of the prizes, a wider margin for rewarding work in various fields than was perhaps previously realized. Such work may, for example concern the management of the world's resources and the protection of the environment in which man lives and will live, notwithstanding the visions of one of this year's prize-winners who has made his imagination take man beyond this sphere.

In order to pursue this philosophy still further, the Nobel Foundation is considering taking up to an increased extent in the form of symposia or lectures questions concerning the care and utilisation of the world's resources and their relationship to a seemingly evergrowing world population. For the Foundation this approach has been regarded as a logical consequence of the desire to keep pace with a changing world and may be considered to be a natural complement to the other duties of the Nobel organisations as set out in Alfred Nobel's will and in the statutes of the Nobel Foundation.

The Foundation hopes in future to be able, on a broader basis than hitherto has been the case, to contribute to measures aimed at serving mankind across national boundaries—in the words of the will—and consequently to function in the spirit of Alfred Nobel.

THE NOBEL PRIZE FOR PHYSICS

Speech by professor HANS WILHELMSSON of the Royal Academy of Sciences
Translation from the Swedish text

Your Majesty, Your Royal Highnesses, Ladies and Gentlemen,
The subject of the Nobel Prize in Physics this year is the science of Astrophysics, the Physics of the stars and galactic systems.

Problems concerning our Universe on a large scale, its constitution and evolution, play an essential rôle in present day scientific discussions.

We are curious about the behaviour of our Universe. In order to draw reliable conclusions regarding cosmological models it is necessary to gather detailed information about conditions in the remote parts of the Cosmos.

Radio-astronomy offers unique possibilities for studying what is taking place, or in reality what occurred very long ago, at enormous distances from Earth, as far out as thousands of millions of lightyears from us. The radio waves now reaching us have been travelling for thousands of millions of years at the speed of light to reach our Earth from those very remote sources.

It is indeed a thrilling fact that the radio signals we record today here on Earth left their cosmic sources at a time when hardly any flowers or living creatures, and certainly no physicists, existed on Earth.

New and epoch-making discoveries have been made in the field of Radio-astrophysics during the last decade, discoveries that are also exceedingly important contributions to modern Physics, for example in establishing through radio-astronomical observations the presence of matter in a superdense state.

One single cubic centimeter of this superdense matter has a weight of thousands of millions of tons. It consists of tightly-packed neutrons. A neutron star appears as a consequence of a star explosion, a so-called supernova event. Neutron stars, with a diameter of about 10 kilometers, are from a cosmic point of view extremely small objects. They represent the final state in the evolution of certain stars.

This year's Nobel Prize winners in Physics, Martin Ryle and Antony Hewish, developed new radio-astronomical techniques. Their observations of cosmic radio sources represent extremely noteworthy research results.

In order to collect radio waves from cosmic radio sources one utilizes radio-telescopes. It is important that a radio-telescope should have a large area, both for highest possible sensitivity and for the high angular resolution that is needed to discriminate among the various cosmic sources of radio radiation.

For observation of exceedingly small sources it is, however, no longer possible to build a single radio-telescope of sufficient size. Ryle and his collaborators therefore developed the method of aperture synthesis. Instead of making one huge aerial, a number of small aerials are used in this method, and the signals received by them are combined in such a way as to provide the necessary extreme accuracy.

Instead of many small aerials, Ryle in fact made use of a few aerials that could be moved successively to different positions on the ground. Ryle also invented the extremely elegant and powerful technique utilizing the rotation of the Earth to move his radio-telescopes. With this technique he obtained a resolution in his observations that corresponded to an aerial of enormous size.

Ryle's measurements enable us to conclude that a steady-state model of the Universe can not be accepted. The Cosmos on a large scale has to be described by dynamic, evolutionary models.

In his latest construction in Cambridge, Ryle obtained an angular resolution permitting the mapping of cosmic radio sources with an error less than one second of arc!

The radio-astronomical instruments invented and developed by Martin Ryle, and utilized so successfully by him and his collaborators in their observations, have been one of the most important elements of the latest discoveries in Astrophysics.

Antony Hewish and his collaborators in Cambridge, in the Autumn of 1967, made a unique and unexpected discovery that has revolutionized Astrophysics. They had constructed new aerials and instruments to study the influence of the outer corona of the Sun on the radiation detected from remote point sources. A special receiver capable of extremely rapid response had been built.

The fast receiver provided a result quite different from its intended purpose. By chance the receiver detected short pulses of radio signals that were repeated periodically about every second, and with exceedingly high precision in the pulse repetition rates.

It was concluded that the radiation originated from cosmic sources of previously unknown type. These sources were subsequently named pulsars.

One has come to the conclusion that the central part of a pulsar consists of a neutron star. The pulsars are also accompanied by magnetic fields many millions of times stronger than those found in laboratories on Earth. The neutron star is surrounded by an electrically-conducting gas or plasma. Each pulsar rotates and emits beams of radiation in the Universe, resembling those from a light-house. The beams strike the Earth periodically with high precision.

These pulsars are indeed the world clocks which our Nobel Prize winner Harry Martinson mentions in his poetry.

Allow me to quote this poet of space:
"World clocks tick and space gleams
everything changes place and order".

Early in the history of pulsar research it was suspected that neutron star matter existed in the centres of supernovas. Radio-telescopes were aimed towards the centre of the Crab nebula, a magnificent glaring gaseous remnant of a supernova event that is known, from Chinese annals, to have occurred in 1054 A.D., and indeed, they detected a pulsar! This pulsar emits not only

20

radio pulses, as expected from a pulsar, but pulses of light and x-rays as well. It is comparatively young, rotates rapidly and is in fact exceptional among pulsars.

Antony Hewish played a decisive rôle in the discovery of pulsars. This discovery, which is of extraordinary scientific interest, opens the way to new methods for studying matter under extreme physical conditions.

The contributions of Ryle and Hewish represent an important step forward in our knowledge of the Universe. Thanks to their work new fields of research have become part of Astrophysics. The gigantic laboratory of the Universe offers rich possibilities for future research.

Sir Martin,

Some of the most fundamental questions in Physics have been elucidated as a result of your brilliant research. Your inventions and observations have brought new foundations for our conception of the Universe.

Professor Antony Hewish,

The discovery of pulsars, for which you played a decisive rôle, is a most outstanding example of how in recent years our knowledge of the Universe has been dramatically extended. Your research has contributed greatly to Astrophysics and to Physics in general.

On behalf of the Royal Academy of Sciences I wish to express our admiration and to convey to you our warmest congratulations.

The Royal Academy of Sciences regrets that Sir Martin Ryle is not here today.

May I now ask you, Professor Hewish, to receive your prize and also the prize awarded to Sir Martin Ryle from the hands of His Majesty the King.

THE NOBEL PRIZE FOR CHEMISTRY

Speech by Professor STIG CLAESSON of the Royal Academy of Sciences
Translation from the Swedish text

Your Majesty, Your Royal Highnesses, Ladies and Gentlemen,
This year's Nobel prize in chemistry has been awarded to Professor Paul Flory for his fundamental contributions to the physical chemistry of macromolecules.

Macromolecules include biologically important materials such as cellulose, albumins and nucleic acids, and all of our plastics and synthetic fibers.

Macromolecules are often referred to as chain molecules and can be compared to a pearl necklace. They consist of long chains of atoms which, when magnified one hundred million times, appear as a pearl necklace. The pearls represent the atoms in the chain. One should realize that this chain is much longer than the necklaces being worn here this evening. To obtain a representative model of a macromolecule all of the necklaces here in this hall should be connected together in a single long chain.

One can readily appreciate that the development of a theory for these molecules presented considerable difficulties. The forms of the chain itself, whether extended or coiled, represents a property difficult to rationalize.

A statistical description is of necessity required, and Professor Flory has made major contributions to the development of such a theory. The problem is more difficult, however. How can one compare different molecules in different solvents?

When chain molecules are dissolved in different solvents they become coiled to different degrees, depending on the interaction between repulsive and attractive forces in the solution. In a good solvent the chain molecules are extended. In a poor solvent, in contrast, the chain molecules assume a highly coiled form.

Professor Flory showed that if one takes a solution of extended chain molecules in a good solvent, and slowly cools the solution, then the molecules become progressively more coiled until they are no longer soluble.

Thus, there must be an intermediate temperature where the attractive and repulsive forces are balanced. At this temperature the molecules assume a kind of standard condition that can be used, generally, to characterize their properties.

This temperature Professor Flory named the theta temperature. A corresponding temperature exists for real gases at which they follow the ideal gas law. This temperature is called the Boyle temperature after Robert Boyle who discovered the gas laws. By analogy, the theta temperature for macromolecules is often referred to as the Flory temperature.

Profssor Flory showed also that it was possible to define a constant for chain molecules, now called Flory's universal constant, which can be compared in significance to the gas constant.

When one, in retrospect, reads about an important scientific discovery, one often feels that the work was remarkably simple. This actually indicates, however, that it was brilliant insight in a new and until then unexplored research area. This is highly characteristic of Professor Flory's scientific discoveries, not only those concerned with the Flory temperature and Flory's universal constant but also many of his other important research studies. Further examples are found in his investigation of the relationship between the reaction mechanism and the length of the chains formed when chain molecules are prepared synthetically, as well as his important contribution to the theory of crystallization and rubber elasticity. These achievements have been of major importance for technological developments in the plastics industry.

In recent years Professor Flory has investigated, both theoretically and experimentally, the relation between rotational characteristics of the chain links and the form of the chain molecules. This is of fundamental significance for the understanding of both biological macromolecules and synthetic chain molecules.

During the time Professor Flory has been active as a scientist, macromolecular chemistry has been transformed from primitive semi-empirical observations into a highly developed science. This evolution has come about through major contributions by research groups from both universities and many of the world's largest industrial laboratories. Professor Flory has remained a leading researcher in the area during this entire period, giving further evidence of his unique position as a scientist.

Professor Flory,

I have tried to describe briefly the fundamental importance of your many contributions to macromolecular chemistry and in particular those concepts introduced by you and now referred to as the Flory-temperature and the Flory universal constant.

On behalf of the Royal Academy of Sciences I wish to convey to you our warmest congratulations and I now ask you to receive your prize from the hands of His Majesty the King.

THE NOBEL PRIZE FOR PHYSIOLOGY
OR MEDICINE

Speech by Professor JAN-ERIK EDSTRÖM of the Royal Caroline Institute
Translation from the Swedish text

Your Majesty, Your Royal Highnesses, Ladies and Gentlemen,
The 1974 Nobel Prize in Physiology or Medicine concerns the fine structure
and the function of the cell, a subject designated Cell Biology. There are no
earlier Prize Winners in this field, simply because it is one that has been newly
created, largely by the Prize Winners themselves. It is necessary to go back to
1906 to find Prize Winners who are to some extent forerunners. In that year
Golgi and Cajal were awarded the Prize for studies of cells with the light
microscope. Although the light microscope certainly opened a door to a new
world during the 19th century, it had obvious limitations. The components of
the cell are so small that it was not possible to study their inner structure,
their mutual relations or their different roles. To take a metaphor from an
earlier Prize Winner, the cell was like a mother's work basket, in that it contained objects strewn about in no discernible order and evidently, for him,
with no recognizable functions.

But, if the cell is a work basket, it is one on a very tiny scale indeed, having
a volume corresponding to a millionth of that of a pinshead. The various
components responsible for the functions of the cell correspond in their turn
to a millionth of this millionth, and are far below the resolving powers of the
light microscope. Nor would it have helped if researchers had used larger
experimental animals: the cells of the elephant are not larger than those of
the mouse.

Progress was quite simply at a standstill during the first few decades of this
century, but then in 1938, the electron microscope became available, an innovation that held out great promise. The difference between this microscope
and the ordinary light microscope is enormous, like being able to read a book
instead of just the title. With such an instrument it should now be possible to
see components almost down to the dimensions of single molecules. But the
early hopes were succeeded by disappointment. It was found impossible to
prepare the cells in such a way that they could be used. The book remained
obstinately shut, even though it would have been possible to read it.

Albert Claude and coworkers were the first to get a glance inside the book.
In the mid-forties they made a break-through and succeeded in preparing
cells for electron microscopy. I say a glance, because much technical development still remained to be done, and *George Palade* should be mentioned foremost among those who developed electron microscopy further, to the highest
degree of artistry.

In addition to form and structure it is necessary to know the chemical composition in order to understand the functions of the cell components. It was

24

hardly possible to analyse whole cells or tissues since these consist of so many different components, and so, one would get a confused picture. Each component has to be studied separately and obviously this is difficult when the components are so small. Here a new art was developed, and again Claude was the pioneer. He showed how one could first grind the cells into fragments and then sort out the different components on a large scale with the aid of the centrifuge. This was an important beginning. Palade made further contributions, but it was above all *Christian de Duve* who introduced brilliant developments within this field.

The functions of the cell could now be mapped with this armoury of methodology. Palade has taught us which components function when the cell grows and produces secretion. The Prize Winner of 1906, Camillo Golgi, discovered a cell component, the Golgi complex. Palade has demonstrated its role and he discovered the small bodies, ribosomes, in which the cellular protein is produced.

Production of organic material must be balanced by scavenging and combustion of waste, even in the tiny world of the cell. de Duve discovered small components, lysosomes, which can engulf and dissolve, e.g., attacking bacteria or parts of the cell itself which are old and worn out. These are real acid baths, but the cell itself is normally protected by surrounding membranes. Sometimes, however, the lysosomes are converted into veritable suicide pills for the cell. This occurs when the surrounding membranes are damaged, e.g. by ionizing radiation. The lysosomes play a role in many clinically important conditions and the foundations laid by the Duve are of the greatest significance for the interpretation of these states, and thus also for prophylactic and therapeutic measures.

To sum up, the 1974 Prize Winners have by their discoveries elucidated cellular functions that are of basic biological and clinical importance. Thus they cover both aspects of the Prize, Physiology as well as Medicine.

Albert Claude, Christian de Duve and George Palade. During the last 30 years a new subject has been created, Cell Biology. You have been largely responsible for this development both by creating the basic methodology and by exploiting it to gain insight into the functional machinery of the cell. On behalf of the Karolinska Institutet, I wish to convey to you our warmest congratulations and I now ask you to receive the prize from the hands of his Majesty the King.

THE NOBEL PRIZE FOR LITERATURE

Speech by KARL RAGNAR GIEROW of the Swedish Academy
Translation from the Swedish text

Your Majesty, Your Royal Highnesses, Ladies and Gentlemen,

Eyvind Johnson's education—i.e. the education provided by society at that time—ended when he was thirteen and was imparted to him at a little village school north of the Arctic Circle. The future awaiting the young Harry Martinson opened up to him when, at the age of six as a so-called child of the parish, he was sold by auction to the lowest bidder—that is, to the person who took charge of the forsaken boy for the smallest payment out of parochial funds. The fact that, with such a start in life, both of them have their places on this platform today, is the visible testimony to a transformation of society, which, step by step, is still going on all over the world. With us it came unusually early; it is perhaps our country's biggest blessing, perhaps also its most remarkable achievement during the last thousand years.

Eyvind Johnson and Harry Martinson did not come alone, nor first. They are representative of the many proletarian writers or working-class poets who, on a wide front, broke into our literature, not to ravage and plunder, but to enrich it with their fortunes. Their arrival meant an influx of experience and creative energy, the value of which can hardly be exaggerated. To that extent they are representative also of the similar breakthrough that has later occurred in the whole of our cultural world. A new class has conquered Parnassus. But if by a conqueror we mean the one who gained most from the outcome, then Parnassus has conquered a new class.

To determine an author and his work against the background of his social origin and political environment is at present good form. And what is good form is seldom particularly to the point. "Eyvind Johnson's literary achievement is one of the most significant and characteristic of a very fruitful period in the whole of Europe." This last sentence is not mine; it was written thirty years ago by Lucien Maury. Even then the boy from a primary school in a remote village in the far north of Sweden was an experienced and self-assured European, never forgetful of his origin (of which his autobiographical stories provide a lasting document), but still less bound and inhibited by the environment where he took his first steps. International perspective distinguished Eyvind Johnson's further writings, and it is matched by an equally wide outlook in time, over the destinies and ages of the human race. The renewal of the historical novel, which he has carried out on his own and perhaps exemplified most clearly in great works like *Days of His Grace* and *Steps Towards Silence,* is based not only on extensive research but also on a clear-sightedness which, expressed briefly, sets out to show that everything that happens to us has happened before, and everything that took place once in the world is still taking place, recognizable under changed signs, a constant simultaneity of epochs which may be the only wisdom the past can teach us in our attempts to survey the present and divine an era which we have not yet seen.

If, nevertheless, we are to point to a special phase and one particular mental environment whose traces are ineffaceable in Eyvind Johnson's work with his pen, it is that very period when Lucien Maury discovered that in this Nordic writer Europe had one of its important intellectuals. The French time-analyst described this epoch as very fruitful. What was it that made it so productive? Not favourable conditions, but the indomitable resistance to the conditions that prevailed. D-day had not yet dawned; nazism still had a stranglehold on Europe. It was in that predicament that Eyvind Johnson spoke out. His attitude was so passionate that its fervour has never since vanished from what he wrote. He retained his European perspective, but naturally it was Scandinavia's liberty that was dearest to him just then. He endorsed his conviction with a handshake across the border. Together with a co-editor on the Norwegian side he was responsible during the occupation years for a mouthpiece of the new Scandinavianism, called—"A Handshake". As from today the two publishers of that little paper are both Nobel prize-winners. The name of Eyvind Johnson's co-editor on the Norwegian side of the frontier was Willy Brandt.

Both Eyvind Johnson and still more Harry Martinson have a lot in common with the oldest and perhaps greatest of all proletarian writers, the subtly wise and charming author of ingenious fables, Aesop. Like him, they spin webs, capturing you with beguiling words that always contain other and more than what they literally say. But the differences between this year's two literary prizewinners are greater than the similarities. Beside Eyvind Johnson, whose writing is based so very much on his fiercely defended citizenship in a free society, Harry Martinson may appear to be almost a purely asocial individual, the incorrigible vagrant in our literature. No one has succeeded in putting him under lock and key. The philosophic tramp Bolle in *The Road* is in many ways the author's spokesman, and he is not homeless at the gate. He is home-less only when he gets inside four walls. He is the bearer of asocialism as a wish and a principle that brings good luck; he is a vagabond of his own free will, in agreement with life's sound instincts and in spontaneous revolt against what is trying to stifle them—that which is governed by calculation and established by force. He already has his home; it is beyond and outside, and he is always on the way towards it. From this starting point, though in a different key, we can also conceive the tragically beautiful vision of Aniara, of the spaceship which heads away from an increasingly hostile existence on a frozen earth and itself loses its rudder, cut off from its home port and with its destination lost.

"I don't want to have real that most people want to have real", Bolle re-marks. In saying this he has also said quite a lot about Harry Martinson's writing. Realism is to be found there to the extent that it can be called elemental: it is based on the closest familiarity with the four elements.

Harry Martinson got to know earth and air as a tramp on the roads, fire and water as a stoker at sea. Yet the world of imagination is more important and more real to him than that of reality. Where realism plods methodically along, his imagination races with the swallow-winged glide of the skater. However, it is not a flight from truth; on the contrary. "We must learn the essential difference between what is factual and what is truth", he has said. "We have facts everywhere. They whirl in our eyes like sand." But it is truth we are concerned with, and that is something else, it is a state in nature and in the receptive human being; it is

     the good will with presence and peace of mind
     to keep watch and to be.

For Harry Martinson fact and fiction are one, and without any aphoristic hair-splitting an entire outlook on life is summed up in these pregnant words. The last two, most emphasized, form the simple verb of mere existence: to be. But existence is only fit for human beings if it gives them pleasure, and for that, good will and vigilance are needed. So, in the end, the truth to which this wanderer's path has led him is a gratitude, round-eyed as a child's, for the generous life that has constantly given him trials, riddles and joy in good measure.

After this quickly cut-out silhouette of two remarkable literary profiles, it is my very pleasant duty to express the heartfelt congratulations of the Swedish Academy to Eyvind Johnson and Harry Martinson and to ask them to receive the emblems of the 1974 Nobel Prize for Literature from the hands of His Majesty the King.

THE NOBEL PRIZE FOR LITERATURE 1970

Address to ALEXANDER SOLZHENITSYN by KARL RAGNAR GIEROW
of the Swedish Academy

Not only for the Swedish Academy but for all of us the ceremony today has its particular significance: we can, finally, hand over to the laureate of 1970 the insignia of his award.

Mr Alexander Solzhenitsyn: I have already made two speeches to you. The first one you couldn't listen to, because there was a frontier to cross. The second one I couldn't deliver, because there was a frontier to cross. Your presence here today doesn't mean that the frontiers have at last been abolished. On the contrary, it means that you are now on this side of a border that still exists. But the spirit of your writings, as I understand it, the driving force of your work, like the spirit and force of Alfred Nobel's last will and testament, is to open all frontiers, to enable man to meet man, freely and confidently.

The difficulty is, that such a confidence can only be built on truth. And nowhere in this world of ours is truth always greeted with pure pleasure. Truth goes from house to house, and the dog barks at whom he does not know, says a stern old philosopher. But all the more happy and grateful are those who recognize the wandering stranger and ask him to spend the night and his life with them, in the deep, even desperate hope that the day may not be far off when a frontier is, as it should be, merely a line on the map, which we pass on our way to friends. Such should be, and could be, the case all around the prospering and tormented planet which we inhabit.

Alexander Solzhenitsyn, my dear friend, with these few words I convey to you the warm congratulations of the Swedish Academy and ask you to receive from the hands of His Majesty the King the insignia of the prize to whose value you have added your honour.

BANQUET NOBEL A STOCKHOLM

Après la remise solennelle des prix, une brillante société se réunit dans la Salle dorée de l'Hôtel de Ville. Parmi les personnes présentes on remarquait tout particulièrement :

SA MAJESTÉ le ROI
Leurs Altesses Royales
la Princesse Margaretha de Danemark et le Prince Bertil, duc de Halland
Ensuite :
Les lauréats de l'année MM. Hewish, Flory, Claude, de Duve, Palade, Johnson, Martinson, von Hayek et Myrdal (*prix de sciences économiques en mémoire d'Alfred Nobel*), et les lauréats des années précédentes déjà nommés.

Étaient également présents des membres du Gouvernement et du Parlement ainsi que les Chefs de Mission diplomatique des pays des lauréats, et un très grand nombre de savants, de hauts fonctionnaires suédois et d'autres personnalités de marque.

Le Président de la Fondation invita l'assistance à porter un toast en l'honneur de Sa Majesté le Roi. Les convives se levèrent pour porter ce toast, qui fut suivi de fanfares et de l'hymne royal suédois. Quelques instants plus tard, Sa Majesté proposa un toast silencieux à la mémoire du grand donateur et philanthrope Alfred Nobel.

Après le dîner, un *toast aux lauréats de l'année* fut porté par M. le professeur Erik Lönnroth, membre de l'Académie suédoise et de l'Académie Royale des Sciences.

Your Majesty, Your Royal Highnesses, Nobel Laureates, Ladies and Gentlemen,

Alfred Nobel endowed mankind with two gifts: the awards and dynamite. The latter belonged to a group of inventions, some of which were to be the most destructive mankind has ever known: instruments of aggressive folly and of ruthless tyranny. Nobel's dynamite was made for peaceful purposes— mining and ground levelling—but you could say that he just brushed against the infernal witchcraft of armament industry. He must at least have had an expert knowledge of its capacity as an instrument of power and thus of the possibility of the world changing for the worse. This knowledge may have been one of the main reasons for his instituting the awards.

Alfred Nobel was destined to live at the high tide of rational idealism, and the idealistic purpose of his awards was meant to balance the destructive powers he saw emerging. The endowment of his wealth under his will was one of the typical Swedish grand gestures of the late 19th century, the most famous of all and perhaps the most farsighted. As is mirrored in Nobel's own life the constant conflict between power exercised through instruments of power and the potential power embodied in the thoughts of scientists and poets is everlasting. The awards were to incite the best brains of each generation to serve mankind, to ease its burdens of heavy work and illness and guide it towards noble aims. The ideals of the Nobel award system have faded more or less with the passage of time. Are they obsolete to-day?

I should say no. They are coming back with renewed force, as a consequence of the situation mankind is in today. The power of science is multiplied by the swiftness of its application to industrial processes and consequently to political planning. The power of words is multiplied by the growing efficiency of mass communications. And with the growth of efficiency, the responsibility scientists and writers have to mankind has become a matter of conscience of overwhelming importance. All kinds of demands, economic and political demands, are forced upon them. These demands may be in accordance with the genuine interests of man, but they may also be quite contrary to them. Of what kind they are, is up to the judgement of scientists who have the right combination of specialized knowledge and general outlook to enable them to see what trends of development are constructive or destructive in their far-reaching consequences. And it is up to the judgement of writers with the right combination of moral integrity and insight in the elementary needs of men, material and spiritual needs, to decide whether the slogans ringing out of the giant megaphones of mass media are spurring us on to the right way or enslaving us with superstitious beliefs.

To-day time seems to be ripe for a global appeal: men of intellectual power in all countries, unite—not in a mass movement, but in a common determination not to be domesticated, to follow the lines of thought and research which your own consciences tell you will serve the interests of mankind.

This evening we pay homage to one laureate of chemistry and three laureates of physiology or medicine, whose discoveries concerning macromolecular chemistry and the structural and functional organization of the cell may be of eminent practical importance. But also to two economists, who have used their genius to be inopportune in quite different ways and two astrophysicists who may not at all have contributed to profitable factory processes but to our view of the universe and thus to our conception of limitation and infinity of space and ages. The link is obvious between their visions and those of the poet of "Aniara" and of the conqueror of chronological distances in "The Age of His Grace" and "A Few Steps towards Silence". All of them masters of their own visions, and in this, akin to the literary laureate of 1970, whom we are happy to see among us after having at last received the outward tokens of his imperishable honour to be a man of unique and solitary power to strike at the very roots of injustice.

RÉPONSES DES LAURÉATS
Eyvind Johnson

På Harry Martinsons och mina egna vägnar skall jag yttra mig så kortfattat som möjligt om den situation som han och jag just nu råkar befinna oss i.

En poet eller prosaberättare brukar, mot de gångna årens bakgrund, betrakta vad han har åstadkommit och vanligen finna att något troligen duger, men att annat är svagare. Den självkritiken är oftast nyttig; den kan ge en bild av ett livssammanhang. Den framkallar eller stärker minnet av de lärare som har varit av betydelse. Det kan gälla för länge sedan ur sin fysiska tillvaro utvandrade tänkare och diktare, som dock lever kvar genom sina verk. Det kan också vara samtida äldre eller yngre diktare, som har givit impulser till en inriktning att känna tacksamhet för, en väg som har kunnat bli den för sökaren mest lockande.

Och man kan med tacksamhet minnas goda lärare i den tidigaste, viktiga skolan, där den sjuårige eleven, kanhända på griffeltavlan, har övat sig i skrivtecknens form och ordning för att så småningom få ett klarare begrepp om alfabetets bättre eller sämre användning.

Författaren speglar inte sällan i sitt verk livserfarenheterna som är grunden för dikten, för berättelsen. Diktaren och berättaren fabulerar för att kunna ge sanna bilder ur verkligheten, så som den är eller förefaller att vara. Diktaren kan i inspirationens, i tankens yrsel, uppnå att ge och förmedla de rätta ordens sammansättning och innehåll. Och poeten eller berättaren kan stundom förnimma en djup egoistisk lycka i det han sysslar med att tänka ut, känna sig fram till och skriva.

I centrum av den diktning, som har skapats och skapas, står ju Människan, omgiven av sina likar och av den natur och den teknik, det våld och den barmhärtighet som hon kan möta i de lidanden och den lycka som avgör hennes personliga eller samhälleliga öde. I nuets värld, i vår tid, tycker vi oss veta att lidandet, ångesten, kroppens och själens plågor, har större utbredning än någonsin tidigare i mänsklighetens historia. Många forskare och många diktare har på olika sätt och med skiftande verktyg och medel oavbrutet försökt att med många hjälpares bistånd skapa en drägligare värld för alla människor. Och vi bör tro detta: att hoppet och viljan kan föra oss närmare de mål som heter: Rätt åt alla, orätt åt ingen!

Harry Martinson och jag tackar Svenska Akademien för den ära som har vederfarits oss genom att denna Akademi haft oförsyntheten att utan vårt eller utomståendes hörande placera oss i den situation där vi alltså befinner oss nu.

Och vi tackar samtidigt den Stiftelse, som i Alfred Nobels aktade namn utan protester har godtagit, ja, vänligt har godkänt vår närvaro här på ett sätt, som gör att vår nyssnämnda personliga situation inte kan betraktas som alldeles mörk.

Translation
On behalf of Harry Martinson and myself I will speak as briefly as possible on the situation in which we now find ourselves.

A poet or prose narrator usually looks back on what he has achieved against a backdrop of the years that have passed, generally finding that some of these achievements are acceptable while others are less so. Such a form of self-criticism is often valuable in that it lends perspective to our lives. It evokes or fortifies recollections of those teachers who have been important to us. These may be long departed thinkers and poets who nonetheless live on by virtue of their work, or contemporary writers, young and old, who have been a source of gratifying inspiration to us and led us along the paths of promise.

We can recall with profound gratitude the fine teachers of our earliest, important schooldays when as youngsters—some of us on slates—we practiced the form and order of letters; in due course to acquire a clearar sense for the better or worse use of the alphabet.

A writer's work often reflects what he or she has been exposed to in life; experiences which are the groundwork of a poem or a story. Poet and story-teller both fabulate in order to produce true pictures of reality—reality as it is, or as it seems to them to be. From the throes of inspiration and the eddies of thought the poet may at last be able to arrive at, and convey the right admixture of words and meaning. And your poet or storyteller may sometimes experience a sense of profound egotistical joy in the function of musing, solving and composing.

And at the centre of all the good writing that has been, and is being created stands Man, in the midst of his own kind and surrounded by the technology, violence and compassion that he may encounter in the suffering and happiness which constitutes his individual or social destiny. In the world of the present, in our time, we feel that suffering, anguish, the torments of body and soul, are greater than ever before in the history of mankind. Many men of science and poets have in their own manner, by various ways and means, and aided by others, sought unceasingly to create a more tolerable world for everyone. And this we should believe: that hope and volition can bring us closer to our ultimate goal: justice for all, injustice for no-one.

Harry Martinson and I would like to thank the Swedish Academy for the honour which it has done us in having the temerity, without consulting us or anyone else, to have placed us in the situation in which we now find ourselves.

At the same time we should like to thank the Foundation which, in the esteemed name of Alfred Nobel, has without protest accepted—indeed been kind enough to approve our presence here today, thereby bestowing upon us something which makes our personal situation—the one to which I have just referred—rather less disagreeable than I have perhaps pretended it to be.

Alexandre Soljenitsyne

Ваше королевское Величество! Дамы и господа!

Много нобелевских лауреатов выступало перед Вами в этом зале, но, наверно, ни с кем не бывало Шведской Академии и Нобелевскому Фонду столько хлопот, сколько со мной. По крайней мере один раз я уже здесь был, хотя и не воплоти; и один раз досточтимый Карл Гиров уже собирался ко мне; и вот, наконец, я приехал не в свою очередь занимать лишний стул. Четырем годам надо было пройти, чтобы дать мне слово на три минуты, а секретарь Академии вынужден обращаться всё к тому же писателю вот уже с третьей речью.

И потому я должен просить извинения, что так много забот доставил всем вам и особо благодарить за ту церемонию 1970 года, когда ваш король и вы все тепло приветствовали здесь пустое кресло.

Но согласитесь, что и для лауреата это тоже не так просто: четыре года возить с собой трехминутную речь. Когда я собирался ехать к вам в 70-м, не хватало никакого объема в груди, никаких листов бумаги для того, чтобы высказаться на первой вольной трибуне моей жизни. Для писателя подневольной страны первая же трибуна и первая речь есть речь обо всём на свете, о всех болях своей страны, — и при этом простительно забыть цель церемонии, состав собравшихся и влить горечь в стаканы торжества. Но с того года, не поехав сюда, я научился и у себя в стране говорить открыто почти всё, что я думаю. А изгнаньем оказавшись на Западе, тем более я приобрел эту неоттеснённую возможность говорить сколько угодно, где угодно, чем здесь и не дорожат. И нет мне уже необходимости перегружать это короткое слово.

Нахожу однако и особое преимущество в том, чтобы ответить на присуждение Нобелевской премии лишь через 4 года. Например, за 4 года можно испытать, какую роль уже сыграла эта премия в твоей жизни. В моей — очень большую. Она помогла мне не быть задавленному в жестоких преследованиях. Она помогла моему голосу быть услышанному там, где моих предшественников не слышали десятилетиями. Она помогла произвести вовне меня такое, чего б я не осилил без нее.

Со мной Шведская Академия совершила одно из исключений, довольно редких: присудила мне премию в среднем возрасте, а по моей открытой литературной деятельности даже во младенческом — всего на 8-м году ее. Для Академии тут крылся большой риск: ведь была опубликована лишь малая часть написанных мною книг.

А может быть лучшая задача всякой литературной и научной премии именно — содействовать движению на самом пути.

И я приношу Шведской Академии мою сердечную благодарность за то, что своим выбором 1970 года чрезвычайно поддержала мою писательскую работу. Осмелюсь поблагодарить ее и от той обширной неказённой России, которой запрещено выражать себя вслух, которую преследуют и за написание книг и даже за чтение их. Академия выслушала много упреков за это свое решение — будто такая премия служила политическим интересам. Но то выкрикивали хриплые глотки, которые никаких других интересов и не знают.

Мы же с вами знаем, что работа художника не укладывается в убогой политической плоскости, как и вся наша жизнь в ней не лежит и как не держать бы нам в ней наше общественное сознание.

Translation
Your Majesty, Your Royal Highnesses, Ladies and Gentlemen,
Many Nobel Prize laureates have appeared before you in this hall, but the

Swedish Academy and the Nobel Foundation have probably never had as much bother with anyone as they have had with me. On at least one occasion I have already been here, although not in the flesh; once the honorable Karl Ragnar Gierow was already on his way to meet me; and now, at last, I have arrived out of turn to occupy an extra seat. Four years had to pass to give me the floor for three minutes, and the secretary of the Academy is being forced now to address the third speech to the same writer.

I must ask your forgiveness, therefore, for having caused all of you so much trouble, and thank you especially for the ceremony in 1970, when your king and all of you welcomed here an empty chair.

But you will agree that it has not been so simple for the prizewinner, either: carrying his three-minute speech around with him for four years. When I was preparing to come to you in 1970 no room in my breast, no amount of paper was sufficient to let me speak my mind on the first free tribune of my life. For a writer from a land without liberty his first tribune and his first speech is a speech about everything in the world, about all the torments of his country,—and it is pardonable if he forgets the object of the ceremony, the persons assembled there and fills the goblets of joy with his bitterness. But since that year when I was unable to come here, I have learned to express openly practically all my thoughts in my own contry as well. So that finding myself expatriated to the West, I have acquired all the better this unhindered possibility of saying as much as I want and where I want, which is something not always appreciated here. I needn't, therefore further burden down this short address.

However, I find a special advantage in not responding to the award of the Nobel Prize until four years later. For example, in four years it is possible to experience the role this prize has already played in your life. In my life it has been a very large one. It has prevented me from being crushed in the severe persecutions to which I have been subjected. It has helped my voice to be heard in places where my predecessors have not been heard for decades. It has helped me to express things that would have otherwise been impossible.

In my case, the Swedish Academy have made an exception, and a rather rare one, awarding me the prize when I am middleaged and my open literary activity is a mere child of some eight years. For the Academy there was a great hidden risk in doing so: after all, only a small part of the books I had written had been published.

But perhaps the finest task of any literary or scientific prize lies precisely in helping to clear the road ahead.

And I would like to express my heartfelt gratitude to the members of the Swedish Academy for the enormous support their choice in 1970 has given my works as a writer. I venture to thank them on behalf of that vast unofficial Russia which is prohibited from expressing itself aloud, which is persecuted both for writing books and even for reading them. The Academy have heard for this decision of theirs many reproaches implying that such a prize has served political interests. But these are the shouts of raucous loudmouths who know of no other interests.

We all know that an artist's work cannot be contained within the wretched dimension of politics. For this dimension cannot hold the whole of our life and we must not restrain our social consciousness within in its bounds.

George E. Palade
Your Majesty, Your Royal Highnesses, Ladies and Gentlemen,

In the large domain of life sciences, Cell Biology is a field reborn. The last period in which it flourished was at the end of the last century, when light microscopes were brought up to the limit of their power of resolution. That development increased our information, but left a large and deep gap between the world of structures—the domain of the anatomists, histologists and pathologists—and the world of molecules—the province of the chemists and biochemists.

With the rebirth that occurred in our time, the situation was significantly changed. The gap was bridged mainly with the help of two major techniques: electron microscopy and cell fractionation. These two techniques led to many new findings and, more importantly, to a satisfactory correlation of structure and function at the subcellular level of biological organization. In the process, most of the boundaries that used to separate morphologists from physiologists and biochemists have been removed: these scientists can now converse and understand each other over the few lingering barriers.

Cell Biology, reborn, has created a new meeting ground in basic life sciences for it showed that the unity of organization of living matter extends well beyond the level of molecules—that was already known—to the level of macromolecular assemblies, cell organs and cells. A remarkable uniformity of organization applies for all living beings at the subcellular level—as if formulae tested very early in evolution for every cell organ—from ribosomes to the cell membrane—have been vertically transmitted for eons with only minor adjustments, attesting in this way to one of the main characteristics of living forms—their never interrupted continuity from their inception to this very day.

We finally understand in general terms how a cell is organized, how its specialized organs function in a well integrated manner to insure its survival and replication. This new knowledge has already begun to be put to good use in understanding abnormal cell function. Many of the major medical problems of our day are degenerative diseases which can be traced to malfunctions in the regulatory mechanisms of cellular activities. Cell Biology finally makes possible a century old dream: that of analysis of diseases, at the cellular level —the first step towards their final control.

We never truly touch or see these wonderful tiny devices that keep every cell and every being alive—since they are far beyond what our senses can perceive unaided. But for us they are alive in our minds, close to our hearts, very much parts of the real world, just like the galaxies with their neutron stars and their pulsars are at the other end of the spectrum of dimensions of matter for our colleagues, the radioastronomers.

For a scientist, it is a unique experience to live through a period in which his field of endeavour comes to bloom—to be witness to those rare moments when the dawn of understanding finally descends upon what appeared to be confusion only a while ago—to listen to the sound of darkness crumbling.

Claude, de Duve and I have lived through such a period and have already enjoyed the intimate rewards that are part of this rare experience. Now, when we are singled out for this highest of all scientific prizes, we feel that the new distinction acknowledges beyond us, beyond our personal achievements, the rebirth of our field of knowledge and the vistas it has opened for the medicine of tomorrow. We accept the distinction with the deepest gratitude

— for the workings of fate—which we do not control—and which made our achievements possible,

— for the great institutions that have supported our work,

— for our many devoted, skilled, and less recognized coworkers without whom our advances would have been less impressive,

— and, finally, for the noble institutions of your Swedish Kingdom which have nurtured Alfred Nobel's dream and made out of it a wonderful means to affirm that—at their best—human minds belong to mankind, above nations and above any frontier.

Paul J. Flory

Your Majesty, Your Royal Highnesses, Ladies and Gentlemen,

Acknowledgment of the privilege of receiving the Nobel Prize in words commensurate with the distinction it conveys oxertaxes the resources of language. It must suffice to say that I am profoundly grateful to the Royal Swedish Academy of Sciences for their gracious decision in my favor. I take genuine pleasure in being afforded the opportunity to express my highest thanks to them and to the Nobel Foundation for this, the ultimate prize in science.

Perhaps I may be permitted to reflect briefly on Alfred Nobel the man vis-à-vis the prizes that bear his name. Lest it seem presumptuous of me to comment on that great but little appreciated man, may I remind you that I too am a chemist. In fact, my researches have touched upon one of the principal ingredients of his epochal discoveries and inventions. I refer to nitrocellulose. To be sure, our interests in this substance differed: his of a scope leading to developments warranting world-wide fame, mine obscure by comparison. Be this as it may, nitrocellulose is a duly respected member of the family of macromolecules, and I take pride in laying claim to scientific kinship to Alfred Nobel through an interest in this substance, however tenuous the connection may be.

The Nobel Prizes have gained universal recognition as pre-eminent symbols of the importance and significance of intellectual achievement. They are much better known than the man who founded them. Yet, that wise but modest man, whose extraordinary vision and perception were obscured by a self-effacing manner, would not be offended, I believe, by the contrast between his own fame in the world of 1974 and that of his prizes. He founded them from the purest of motives, not as a means of memorializing himself. His will does not suggest, much less require, that the prizes bear his name; this was a decision of his executors, a well reasoned one to be sure. Alfred Nobel appears to have been motivated by the conviction that science and learning should be encouraged and more widely appreciated.

And so, on this spendid occasion, I am persuaded to pay tribute to Alfred Nobel, inventive genius, humanitarian and scholar, who had both the foresight and the magnanimity to commit his fortune for the encouragement of future generations to devote themselves to the cause of Peace, to the cultivation of science and to the enrichment of literature, endeavors which the burdens of his other responsibilities allowed him far too little time to pursue and enjoy. To this I should like to add a word in tribute to the executors of his estate and to the Nobel Foundation for implementing Alfred Nobel's intentions and desires with such remarkable success.

Again, my best thanks!

Antony Hewish
Your Majesty, Your Royal Highnesses, Ladies and Gentlemen,

The world of man lies midway in scale between the inner space of atoms and particles, and the outer space of stars and galaxies. The exploration of both these regions stretches our imagination to its limits.

In deciding to honour the field of Astrophysics the Nobel Foundation, and the Royal Academy of Sciences, have given great encouragement and delight to all astronomers who share with us this proud moment. Sir Martin Ryle and I know this well from the countless messages that we have received from all over the world.

There is, I think, some special benefit for mankind in the realm of astrophysics. It is impossible to witness the interplay of galaxies without a sense of wonder, and looking back at Earth we see it in its true perspective, a planet of great beauty, an undivided sphere. Let us try and keep this image always in our view.

F. A. von Hayek
Your Majesty, Your Royal Highnesses, Ladies and Gentlemen,

Now that the Nobel Memorial Prize for economic science has been created, one can only be profoundly grateful for having been selected as one of its joint recipients, and the economists certainly have every reason for being grateful to the Swedish Riksbank for regarding their subject as worthy of this high honour.

Yet I must confess that if I had been consulted whether to establish a Nobel Prize in economics, I should have decidedly advised against it.

One reason was that I feared that such a prize, as I believe is true of the activities of some of the great scientific foundations, would tend to accentuate the swings of scientific fashion.

This apprehension the selection committee has brilliantly refuted by awarding the prize to one whose views are as unfashionable as mine are.

I do not yet feel equally reassured concerning my second cause of apprehension.

It is that the Nobel Prize confers on an individual an authority which in economics no man ought to possess.

This does not matter in the natural sciences. Here the influence exercised by an individual is chiefly an influence on his fellow experts; and they will soon cut him down to seize if he exceeds his competence.

But the influence of the economist that mainly matters is an influence over laymen: politicians, journalists, civil servants and the public generally.

There is no reason why a man who has made a distinctive contribution to economic science should be omnicompetent on all problems of society—as the press tends to treat him till in the end he may himself be persuaded to believe.

One is even made to feel it a public duty to pronounce on problems to which one may not have devoted special attention.

I am not sure that it is desirable to strengthen the influence of a few individual economists by such a ceremonial and eye-catching recognition of achievements, perhaps of the distant past.

I am therefore almost inclined to suggest that you require from your laureates an oath of humility, a sort of hippocratic oath, never to exceed in public pronouncements the limits of their competence.

Or you ought at least, on confering the prize, remind the recipient of the sage counsel of one of the great men in our subject, Alfred Marshall, who wrote:

"Students of social science, must fear popular approval: Evil is with them when all men speak well of them".

Plus tard, au cours de la soirée, les organisations *d'étudiants de Stockholm* vinrent présenter leur hommage aux lauréats. Le président de l'Association Centrale des Étudiants de Stockholm, M. Jan Martin, leur adressa ces paroles: Your Majesty, Your Royal Highnesses, Nobel Prize Winners,

Today, if only for a moment, we, the students of Stockholm, represent the youth of the world.

Today is a day when we have been given the opportunity and the privilege of honouring the foremost representatives of science and art.

You have today been rewarded for contributions which have been and will continue to be of great importance for the future of mankind.

This is the day in your life when you stand before the world; your devotion and ambition to carry on your quest, despite disappointments and set-backs, are taken as models for mankind to follow.

The possibilities for the future we see in your work, give us courage to meet the future.

The goals that we in our optimism try to reach may at times seem utopian. The progress of time cannot be affected, but it is we who give time its substance. Therefore we must not allow the vastness of time to prevent us from seeking the truth. We will not find the perfect world we seek, but for that reason we must not give up hope of creating a better world.

At the same time as we constantly look forward, we must not forget our history, not to pass judgement, but to learn for the future.

We must always defend the fundamental values of progress—freedom of thought and speech. You have through your untiring search for the truth shown that these values are worth defending.

Honoured Nobel Prize Winners,

On behalf of the youth of the world, we, the students of Stockholm thank you for your contributions and your stimulating example and convey our most cordial and sincere congratulations.

Christian de Duve

Your Majesty, Your Royal Highnesses, Ladies and Gentlemen, Fellow Students,

I hope I may still be allowed to use the term *fellow* students. For we know that once we stop learning and call ourselves learned, we become useless members of the scientific society. On behalf of my fellow Nobel laureates and on my own, thank you for your kind words, and for your beautiful songs.

To me personally, they have been a reminder of my long association with Sweden and Swedish students. It started 35 years ago, when I attended a summer course at the University of Lund. I followed lectures on the history, geography, economy and political organization of Sweden. And I received a book called *Ett år med Familjen Biörck* to learn Swedish.

Efter tre veckor talade jag svenska flytande och reste till Stockholm. Där kommer jag ihåg ett skräckinjagande möte med en ung man som tog emot mig i ett tjänsterum som såg ut som det tillhörde minst ett statsråd. Den unge mannen var ordförande i medicinska föreningen. Jag skall inte säga hans namn, eftersom han numera är en framstående professor och ikväll finns här i Blå Hallen.

Sedan bröt kriget ut, och under några år levde jag i mörker med minnet av Sveriges sjöar, träd och biåa himmel. Det dröjde till 1946 innan jag kunde återvända och få tillbringa två oförglömliga år tillsammans med professor Hugo Theorell i hans laboratorium.

Vintern gick mot sitt slut när jag kom till Sverige, och utan att riktigt förstå det hela deltog jag i alla riter och hyllningar till vår och sommar; eldarna på Valborgsmäss, Midsommaraftonens dans till gryningen, solnedgången i skärgården när vattnet skimrade i alla regnbågens färger.

Sedan blev dagarna allt kortare, nätterna syntes utan slut, dagsljuset blev matt och grått. Vännerna omkring mig tycktes också med ens matta och gråa. Själv kände jag mig lite apatisk och nedstämd. Så en dag, just vid den här tiden på året, uppenbarade sig i laboratoriets mörker en otroligt vacker flicka, klädd i ett spökes vita dräkt, med långt gyllene hår och på huvudet bar hon en krona med brinnande ljus. Hon hette Brita och henne träffade jag varje dag. Men den kvällen var hon Lucia — en fe och gudinna. Hon lärde mig hur viktigt ljuset var: kunskapens ljus, fredens ljus, frihetens ljus, kärlekens ljus och det som har att göra med ömsesidig förståelse.

Jag vill gärna tro att just detta är budskapet från Ert land och från dessa storartade högtider. Tack.

English version of Swedish part

After three weeks, I spoke Swedish fluently and came to Stockholm, where I remember being admitted in the awesome presence of a young man, who was sitting in an office resembling that of a Minister of State. He was the President of the Medical Students Association. I will not name him, since he is now a famous professor and in this banquet hall to night.

Then the war broke out, and for a number of years I lived in darkness, with the memory of the lakes, the trees and the skies of Sweden, until I returned in 1946 to spend two unforgettable years in the laboratory of Hugo Theorell.

I arrived at the end of the winter and joined, without quite understanding, in the rites of spring and of summer: lighting fires and waiting for the sun to rise on *Valborgsmässoafton;* dancing all night on *Midsommarafton;* watching the slow fractional distillation of all the colours of the spectrum as the sun came down over the shimmering waters in the Skärgård. Later the days became shorter, the nights interminable, the light grey and dim. Like all my friends around me, I felt a little lethargic and depressed, until one day at just about this time of the year, in the darkness of the laboratory, I saw an extraordinary apparition: an unbelievably beautiful girl, in a ghostly white gown, with long golden hair, and on her head a crown of glowing candles. Her name was Brita and I saw her everyday. But that night she was Lucia, a magician and a goddess. And she told me the importance of light: The light of knowledge, the light of peace, the light of freedom, the light of love and of mutual understanding.

This, I believe, is the message of your country and of these marvellous celebrations. Thank you.

REMISE DU PRIX ET BANQUET A OSLO

Le Prix Nobel de la Paix pour 1974 fut décerné à M. Eisaku Sato et à M. Seán Mac Bride. La distribution de prix fut célébrée le 10 décembre par une séance solennelle dans l'Aula de l'Université d'Oslo. Sa Majesté le Roi, le Prince Royal Harald et la Princesse Royale Sonje honoraient la cérémonie de leur présence. Aussi de nombreux représentants du Gouvernement, dont Son Excellence M. Trygve Bratteli, Premier Ministre, les Chefs de Mission et d'autres membres du corps diplomatique honoraient la cérémonie de leur présence. La Fondation Nobel était représentée par M. Arne Fredga. Un orchestre dirigé par M. Öivind Bergh ayant ouvert la cérémonie par « Intrata » de Johan Halvorsen, la présidente du Comité Nobel, Mme Aase Lionæs, a fait le discours suivant en l'honneur des lauréats 1974 :

Deres Majestet, Deres Kongelige Høyheter, Deres Eksellenser, Mine Herrer og Damer,

Noen år før Alfred Nobel skrev sitt testamente bemerket han i et brev til Bertha von Suttner at hans dynamittfabrikker ville kunne gjøre slutt på krigene atskillig raskere enn fredskongressene noensinne ville klare det.

"Den dag da to hærstyrker kan tilintetgjøre hverandre i løpet av et sekund, er det håp om at alle siviliserte nasjoner vil demobilisere sine styrker og avholde seg fra å gå til krig." Det var en slags total gjengjeldelse Alfred Nobel forutså allerede i midten av 1890-årene.

Etter at den første atombombe var blitt prøvet i New Mexico i juli 1945, mente de som hadde gjennomført eksperimentet at verden stod overfor en ny mulighet til å få slutt på alle kriger. Med et slikt våpen i hendene hadde menneskeheten nådd til en terskel. Ble den overskredet, ville både angriper og forsvarer være dømt til undergang.

Den totale utslettelse ble alternativet til fred. Midt i den grusomme frykt, som også fikk kjernefysikerne til å mane verden til fornuft, spirte et håp om at det nå var mulighet for avvæpning og fred.

Det gikk som det måtte gå i en verden splittet av indre motsetninger, verdensfreden ble gjort avhengig av at en uhyggelig terrorbalanse ble opprettet mellom øst og vest.

Selv på randen av undergangen lot krigene seg ikke stanse. Det gamle mønstret ble opprettholdt, også i det vi feilaktig har kalt etterkrigstiden. Liv utslettes, verdier ødes, sinn formørkes og frykten næres i alle verdensdeler. Kanskje har vi etterhvert lært noe mer om *årsakene* til krig og ufred, kanskje er vi etterhvert blitt mer oppmerksomme på vårt medansvar også for tragedier som utspiller seg fjernt fra våre egne grenser. Det er en slags trøst å tro det.

Men vi er ikke kommet særlig meget lengere når det gjelder tiltak for å fjerne disse årsakene, trass i alle anstrengelser.

På en dag som denne — ved utdelingen av Nobels fredspris — kan det likevel være grunn til å nevne positive trekk i utviklingen. I de siste år er det kommet i stand både multilaterale og bilaterale forhandlinger med sikte på å fremme avspenning og praktisk samarbeid. Vi opplever en periode der dialogen stort sett har erstattet konfrontasjon og isolasjon. For bare noen få år siden ville et slikt forhandlingsmønster som vi nå skimter konturene av, vært ganske utopisk. En hel verden knytter håp og forventninger til denne meningsutveksling.

Jeg ser et lyspunkt i det faktum at en sterk og levende opinion over hele verden vender seg mot vold og maktmisbruk. Det er tale om en bred internasjonal stemningsbølge. Kall det ikke krigstretthet, for ofte er det kvinner og menn som ikke selv har opplevd krig som bærer denne bølgen frem. Kall det isteden en ekte fredstro. Den opinion jeg tenker på, begrenser ikke sin kamp til å gjelde krigen alene. I stor grad rettes oppmerksomheten mot sosial, politisk og økonomisk undertrykkelse. Og det er riktig. Kampen mot urett er blitt innsats for fred.

Den urett som begås mot andre, begås også mot hver enkelt av oss, som medmennesker. En av vår tids lysbærere i kampen for menneskerettighetene, nobelprisvinneren Aleksander Solsjenitsyn har sagt at: Oppgaven må være å bortvise fra menneskeheten selve den idé at noen har tillatelse til å bruke makt mot rettferdigheten, retten, og mot gjensidige avtaler.

Aldri har vel denne tanke blitt mer forstått og godtatt i bredere kretser rundt om i verden enn nettopp i vår tid. Det er løfterikt — i en verden full av uhyggelige fremtidsperspektiver. Ingen statsmann og intet regime vil ustraffet kunne handle uten hensyn til denne opinion.

Det norske Stortings Nobelkomite er pålagt det vanskelige verv å peke ut personer eller institusjoner som har gjort seg fortjent til årets fredspris.

Det ville være usannsynlig at komiteens avgjørelse ikke skulle vekke debatt. Slik har det vært siden den første pris ble utdelt for over 70 år siden. Det er et vitnesbyrd om hvor vanskeli fredsbegrepet er å definere. Nobelkomiteen har ved sine tildelinger funnet frem til vinnere som har gjort en innsats på høyst ulike felter. Det er politikere ved forhandlingsbordet, forsvarere av menneskerettighetene, folkerettseksperter, opprøreren, humanisten, idealisten, pragmatikeren, drømmeren. Det er alle personligheter det har stått strid om.

Prisvinnere i år kommer begge fra land som aldri tidligere har hatt vinnere av Nobels fredspris. Ja, Eisaku Sato er samtidig den første asiat som har mottatt prisen. Han står idag som representant for et folk som er det eneste som har opplevd atomkrigens ufattelige redsler. De uhyggelige erfaringer har satt dype spor i det japanske folk. Men også for oss andre er navn som Hiroshima og Nagasaki blitt stående som symboler på noe vi alle må sette kreftene inn for å forhindre for all fremtid.

Seán Mac Bride kommer fra et land som gjennom mange år har vært skueplassen for ulykkelig, bitter strid. Hans erfaringer har virket som en spore for ham i hans mangesidige innsats i mellomfolkelig arbeid.

Hver for seg representerer de to fredsprisvinnere forskjellige sider ved fredsarbeidet. Gjennom pragmatisk innsats har de ved hjelp av politikkens og forhandlingenes vanskelige kunst søkt å fremme sine idealer. De mål de har nådd, må stadig erobres på nytt fordi den fred og den rettferd verden trenger stadig er truet.

Eisaku Sato var Japans statsminister lenger enn noen før ham, i nesten åtte år, fra november 1964 til juni 1972. Stillingen som regjeringssjef er utsatt i alle demokratier, og Sato har ofte måttet tåle skarp kritikk.

Ved sin tiltreden som statsminister sa Sato at han ville gå inn for å sikre Japan en innflytelse i internasjonal politikk som stod i forhold til landets stilling som økonomisk stormakt. I andre land hadde man all grunn til å følge med i hvordan dette program skulle innfries. Ville Japan i sin mer aktive utenrikspolitikk søke tilbake til en nasjonalistisk preget linje? Det var mange som fryktet det. Øket selvfølelse som følge av økonomisk styrke, nasjonale prestisjehensyn og innenrikspolitiske hensyn kunne ha dominert i Japan som det har gjort i andre stormakter.

Det ble tidlig klart at Japan fulgte en utenrikspolitisk kurs som tok sikte på å skape vennskap til andre land.

For mange land var minnene om det aggressive og militariske Japan levende etter krigen. Ikke minst i de land som hadde gjennomlevd den japanske okkupasjon, var mistilliten stor. Med stor forventning fulgte verden med i det forsoningsarbeid Japan gikk inn for.

Landets utenrikspolitiske og sikkerhetspolitiske utgangspunkt var preget av de forpliktelser landet var pålagt etter den annen verdenskrig. Den forfatning Japan fikk i 1947 hadde uttrykkelig slått fast at det japanske folk fraskrev seg rettigheter som tidligere ble betraktet som vesentlige for et selvstendig folk. "Krig og trusel om, eller bruk av makt oppgis som middel til å avgjøre stridigheter med andre nasjoner." Dette er en enestående bestemmelse i et lands forfatning. Hovedprinsippene var fastlagt av de amerikanske okkupasjonsmyndigheter og ble sterkt preget av det. I Japan var militarismen knust i 1945 og sterke pasifistiske stemninger gjorde seg gjeldende i folket.

Som regjeringssjef minte Sato ofte om at Grunnlovens antikrigsbestemmelse måtte tjene som grunnlag for landets politikk. Han understreket tre prinsipper som hans regjering ville bygge på når det gjaldt de kjernefysiske våpen: "Aldri å produsere slike våpen, aldri å eie dem — og heller aldri å bringe dem inn i Japan."

Det japanske folk har stått bak denne Satos fredslinje og har reagert meget sterkt mot ethvert tegn til at utviklingen skulle ta en annen retning. Man har stundom talt om at det japanske folk har utviklet en allergi mot kjernefysiske våpen. En slik allergi er et sunnhetstegn, og andre land kunne ha meget å lære av det.

Når Eisaku Sato som statsminister understreket — ved mange anledninger — at det bare var med fredelige midler at Japan ville fremme sine mål — ga han utvilsomt uttrykk for den helt dominerende oppfatning i sitt folk.

Kort tid etter at Sato hadde overtatt som statsminister gikk han inn for å bedre forholdet til Sør-Korea. En vennskapsavtale ble undertegnet mellom de to land og ratifisert høsten 1965. Det ble også straks opprettet diplomatisk forbindelse mellom Sør-Korea og Japan.

Denne avtale ble innledningen til et planmessig arbeid for å bedre forholdet mellom Japan og en rekke andre stater i Stillehavsområdet. Høsten 1967 reiste Sato på en omfattende tur, som brakte ham bl. a. til Burma, Malaysia, Singapore, Thailand, Laos, Indonesia, Australia, New Zealand, Filippinene og Sør-Vietnam. Hensikten var å styrke de vennskapelige forbindelser, øke samhandelen og få istand utvidede konsultasjoner med sikte på politisk samarbeid og mer aktiv kulturutveksling. Det er en utbredt oppfatning at veien til økt forståelse mellom nasjonene nettopp går gjennom økt handelssamkvem. Kan man begynne på dette praktiske felt, finne frem til felles interesser, kan det bane veien til utvidet kontakt også på andre områder. Denne problemstilling har som kjent spilt en stor rolle i forholdet mellom øst og vest i de senere år. I Asia søkte Japan under Satos ledelse å styrke handelsforbindelsene, øke hjelpen til utviklingslandene og oppmuntre til økt regionalt samarbeid. Japan tok initiativet til en ministerkonferanse for økonomisk utvikling av Sør-Øst Asia og var meget aktiv for å sikre at Den Asiatiske Utviklingsbank skulle bli virkeliggjort. Japan har vært blant de største bidragsytere til banken, ut fra det syn at landet har et særlig ansvar for at freden kan bli styrket i området. En viktig forutsetning for dette var etter Satos mening at landene ble bedre istand til å utnytte sine materielle og kulturelle ressurser.

Utgangspunktet for den japanske vennskapspolitikk var vanskelig bl. a. fordi Japans nære allianseforhold med USA ble kritisert, særlig under Vietnamkrigen. Japan deltok ikke i krigføringen i Vietnam. Eisaku Sato henstilte til partene i striden å komme sammen, uten vilkår av noe slag, for å drøfte våpenhvile og fred. Krigen kunne ikke løse de politiske problemer sa Sato i sin tale i den japanske nasjonalforsamling i juli 1965. Et forsøk fra den japanske regjerings side på å sondere mulighetene for et fredsinitiativ førte ikke frem våren 1966.

Som regjeringssjef ble det Satos oppgave å balansere de forskjellige hensyn. Han holdt fast ved avtalen med USA — men han krevde også større selvstendighet. Særlig viktig for det japanske folk var det å komme til enighet med USA om tilbakelevering av de øygrupper USA hadde holdt okkupert siden den annen verdenskrig. Etter fem års kontinuerlig arbeid lyktes det Sato å få i stand en ordning som igjen ga Japan suverenitet over Okinawa og Ogasawara-øyene. Resultatet bidro til å fjerne et alvorlig friksjonsmoment i forholdet mellom de to land. Men det tjente også til å styrke stabiliteten i hele området og til å overbevise det japanske folk om at de utenrikspolitiske mål best kunne nås ved forhandlinger, ikke gjennom aggressive handlinger og trusler. For Japan var det av særlig betydning at avtalen sikret at det ikke skulle være kjernefysiske våpen på de amerikanske basene på Okinawa. Den gang avtalen ble inngått i 1951 var det som et ledd i Japans ønske om å få sitt territorium trygget. Både denne sikkerhetsavtale og selve fredsavtalen forutsatte at Japan skulle ha rett til selvforsvar og rett til å delta i kollektive sikkerhetssystemer i henhold til FN-pakten. På dette grunnlag bygger det japanske forsvar. Det er alminnelig erkjent at Japan i de år som er gått har vist til-

bakeholdenhet på dette felt. Ingen stormakt har vist tilsvarende modera-
sjon, ja mange små land har et forsvar som er sterkere enn det japanske.
Ingen enkelt politiker i Japan skal ha æren for dette. Motstanden i det japanske folk mot enhver form for militaristisk renessanse er så sterk at noen
annen politikk ikke ville ha vært mulig.

Også i forholdet til Sovjetunionen ble det i Satos tid gjort positive fremskritt. Noen fredsavtale med russerne kom ikke i stand, fordi russerne in-
sisterte på retten til øyene i Nord-Kurilene. Dette har ingen japansk regjering
kunnet godkjenne. Men i Satos tid ble det utenrikspolitiske og handelspolitiske
samarbeid ført videre, ikke minst etter at de to lands utenriksministre hadde
avlagt flere besøk hos hverandre.

I Satos tid ble det ikke opptatt diplomatiske forbindelser mellom folkerepublikken China og Japan. Den japanske regjering fulgte — i likhet med mange
andre land — en politikk som innebar anerkjennelse av Taiwan. Det hindret
ikke at det likevel ble etablert flere viktige kontakter mellom Tokyo og
Peking. I forbindelse med Bandung-konferansen i april 1965 hadde statsminister Satos spesielle utsending en samtale med statsminister Chou En-lai og
forsikret om japanernes ønske om nærmere kontakt med folkerepublikken.
Trass i politiske vansker økte samhandelen mellom de to land og verden la
bl. a. merke til at japanske journalister fikk tillatelse til å arbeide i Peking
under kulturrevolusjonen. Journalister fra de fleste andre land måtte forlate
folkerepublikken. Ved en rekke anledninger talte Sato om nødvendigheten av
å holde døren åpen mot Peking. Så lenge Japan imidlertid holdt fast ved sin
anerkjennelse av regimet i Taiwan var det umulig å få i stand diplomatiske
forbindelser med Peking. Det fikk imidlertid betydning for den internasjonale
atmosfære at forholdet mellom de to stater hele tiden var preget av modera-
sjon.

I flere konflikter i Asia, spesielt striden mellom India og Pakistan og kon-
flikten mellom Malaysia og Indonesia søkte Sato personlig å få partene til å
inngå forlik. At Japan under Satos regjeringstid betalte betydelige erstat-
ninger til land som hadde lidt under den japanske okkupasjon bidro vesentlig
til å bedre forholdene til omverdenen. Gamle motsetninger ble dempet, og
nye interessefellesskap ble skapt. Den gode naboskapspolitikk som Sato stod
som leder for, ble godt mottatt i store deler av Asia. At japanernes økono-
miske innflytelse skapte strid og møtte motstand, endrer ikke dette hoved-
inntrykk.

Nobelkomiteen har ved å gi fredsprisen for 1974 til Eisaku Sato villet fremheve den viktige rolle det japanske folk har spilt for å fremme et vennskape-
lig samarbeid med andre nasjoner. Japans holdning har bidratt til å styrke
freden i Øst-Asia og til å legge grunnen for økonomisk vekst og fremgang for
mange land. Ved å gå imot tendensene til en nasjonalistisk preget politikk i
Japan etter krigen, ved stadig å fremheve nødvendigheten av internasjonalt
samarbeid og forståelse, ved å opptre som mekler og en som kunne utjevne
motsetninger, ytet Sato en innsats for freden.

Nobelkomiteen har lagt stor vekt på de erklæringer som Eisaku Sato har
avgitt om å holde fast ved sin doktrine at Japan ikke skal eie, fremstille eller

bringe kjernefysiske våpen inn i landet. I en tid med voksende risiko for at flere stater skaffer seg slike våpen, er det viktig at Japan under Satos ledelse, undertegnet avtalen om ikke-spredning av kjernefysiske våpen i februar 1970.

Sato sa den gang at det var i pakt med Japans nasjonale mål å hindre at slike våpen ble gitt til flere stater. Målet var å dempe den internasjonale spenning, opprette vennskapelige forbindelser med alle land og bidra til å få istand internasjonale ordninger som tjente fredens sak. Satos håp var at ikke-spredningsavtalen måtte bli fulgt opp med effektive tiltak som førte til en reduksjon av antall atomvåpen i verden. Han la vekt på at avtalen også måtte bli innledningen til praktiske fremskritt når det gjaldt den alminnelige ned-rustning.

Ikke-spredningsavtalen er ennå ikke blitt ratifisert av Japan, skjønt den regjering som fulgte etter Sato, senest i FN's hovedforsamling i år bekreftet at den ville arbeide for dette mål. Ansvaret for den fremtidige avgjørelse påligger ingen enkelt person. Men jeg vil understreke at det japanske folks standpunkt kan bli avgjørende for den fremtidige utvikling i Asia. Det er Nobelkomiteens håp at årets tildeling vil bli oppfattet som en støtte til alle som arbeider for at ikke-spredningsavtalen skal få bredest mulig oppslutning.

Alle fredselskende krefter i verden håper at den videre utvikling i Asia må kunne foregå uten frykt for krig og maktbruk. Måtte Stillehavets muligheter til å bli et virkelig fredens hav bli realisert.

Japans rolle i denne utvikling er av avgjørende betydning.

Årets andre fredsprisvinner er iren Seán Mac Bride som ble født i Paris den 26. januar 1904. Som ganske ung opplevde han den irske uavhengighetskamp, med all dens brutalitet. Erfaringene måtte komme til å sette sitt sterke preg på ham — på mange måter. Etter å ha virket som journalist i noen år, utdannet han seg som advokat i 1937. På denne måten ble han bedre i stand til å arbeide for forfulgte menneskers rettsvern. Etter den annen verdenskrig kom han inn i det irske parlament, der han satt fra 1947 til 1958. Fra 1948 til 1951 var han Irlands utenriksminister. Det var på et tidspunkt da Europarådet arbeidet med å få i stand den europeiske menneskerettighetskonvensjon. Siktemålet for dette arbeid var å få vedtatt en konvensjon der menneskerettighetene for første gang blir gitt en alminnelig internasjonal beskyttelse. Det var en stor dag i europeisk historie, da konvensjonen kunne undertegnes av medlemslandenes utenriksministre i Roma den 4. november 1950. Mac Bride spilte en fremtredende rolle i tilblivelsen av denne konvensjon. Fra nå av skulle han komme til å vie hele sitt liv til arbeidet for større respekt for menneskerettighetene, ikke bare i Vest-Europa, men i hele verden. Gjennom taler og artikler mante han myndighetene i alle land til å inngå og etterleve internasjonale avtaler som garanterte individenes rettigheter.

I 1961 ble han formann i det internasjonale styre i Amnesty International og i en rekke år var han denne organisasjons uredde og aktive leder. Han besøkte mange land for å tale de forfulgte menneskers sak, for å kjempe mot tortur og for å oppfordre til større humanitet og nestekjærlighet. Han var virksom i Asia, Afrika, Europa og Amerika. Den viktigste ressurs han hadde å sette inn i denne kampen var sin egen arbeidskraft og oppslutningen fra utallige frivillige hjelpere i mange land. Han mobiliserte verdens samvittighet i kampen mot urett. Den organisasjon han stod i spissen for, vokste gradvis frem til større anerkjennelse og innflytelse. Utrettelig tok han fatt på stadig nye arbeidsoppgaver. Mac Bride vet selv at det kan komme til å ta lang tid å skape den mentalitetsendring som til syvende og sist er den eneste sikre garanti mot vilkårlige overgrep og brutalitet. Men han vet også at det er utallige mennesker rundt om på kloden som føler det som en samvittighetssak å være med i denne strid.

Mac Bride har arbeidet både på det prinsipielle, ideologiske plan og på det praktiske område. Han har vært en organisasjonsleder og feltarbeider i en og samme person. I arbeidet for å styrke og verne menneskerettighetene inntar han en enestående posisjon. Som generalsekretær for Den internasjonale juristkommisjon fra 1963 til 1970 var han også meget aktiv.

Denne kommisjon ble opprettet i Vest-Berlin i 1952 og hadde opprinnelig til formål å registrere rettskrenkelser som fant sted i Øst-Tyskland og andre øst-europeiske land. Men etter hvert kom kommisjonen til å arbeide mot krenkelser av menneskerettighetene i alle land. En rekke fremtredende jurister fra forskjellige stater ble med i kommisjonen. Fra Norge deltok Terje Wold som den gang var høyesterettsjustitiarius. Den internasjonale juristkommisjon har oppnådd stor respekt for sin virksomhet og har opprettholdt nær kontakt med FN. Det er uttrykk for den anseelse kommisjonen nyter at over 50 land, deriblant Norge, yter frivillige bidrag til dens virksomhet. Seán Mac Bride var en energisk generalsekretær, og bidro til å styrke kommisjonens rennomé.

Mac Bride har alltid lagt stor vekt på arbeidet med å få utbygget de lovmessige forpliktelser til vern om rettighetene. Den enkelte stat må påta seg slike forpliktelser både i den nasjonale lovgivning og som part i internasjonale konvensjoner. På denne måten mener han at folkeretten kan utbygges for å gi sikrere garantier for det enkelte individ. Da Seán Mac Bride deltok på et Nobelsymposium i Oslo i september 1967, tok han f. eks. til orde for å få opprettet en konvensjon mellom de øst-europeiske stater til beskyttelse av menneskerettighetene og de fundamentale friheter. Mønster for en slik konvensjon skulle være den konvensjon som Europarådets medlemsstater hadde inngått. Gjennom slike regionale avtaler håpet han å kunne bringe arbeidet for å sikre rettighetene et vesentlig steg videre. Han hevdet også at meget kunne gjøres for å få FN's rettighetserklæring til å bli en levende realitet. Hans ideal ville være å få opprettet en universell menneskerettighetsdomstol, med myndighet til å behandle klager fra enkeltmennesker som ble forfulgt i strid med de alminnelig aksepterte rettsprinsipper. Seán Mac Bride mener at ikke noen stat kan gjøre krav på absolutt nasjonal suverenitet når det gjelder menneskerettigheter som er universelt anerkjent. De er menneskehetens felleseie; myndighetene i et land har ikke rett til å krenke de fundamentale individuelle rettigheter. Vi er ennå langt fra å kunne realisere dette mål. Men Mac Bride har pekt på verdien av å drøfte tanken, fordi en slik prosess i seg selv tjener til å gjøre nestekjærligheten og respekten for våre medmennesker mer levende blant oss.

Hver krenkelse av menneskeverdet — uansett hvor det skjer — er en urett

mot selve menneskeheten. At Mac Bride har vært aktiv i det organiserte fredsarbeid på mange måter, bl. a. i det internasjonale fredsbyrå, er kjent av mange.
Fredsbyråets historie går helt tilbake til 1892. Det ble opprettet som et felles-
organ for de mange fredsforeninger som fantes rundt om i verden, og fikk
Nobelprisen så tidlig som i 1910. Det kom til å spille en viktig rolle ved opp-
rettelsen av Folkeforbundet. Etter den annen verdenskrig er byrået omorga-
nisert. Dets mål er det samme, nemlig å fremme internasjonal forståelse og
ikke-voldelige løsninger på internasjonale konflikter. Mac Bride har gjennom
årene hatt flere ledende tillitsverv i byrået.

I pakt med hele sitt syn på det forpliktende internasjonale samarbeid tok
Mac Bride tidlig til orde for å få opprettet et Høykommissariat i De forente
nasjoner til beskyttelse av rettighetene. Dette spørsmål har i flere år vært
drøftet i FN's komiteer og i Generalforsamlingen. Norge har vært blant de
land som mest aktivt har støttet forslaget. Drøftelsene i FN i fjor og i år viser
at det ennå dessverre er langt frem før denne idé vil kunne realiseres. I mel-
lomtiden vil arbeidet måtte gå videre med sikte på stadig nye små skritt mot
målet.

Under FN's menneskerettighetsår i 1968 tok Mac Bride initiativet til dan-
nelsen av en felleskomite for de forskjellige ikke-statlige organisasjoner som
kjempet for menneskerettighetene. Han ble selv leder for dette samarbeidet
som ble i stand til å øve større innflytelse ved å forene kreftene. Hans evner
som praktisk forhandler er anerkjent og respektert, og ved utallige møter og
konferanser har man opplevd hans overbevisningskraft og idealisme.

I over tyve år har Mac Bride stått helt sentralt i arbeidet for menneskerettighetenes sak. Han har sett at innsatsen har båret frukter. Over hele verden
har han nådd frem med sitt krevende budskap, som i sin enkleste form er
beslektet med det klassiske "Elsk din neste". Når respekten for menneskerettighetene er i vekst, på tross av alt det vi vet ennå er ugjort, er dette ikke
minst Mac Brides verk.

Det norske Stortings Nobelkomite har ved å gi årets fredspris til Seán Mac
Bride villet anerkjenne en forkjemper for dette viktige fredsarbeid. Komiteen
vet at i alle deler av verden har Mac Bride venner og tilhengere som deler
gleden med ham idag på selve menneskerettighetenes dag. Nobelkomiteen har
tidligere hatt anledning til å gi prisen til fremtredende forkjempere for de
menneskelige rettigheter. Seán Mac Brides navn hører hjemme i denne krets
av fredsprisvinnere, som har vist menneskeheten vei i mørket.

Nå står Mac Bride midt oppe i et nytt og krevende arbeid, som FN's Høy-
kommissær for Namibia. Han har selv uttalt seg optimistisk om mulighetene
for sitt virke. Verden vil følge hans videre gjerning i FN's tjeneste med spenning og forventning.

49

THE NOBEL PRIZE FOR PEACE

Speech by Mrs. AASE LIONÆS, chairman of the Nobel Committee of the Norwegian Storting
Translation

Your Majesty, Your Royal Highnesses, Your Excellencies, Ladies and Gentlemen,

A few years before he drew up his last will and testament, Alfred Nobel observed in a letter to Bertha von Suttner that his dynamite factories would be able to bring wars to an end a great deal more rapidly than peace congresses would ever succeed in doing.

"The day two armies can destroy one another in the course of a second there will be hope that all civilised nations will demobilise their forces and refrain from waging war." Thus as far back as the mid-1890s Alfred Nobel foresaw a kind of total retaliation.

After the first atom bomb had been tried out in New Mexico in July 1945 the scientists who had carried out the experiment believed that the world was faced with a new opportunity of putting and end to all wars. Armed with a weapon of this kind humanity had reached a threshold: if this threshold were crossed, both aggressor and defender would be doomed to destruction.

Total annihilation was the alternative to peace. Amid the awful terror which compelled nuclear physicists too to urge the world to come to its senses, a hope was born that disarmament and peace would have a chance.

Inevitably, in a world rent by internal dissension, world peace was made dependent on the establishment of a fearsome balance of terror between East and West.

Even on the brink of disaster wars could not be brought to an end. The old pattern was maintained in a period we have erroneously called the post-war period as well. Lives are being destroyed, property laid waste, minds darkened, and fear fermented in every corner of the world, Maybe we have gradually come to know more about the *causes* of war and discord; maybe we have gradually realised our share of responsibility, too, for tragedies enacted far from our own borders. It is comfort of a kind to believe this. But we have not made any appreciable progress in introducing measures to remove these causes, despite all our efforts.

On a day such as this, with the award of the Nobel Peace Prize, there are nevertheless good grounds for mentioning some of the favourable aspects of the development. In recent years both multilateral and bilateral negotiations have been initiated, with a view to promoting détente and practical cooperation. We are living in an era in which dialogue has largely replaced confrontation and isolation. Only a few years ago a negotiating pattern of this kind, of which we can now observe the contours, would have been considered entirely utopian. The whole world pins its hopes and expectations on this exchange of views and ideas.

I can see a ray of hope in the fact that a strong and vital body of public opinion all over the world rejects violence and the abuse of power. We are witnessing a world-wide wave of opinion. Do not be misled into attributing this to war weariness, because frequently men and women who have no personal experience of war are in the forefront of this wave. Call it rather a genuine belief in peace. The climate of opinion of which I am speaking does not restrict its efforts to combating war alone. In large measure attention is drawn to social, political, and economic oppression. And this is just and right: the struggle against injustice is a blow struck in the cause of peace.

The injustice inflicted on other strikes every one of us, as fellow humans. One of the great torchbearers of our age in the struggle for human rights, the Nobel Prize winner Alexander Solzhenitsyn, has said that our aim must be to eliminate from mankind the very idea that anyone is allowed to use force against justice, law, and mutual agreements. At no time surely has this idea been more accepted and understood in ever-widening circles throughout the world than precisely in our own age. This is a hopeful sign, in a world full of terrifying future prospects.

No statesman, no government, will be in a position to act with impunity without taking this body of opinion into account.

The Nobel Committee of the Norwegian Storting is charged with the onerous task of selecting persons or institutions that merit the award of the year's Peace Prize.

It could hardly be expected that the decisions of the Committee would not give rise to discussion. This has been the case ever since the first award was made over seventy years ago. This eloquently proves how difficult it is to define the concept of peace. On previous occasions of this nature the Nobel Committee has selected laureates whose efforts on behalf of peace have covered a great many varied fields: they have included statesmen negotiating round the conference table, defenders of human rights, experts on international law, rebels, humanists, idealists, pragmaticists, dreamers. They have all been controversial figures.

On this occasion both laureates are from countries that have previously not produced winners of the Nobel Peace Prize. In fact, Eisaku Sato is at the same time the first Asiatic who has received this prize. He comes before us today as a representative of the only nation that has experienced the unspeakable horrors of nuclear warfare. This terrible experience has left a deep imprint on the Japanese nation. But for the rest of us, too, names such as Hiroshima and Nagasaki are permanent symbols of something that we must all strive to prevent for all future time.

Seán Mac Bride is a citizen of a country that for many years has been the scene of bitter, grievous conflict. His experience has acted as a spur, urging him on in his many and varied efforts to promote international cooperation.

Each of these two Peace Prize winners represents different aspects of peace work. With the aid of the difficult art of politics and negotiation, they have endeavoured by practical means to promote their ideals. The goals they have reached must constantly be achieved afresh, since the peace and the justice that the world so sorely need are constantly threatened.

Eisaku Sato was prime minister of Japan for nearly eight years, from November 1964 to June 1972, a longer span than any of his predecessors. In all democracies the position of head of government is subject to attack from many angles, and Sato was frequently the object of violent criticism. Upon assuming the post of prime minister Sato declared that he would aim to secure for Japan an influence in international politics consistent with the country's status as a major economic power. Observers in other countries had every reason to watch how this programme would be implemented. Would Japan, in her more active foreign policy, revert to a nationalistic approach? There were many who feared this. Increased self-assurance, resulting from economic strength, considerations of national prestige and domestic policy might well have dominated in Japan, as has been the case with other great powers.

It soon became clear that Japan would pursue a foreign policy that aimed at promoting friendhip with other countries.

After the war, many nations still had vivid memories of an aggressive and militaristic Japan. Not least in countries that had experienced Japanese occupation the feeling of distrust was considerable. With a sense of great expectation the world followed the work of appeasement on which Japan had embarked.

The basis of Japan's foreign policy and security policy was conditioned by the obligations imposed on the country after the Second World War. The constitution Japan adopted in 1947 had expressly stated that the Japanese people renounced rights that had previously been regarded as essential to an independent nation. "War and the threat or use of force are renounced as means of deciding conflicts with other nations." This is a unique provision in a country's constitution. This principle was established by the American occupation authorities, and was markedly influenced by this fact. In Japan militarism was crushed in 1945, and strong pacifist tendencies made their influence felt among the people.

As head of government Sato frequently recalled that the anti-war provision in the Constitution must serve as a basis for the country's policy. He emphasised three principles upon which his government would base itself as far as nuclear arms were concerned:

"Never to produce arms of this nature, never to own them, and never to introduce them into Japan."

The Japanese people have supported this peace policy laid down by Sato, reacting very forcefully to any indication that developments might proceed in another direction. From time to time it has been said that the Japanese people have developed an allergy against nuclear arms. An allergy of this kind is a healthy sign, and other countries might well learn a lesson from this.

Whenever Eisaku Sato, in his role of prime minister, emphasised, as he did on many occasions, that Japan would only pursue its goals by peaceful means, he undoubtedly expressed an opinion that had the overwhelming support of the great majority of his people.

Shortly after Sato had taken office as prime minister he set out to improve relations with South Korea. A friendship pact was signed between the two countries, and ratified in the autumn of 1965. Diplomatic relations were also immediately established between the two countries.

This agreement proved the prelude to a systematic plan for improving relations between Japan and a number of other states in the Pacific area. In the autumn of 1967 Sato set off on a protracted tour, in the course of which he visited, among other countries, Burma, Malaysia, Singapore, Thailand, Laos, Indonesia, Australia, New Zealand, the Philippines, and South Vietnam. The objects of his journey were to strengthen friendly relations, stimulate trade, and inaugurate discussions, with a view to promoting political cooperation and a more active cultural exchange. It is widely accepted that increased trade is one of the best ways of promoting international understanding. Once a start is made in this practical field, and mutual interests are discovered, the road will be clear for increased contact in other spheres as well. This approach, as we all know, has played a major role in East—West relations in recent years. In Asia Japan, under the leadership of Sato, set out to improve trade relations, increase aid to developing countries, and encourage a greater measure of regional cooperation. Japan was responsible for initiating a ministerial conference for economic development in South-East Asia, as well as actively promoting measures to ensure the realisation of the International Development Bank for Asia. Japan has herself been among the major contributors to this bank, on the assumption that the country carries a special responsibility for the promotion of peace in this area. In Sato's opinion an important factor in this respect was that countries would be in a better position to exploit their material and cultural resources.

The Japanese friendship policy was faced with a fundamental difficulty from the very start, inter alia because Japan's close treaty relations with the USA were criticised in certain quarters, particularly during the Vietnam war. Not only did Japan refrain from any military participation in Vietnam, but Eisaku Sato urged the belligerents to come together, without imposing conditions of any kind, in order to discuss a truce and peace. War would never solve the political problems, Sato declared in his speech to the Japanese National Assembly in July 1965. An attempt on the part of the Japanese Government to investigate the possibilities for a peace initiative proved abortive in the spring of 1966.

As head of government it fell to Sato's lot to maintain a balance between conflicting interests. While adhering to the treaty with the USA, he also demanded greater independence. It was particularly important for the Japanese people to reach agreement with the United States on the return of the groups of islands that the USA had occupied since the end of the Second World War. After five years of ceaseless endeavour Sato succeeded in coming to an arrangement whereby Japan was given sovereignty over Okinawa and the Ogasawara Islands. His success in doing so helped to remove a serious source of friction in relations between the two countries; at the same time it also helped to strengthen stability throughout this area, and to convince the Japanese people that their foreign political aims could best be achieved through the medium of negotiation, and not by aggressive acts or threats. It was of particular importance to Japan that the agreement ensured that no nuclear arms would be stationed on the American bases on Okinawa. The agreement, when it was negotiated in 1951, could be hailed as a step in the direction of fulfilling the Japanese wish to safeguard its national security. Both the security agreement and the actual peace pact presupposed that Japan would have the right to self-defence, and the right to participate in collective security compacts in accordance with the United Nations Charter. It is on this basis that Japan's defence system is founded. It is generally accepted that during the years that have subsequently elapsed Japan has shown considerable restraint in this field. No great power has shown a corresponding degree of moderation; in fact, a great many small countries maintain military forces that are very much larger and stronger than the Japanese. No single politician in Japan deserves the sole credit for this. The Japanese people's opposition to any form of military resurgence is so strong that no other policy would have been feasible.

In relations with the Soviet Union, too, marked improvements were registered during Sato's term of office. No peace agreement was concluded with the Russians, because the latter insisted on the right to the islands in the North Kurils, a claim no Japanese government could accept. But during Sato's term of office cooperation was continued in the sphere of foreign policy and trade, not least after an exchange of visits by the foreign ministers of the two countries.

No diplomatic relations were established between the Chinese People's Republic and Japan. In common with a great many other countries, the Japanese Government pursued a policy, which entailed recognition of Formosa. In spite of this several important points of contact were established between Tokyo and Peking. In connection with the Bandung Conference in April 1965 Prime Minister Sato's special envoy had a conversation with Prime Minister Chou En-lai in which the Japanese desire for closer contact with the People's Republic was expressed. Despite political obstacles, trade between the two countries increased, and the outside world noted inter alia that Japanese journalists were allowed to work in Peking during the Cultural Revolution, whereas journalists from most other countries were obliged to leave the People's Republic. On a number of occasions Sato spoke of the need to hold the door to Peking open. However, as long as Japan maintained recognition of the regime in Formosa it was impossible to establish diplomatic relations with Peking. Nevertheless it was of importance to the international atmosphere that relations between the two states should all this time have been marked by a sense of restraint.

In several disputes in Asia, particularly in the conflict between India and Pakistan and that between Malaysia and Indonesia, Sato intervened personally in order to persuade the parties involved to settle their differences. The payment of considerable sums, by way of compensation, to countries that had suffered under the Japanese occupation, was another factor that contributed greatly to improving relations with other countries during Sato's ministry. Longstanding differences were mitigated, and new mutual interests were created. The good-neighbour policy, of which Sato was the chief exponent, was well received in large areas of Asia. That the economic influence of the Japanese should have been the source of dispute and have encountered resistance in no way alters the overall impression.

In awarding the Peace Prize for 1974 to Eisaku Sato the Nobel Committee wishes to emphasise the important role the Japanese people have played in promoting close and friendly cooperation with other nations. Japan's attitude has helped to strengthen peace in East Asia, and to lay the foundation for economic growth and progress for many countries. By countering the tendency towards a nationalistic policy in Japan after the war, by constantly emphasising the need for international cooperation and understanding, by playing the role of arbitrator and thus helping to iron out differences, Sato has made a major contribution to peace.

The Nobel Committee has attached considerable importance to the statements Eisaku Sato has made in which he has affirmed his determination to adhere to his doctrine that Japan shall never own, produce, or acquire nuclear arms. At a time of increasing risk that more and more nations will acquire weapons of this kind, it is important that Japan, under Sato's leadership, signed a pact on the non-proliferation of nuclear arms in February 1970.

At that time Sato declared that it was in conformity with Japan's national aims to prevent arms of this kind being acquired by more states. The aim was to ease international tension, establish friendly relations with every country, and help to set up international compacts that would promote the cause of peace. It was Sato's hope that the non-proliferation agreement would be followed up by effective measures resulting in a reduction of the number of nuclear arms in the world. He also emphasised the importance of ensuring that this pact should be the prelude to practical progress in promoting general disarmament.

The non-proliferation agreement has as yet not been ratified by Japan, although the government that succeeded Sato's confirmed as recently as in the meeting of the United Nations General Assembly this year that it would work to achieve this. The responsibility for future decisions is not vested in any one individual; I should like to emphasise that the attitude of the Japanese people may well prove decisive in shaping future developments. It is the hope of the Nobel Committee that this year's award will be interpreted as an encouragement to all who work to ensure that the non-proliferation agreement will receive the widest possible support.

Peace-loving people throughout the world cherish the hope that the future development of Asia will proceed without the fear of war and the resort to force. May the hope that the Pacific Ocean will become a real ocean of peace be realised!

In this development Japan's role is of decisive importance.

The other Peace Prize winner this year is the Irishman Seán Mac Bride, who was born in Paris on January 26, 1904. As a young man he witnessed the Irish struggle for independence, with all its horrors. This experience was in many ways to prove an abiding influence. After working as a journalist for a number of years he studied law, and qualified to practise in 1937. This enabled him to work more effectively for the legal rights of persecuted individuals. After the Second World War he entererd the Irish National Assembly, the Dáil Eireann, of which he was a member from 1947 to 1958. From 1948 to 1951 he was Ireland's foreign minister. This was at a time when the Council of Europe was drafting the European Convention on Human Rights. The object of this work was to secure the acceptance of a convention in which human rights would for the first time be accorded universal international protection. It was a great day in European history when the convention was finally signed by the foreign ministers of member states in Rome on November 4, 1950. Mac Bride played a dominant role in piloting this convention through to a successful conclusion. From now on he was to devote his entire life to the work of promoting greater respect for human rights, not only in West Europe, but throughout the world. In speeches and in articles he urged the authorities of every country to negotiate and abide by international agreements guaranteeing the rights of the individual.

In 1961 he was elected President of the International Board of Amnesty International, and for many years he was active as the fearless and vigorous head of this organisation, visiting a great many countries to plead the cause of persecuted men and women, taking up the cudgels against torture, and urging a sense of greater humanity and neighbourly love. His field of activity covered Asia, Africa, and America. His most important standby in this campaign was his own energy and enthusiasm, and the support he received from countless voluntary helpers in many countries. He mobilised the conscience of the world in the fight against injustice. The organisation of which he was the leader gradually achieved wider recognition and greater influence. With unflagging zeal he tackled new and fresh tasks. Mac Bride himself knows that it may take a long time to create the change in the mental climate which in the last resort will provide the only sure guarantee against brutality and arbitrary encroachment on individual liberty. But he knows, too, that there are countless people all over the world who consider themselves bound by their conscience to play their part in this struggle.

Mac Bride has worked both on the ideological and theoretical plane and in the practical sphere. He has combined the duties of an organisational leader and a field worker. In his work to protect and strengthen human rights he has achieved a unique position. As Secretary General of the International Commission of Jurists from 1963 to 1970 he was also extremely active.

This commission was set up in West Berlin in 1952, its original aims being to record acts of injustice perpetrated in East Germany and other East European countries. But in time the commission became active in the work of countering violations of human rights in every country. A number of leading jurists from various countries joined the commission. Norway was represented by Terje Wold, at that time President of the Norwegian High Court of Justice. The International Commission of Jurists, which issues several valuable publications, has gained great respect for its activities, and has maintained close contact with the United Nations Organisations. An expression of the esteem in which the commission is held is afforded by the fact that over fifty countries, including Norway, make voluntary contributions to its work.

Seán Mac Bride was extremely active as Secretary General, and contributed in large measure to enhancing the reputation of the commission.

He has always emphasised the importance of extending and enforcing the legislative obligations to protect personal rights. The individual state must assume obligations of this kind both in its own national legislation and also as an integrated part of international conventions. In this way, he believes, international law can be developed and extended to provide a guarantee of greater protection for the individual. When Seán Mac Bride participated in a Nobel symposium in Oslo in September 1967, for example, he launched the idea of establishing a convention among the nations of East Europe for the protection of human rights and fundamental freedoms. The convention contracted by the member-states of the European Council was to provide a pattern for a convention of the kind he envisaged. By means of regional agreements of this kind he hoped it would be possible to bring about a real measure of progress in the work of securing such rights. He also maintained that a great deal could be done to ensure that UNO's Declaration of Human Rights became a living reality. His ideal would be the establishment of a universal Human Rights Court, with the authority to deal with complaints from individuals who were being subjected to persecution in violation of the universally accepted principles of justice. Seán Mac Bride is of the opinion that no state can claim absolute national sovereignty where human rights that are universally recognised are concerned. Rights of this kind are the common property of all mankind; the authorities of a country have no right to violate these fundamental individual rights. We still have a long way to go before we can reach this goal; but Mac Bride has emphasised the value of discussing this idea, since a process of this kind in itself serves to stimulate afresh our sense of neighbourly love and respect for our fellow human beings.

Every violation of human dignity, no matter where it occurs, is an affront to humanity itself.

Mac Bride's active participation in organised peace work of a great many kinds, inter alia in the International Peace Bureau, is widely known and recognised. The history of the Peace Bureau goes right back to the year 1892: it was established as a parent body for the many pacifist associations that existed all over the world and was to play an important part in the setting up of the League of Nations. After the Second World War the Bureau was reorganised, but its objectives remain unchanged, viz. to promote international understanding and nonviolent solutions to international conflicts.

The Peace Bureau was awarded the Nobel Prize as far back as 1910. Over the years Mac Bride has occupied various leading positions of trust within this organisation.

True to his entire attitude to the obligations of international cooperation Mac Bride launched at an early stage the idea of establishing a High Commissariat in the United Nations for the protection of individual rights. This question has been debated for a number of years in UNO's committees and in the General Assembly. Norway is one of the countries that has most actively supported this proposal. Discussions in UNO last year and this year unfortunately reveal that we still have a long way to go before it will be possible to realise this idea. In the meantime the work will have to be continued, with a view to making steady if slow progress towards this goal.

During UNO's Human Rights Year in 1968 Mac Bride took the initiative in setting up a joint committee for the various non-governmental organisations that championed the cause of human rights. He himself was placed in command of this cooperative venture, which proved capable of exercising greater influence with its concerted efforts. His skill as a practical negotiator is widely recognised and respected, and his powers of conviction and idealism have been in evidence at countless conferences and meetings.

For over twenty years Mac Bride has occupied a central position in the work of promoting the cause of human rights. He has seen his efforts crowned with success. All over the world his exacting message, which in its simplest form is akin to the classical "Love thy Neighbour", has found an audience. That respect for human rights is growing, despite all that we know still remains to be done, is due not least to the endeavours of Mac Bride.

In awarding this year's Peace Prize to Seán Mac Bride the Nobel Committee of the Norwegian Storting is paying its tribute to an advocate and champion of this important work for peace. The Committee is convinced that Mac Bride's numerous friends and supporters all over the world will share with him his pleasure on this day, which is actually Human Rights Day. On previous occasions the Nobel Committee has had an opportunity of awarding the prize to others who have made a great contribution to the cause of human rights. The name of Seán Mac Bride takes its place in this circle of Peace Prize laureates who have shown humanity the way through the darkness.

Mac Bride is at present facing a new and demanding task as UN's High Commissioner for Namibia. He has personally expressed optimism with regard to the future prospects of this work. The world will follow his future work in the service of the United Nations with anticipation and expectation.

Dans la soirée du même jour, le Comité a offert un banquet au Grand Hôtel. Au banquet ont assisté M. Sato, M. Mac Bride, M. Guttorm Hansen, Président du Storting, M. Rolv Ryssdal, Président de la Cour Suprême, M. Yngve Möller, Ambassadeur de Suède en Norvège, M. T. Yamanaka, Ambassadeur du Japon en Norvège, M. D. P. Waldron, Ambassadeur d'Irlande en Norvège, M. Arne Fredga, Représentant de la Fondation Nobel, des représentants du Storting, du Gouvernement, du monde scientifique, économique et culturel.

INSIGNES NOBEL
ET
MONTANT DU PRIX

Conformément aux statuts de la Fondation Nobel les lauréats ont reçu un *diplôme*, une *médaille d'or* et un *document* indiquant le *montant du prix*.

Le montant de chacun des prix Nobel décernés en 1974 s'élève à 550 000 couronnes suédoises.

La somme disponible à répartir entre les lauréats varie selon les revenus annuels nets du fonds principal de la Fondation Nobel. En 1901, la première fois que les prix furent distribués, chacun d'entre eux se montait à 150 000 couronnes suédoises.

Les diplômes présentés aux lauréats en physique M. Ryle et A. Hewish ainsi que le diplôme présenté au lauréat en chimie P. J. Flory sont exécutés par l'artiste peintre suédois Karl-Axel Pehrson. Les diplômes présentés aux lauréats en littérature E. Johnson et H. Martinson sont exécutés par l'artiste peintre suédois Gunnar Brusewitz.

Les diplômes présentés aux lauréats en physiologie ou médecine A. Claude, C. de Duve et G. E. Palade ne portent d'autre motif qu'une effigie de la médaille Nobel.

Commentaires aux images des diplômes des prix exécutés par Karl-Axel Pehrson :

Martin Ryle
Sous une forme biologique — la coupe d'un fruit imaginaire — l'image transposée d'un radiotéléscope.

Antony Hewish
Un crabe aux tonalités bleues sur un fond dont la structure imaginaire symbolise les études poursuivies par le lauréat sur la nébuleuse du Crabe, où il découvrit les premiers pulsars.

Paul J. Flory
D'une branche jaillissent en chaîne des fruits qui évoquent les longues chaînes moléculaires dont le lauréat a décelé les propriétés.

Commentaires aux images des diplômes des prix exécutés par Gunnar Brusewitz :

Eyvind Johnson

Dominant l'image, une concrétisation de la violence et de l'oppression — un soldat de César coiffé d'un casque de l'époque naziste. On peut voir dans le personnage agenouillé un prisonnier politique, l'un des premiers chrétiens ou un Juif à Belsen.

La partie inférieure de l'image est une allusion au milieu du Norrland où Eyvind Johnson a passé sa jeunesse — flottage de bois, scieries, et les panaches rouges des épilobes. Les rails qui aboutissent à un ciel blanc où une fenêtre grillée est brisée, symbolisent la route vers le sud, vers la liberté et l'Europe.

A gauche, des scènes du Paris et du Berlin de l'entre-deux-guerres. Les autres parties du champ central portent des images inspirées par « Au temps de Sa Grâce » — à gauche — et par « De roses et de feu ».

L'image du champ supérieur est inspirée par « Heureux Ulysse » — le vaisseau d'Ulysse et le mirage d'Ithaque à l'horizon.

Harry Martinson

Au centre, le champ est dominé par une fleur de pissenlit qui forme en même temps un soleil jaune dont les rayons pénètrent le microcosme. Le champ inférieur de l'image s'inspire entièrement des œuvres de l'auteur qui ont la nature pour thème initial, depuis « Nature » et « Papillon de nuit et tipule », jusqu'à « Choses vues d'une touffe d'herbe » et « Mottes et touffes d'herbe ». Là, le crapaud des chansons folkloriques côtoie les représentants de « L'Aventure de la pensée : les insectes », et autres pièces en prose poético-scientifiques. Les orties fleurissent à droite... Au milieu, une alchémille porte la goutte de rosée qui reflète le cosmos.

Derrière le soleil-pissenlit se dresse la tige florifère fanée, qui sème à tout vent ses parasols de graines vers le cosmos, y formant des galaxes et des systèmes planétaires — « Aniara »! A gauche, des images inspirées de « Herbes de Thulé », « Nomade » et « le Vaisseau fantôme ».

A. Hewish

Martin Ryle

Paul J. Flory

E. Johnsson

H. Martinsson

CONFÉRENCES NOBEL

LES LAURÉATS
NOTICES BIOGRAPHIQUES

ANTONY HEWISH

Antony Hewish was born in Fowey, Cornwall, on May 11th, 1924, the youngest of three sons. He grew up in Newquay, on the north Cornish coast, where his father was a banker. He was educated at King's College, Taunton from 1935—1942 and at Gonville and Caius College, Cambridge from 1942—43, and 1946—48.

From 1943—46 he was at the Royal Aircraft Establishment, Farnborough, although he was seconded to the Telecommunication Research Establishment, Malvern, and was concerned with airborne radar-counter-measure devices. It was at Malvern that he met Ryle.

In 1946 he returned to Cambridge, graduating in 1948 and immediately joining Ryle's research team at the Cavendish Laboratory. He obtained his Ph.D in 1952 and was a Research Fellow at Gonville and Caius College from 1952—54; in 1955 he became a Supernumerary Fellow. He was elected a Fellow and Director of Studies in Physics at Churchill College in 1961 and was a University Lecturer in Physics from 1961—69. He was visiting Professor in Astronomy at Yale in 1962. He was a Reader during 1969—71 when he was elected to Professor of Radio Astronomy in Cambridge.

He is a Fellow of the Royal Society (since 1968), and of the Royal Astronomical Society. He is also Foreign Honorary Member of the American Academy of Arts and Sciences. In 1950 he married Marjorie Richards and they have a son and daughter. His relaxations are listening to music, sailing, and almost any manual activity.

1952   Hamilton Prize. University of Cambridge.

1969   Eddington Medal. Royal Astronomical Society.

1970   Charles Vernon Boys Prize. Institute of Physics and the Physical Society.

1972   Dellinger Medal. International Union of Radio Science.

1973   William Hopkins Prize. Cambridge Philosophical Society. Michelson Medal. Franklin Institute. U.S.A.

1974   Holweck Medal. Société Française de Physique.

PULSARS AND HIGH DENSITY PHYSICS

Nobel Lecture, December 12, 1974

by

ANTONY HEWISH

University of Cambridge, Cavendish Laboratory, Cambridge, England

DISCOVERY OF PULSARS

The trail which ultimately led to the first pulsar began in 1948 when I joined Ryle's small research team and became interested in the general problem of the propagation of radiation through irregular transparent media. We are all familiar with the twinkling of visible stars and my task was to understand why radio stars also twinkled. I was fortunate to have been taught by Ratcliffe, who first showed me the power of Fourier techniques in dealing with such diffraction phenomena. By a modest extension of existing theory I was able to show that our radio stars twinkled because of plasma clouds in the ionosphere at heights around 300 km, and I was also able to measure the speed of ionospheric winds in this region (1).

My fascination in using extra-terrestrial radio sources for studying the intervening plasma next brought me to the solar corona. From observations of the angular scattering of radiation passing through the corona, using simple radio interferometers, I was eventually able to trace the solar atmosphere out to one half the radius of the Earth's orbit (2).

In my notebook for 1954 there is a comment that, if radio sources were of small enough angular size, they would illuminate the solar atmosphere with sufficient coherence to produce interference patterns at the Earth which would be detectable as a very rapid fluctuation of intensity. Unfortunately the information then available showed that the few sources known were more than one hundred times too large to produce this effect, and I did not pursue the idea. This was sad because the phenomenon was discovered by chance, about eight years later, by Margaret Clarke long after I had forgotten all about my comment. She was involved with a survey of radio sources at Cambridge and noticed that three particular sources showed variations of intensity. She pointed out that two of the sources were known to have angular sizes of less than 2″ and estimated that a scintillation mechanism required plasma irregularities at distances of thousands of km but she concluded that the fluctuations were an unsolved mystery (3). During a group discussion I suddenly remembered my earlier conclusion and realised that, if the radio sources subtended an angle of less than 1″, they might show the predicted intensity scintillation caused by plasma clouds in the interplanetary medium. With the assistance of Scott and Collins special observations of 3C 48 and other quasistellar radio sources were made and the scintillation phenomenon was immediately confirmed (4).

Since interplanetary scintillation, as we called this new effect, could be detected in any direction in space. I used it to study the solar wind, which had by then been discovered by space probes launched into orbits far beyond the magnetosphere. It was interesting to track the interplanetary diffraction patterns as they raced across England at speeds in excess of 300 km s^{-1}, and to sample the behaviour of the solar wind far outside the plane of the ecliptic where spacecraft have yet to venture (5).

The scintillation technique also provided an extremely simple and useful means of showing which radio sources had angular sizes in the range 0″.1— 1″.0. The first really unusual source to be uncovered by this method turned up in 1965 when, with my student Okoye, I was studying radio emission from the Crab Nebula. We found a prominent scintillating component within the nebula which was far too small to be explained by conventional synchotron radiation and we suggested that this might be the remains of the original star which had exploded and which still showed activity in the form of flare-type radio emission (6). This source later turned out to be none other than the famous Crab Nebula Pulsar.

In 1965 I drew up plans for a radio telescope with which I intended to carry out a large-scale survey of more than 1000 radio galaxies using interplanetary scintillation to provide high angular resolution. To achieve the required sensitivity it was necessary to cover an area of 18,000 m^2 and, because scintillation due to plasmas is most pronounced at long wavelengths, I used a wavelength of 3.7 m. The final design was an array containing 2048 dipole antennas. Lather that year I was joined by a new graduate student, Jocelyn Bell, and she become responsible for the network of cables connecting the dipoles. The entire system was built with local effort and we relied heavily upon the willing assistance of many members of the Cambridge team.

The radio telescope was complete, and tested, by July 1967 and we immediately commenced a survey of the sky. Our method of utilising scintillation for the quantitative measurement of angular sizes demanded repeated observations so that every source could be studied at many different solar elongations. In fact we surveyed the entire range of accessible sky at intervals of one week. To maintain a continuous assessment of the survey we arranged to plot the positions of scintillating radio sources on a sky-chart, as each record was analysed, and to add points as the observations were repeated at weekly intervals. In this way genuine sources could be distinguished from electrical interference since the latter would be unlikely to recur with the same celestial coordinates. It is greatly to Jocelyn Bell's credit that she was able to keep up with the flow of paper from the four recorders.

One day around the middle of August 1967 Jocelyn showed me a record indicating fluctuating signals that could have been a faint source undergoing scintillation when observed in the antisolar direction. This was unusual since strong scintillation rarely occurs in this direction and we first thought that the signals might be electrical interference. So we continued the routine survey. By the end of September the source had been detected on several occasions, although it was not always present, and I suspected that we had located a flare star, perhaps similar to the M-type dwarfs under investigation by Lovell.

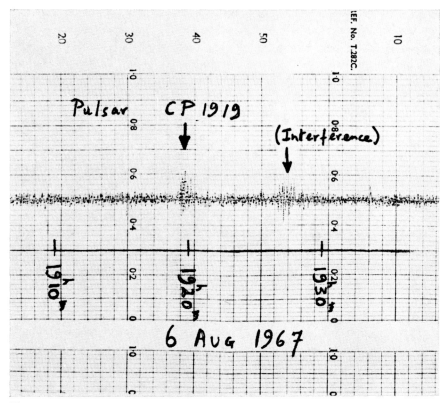

Fig. 1. The first signals from CP 1919.

But the source also exhibited apparent shifts of right ascension of up to 90 seconds which was evidence against a celestial origin. We installed a high-speed recorder to study the nature of the fluctuating signals but met with no success as the source intensity faded below our detection limit. During October

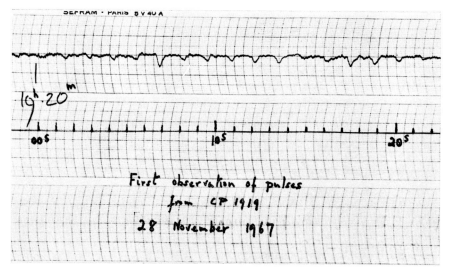

Fig. 2. The first indication of pulsed radio emission from CP 1919.

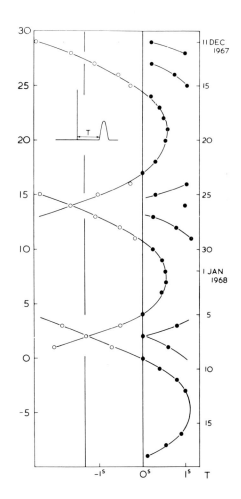

Fig. 3. Timing measurements showing Doppler shift due to the orbital
motion of the Earth.

this recorder was required for pre-arranged observations of another source, 3C 273, to check certain aspects of scintillation theory, and it was not until November 28th that we obtained the first evidence that our mysterious source was emitting regular pulses of radiation at intervals of just greater than one second. I could not believe that any natural source would radiate in this fashion and I immediately consulted astronomical colleagues at other observatories to enquire whether they had any equipment in operation which might possibly generate electrical interference at a sidereal time near 19^h 19^m.

In early December the source increased in intensity and the pulses were clearly visible above the noise. Knowing that the signals were pulsed enabled me to ascertain their electrical phase and I reanalysed the routine survey records. This showed that the right ascension was constant. The apparent variations had been caused by the changing intensity of the source. Still sceptical, I arranged a device to display accurate time marks at one second intervals broadcast from the MSF Rugby time service and on December 11th began daily timing measurements. To my astonishment the readings fell in a regular pattern, to within the observational uncertainty of 0.1s, showing that the pulsed source kept time to better than 1 part in 10^6. Meanwhile my colleagues Pilkington, and Scott and Collins, found by quite independent methods that the signal exhibited a rapidly sweeping frequency of about -5 MHz s^{-1}. This showed that the duration of each pulse, at one particular radio frequency, was approximately 16 ms.

Having found no satisfactory terrestrial explanation for the pulses we now began to believe that they could only be generated by some source far beyond the solar system, and the short duration of each pulse suggested that the radiator could not be larger than a small planet. We had to face the possibility that the signals were, indeed, generated on a planet circling some distant star, and that they were artificial. I knew that timing measurements, if continued for a few weeks, would reveal any orbital motion of the source as a Doppler shift, and I felt compelled to maintain a curtain of silence until this result was known with some certainty. Without doubt, those weeks in December 1967 were the most exciting in my life.

It turned out that the Doppler shift was precisely that due to the motion of the Earth alone, and we began to seek explanations involving dwarf stars, or the hypothetical neutron stars. My friends in the library at the optical observatory were surprised to see a radio astronomer taking so keen an interest in books on stellar evolution. I finally decided that the gravitational oscillation of an entire star provided a possible mechanism for explaining the periodic emission of radio pulses, and that the fundamental frequency obtainable from white dwarf stars was too low. I suggested that a higher order mode was needed in the case of a white dwarf, or that a neutron star of the lowest allowed density, vibrating in the fundamental mode, might give the required periodicity. We also estimated the distance of the source on the assumption that the frequency sweep was caused by pulse dispersion in the interstellar plasma, and obtained a value of 65 parsec, a typical stellar distance.

While I was preparing a coherent account of this rather hectic research, in January 1968, Jocelyn Bell was scrutinising all our sky-survey recordings with her typical persistence and diligence and she produced a list of possible additional pulsar positions. These were observed again for evidence of pulsed radiation and before submitting our paper for publication, on February 8th, we were confident that three additional pulsars existed although their parameters were then only crudely known. I well remember the morning when Jocelyn came into my room with a recording of a possible pulsar that she had made during the previous night at a right ascension 09^h 50^m. When we spread the chart over the floor and placed a metre rule against it a periodicity of 0.25s was just discernible. This was confirmed later when the receiver was adjusted to a narrower bandwidth, and the rapidity of this pulsar made explanations involving white dwarf stars increasingly difficult.

The months that followed the announcement (7) of our discovery were busy ones for observers and theoreticians alike, as radio telescopes all over the world turned towards the first pulsars and information flooded in at a phenomenal rate. It was Gold (8) who first suggested that the rotation of neutron stars provided the simplest and most flexible mechanism to explain the pulsar clock, and his prediction that the pulse period should increase with

Fig. 4. Radiation from a typical pulsar.

time soon received dramatic confirmation with the discovery of the pulsar in the Crab Nebula (9, 10). Further impressive support for the neutron star hypothesis was the detection of pulsed light from the star which had previously been identified as the remnant of the original explosion. This, according to theories of stellar evolution, is precisely where a young neutron star should be created. Gold also showed that the loss of rotational energy, calculated from the increase of period for a neutron star model, was exactly that needed to power the observed synchrotron light from the nebula.

Now, in 1974, with more than 130 pulsars charted in the heavens, there is overwhelming evidence that the neutron star "lighthouse" model is correct. No other star could spin fast enough, without fragmenting, to account for the most rapid pulsars yet periods ranging from 33 ms to 3.5 s are readily accommodated by the rotation theory. At the same time there is unfortunately no satisfactory theory to account for the radio emission generated by these tiny stars which have radii of only 10 km.

HIGH DENSITY PHYSICS INSIDE NEUTRON STARS

The prediction that matter at the almost unimaginable density of 10^{18} kg m^{-3} might be formed under gravitational compression inside stars was first made by Baade and Zwicky (11) in 1934, soon after Chadwick's discovery of the neutron. At this density only a small fraction of the original protons and electrons could exist and matter would consist predominantly of neutrons. It is the denegeracy pressure arising from the neutrons, which obey Fermi statistics, that balances further gravitational compression, alhough finally the Fermi energy becomes relativistic and further gravitational collapse ensues. Since complex nuclei are generated by nuclear fusion inside hot stars, where there is a large thermal pressure, the degenerate neutron state can only be found when fusion ceases and we deal with the cooling "ashes" of stellar evolution. The stars that give rise to neutron stars are more massive than the Sun, and it is believed that the formation of neutron stars is associated with supernova explosions.

Since the discovery of pulsars there has been great activity amongst solid-state physicists around the world because neutron matter, at any temperature less than about 10^9 K, behaves rather like ordinary matter close to the absolute zero of temperature. The generally agreed model of a neutron star consists of concentric shells with very different physical properties as reviewed by Ruderman (12).

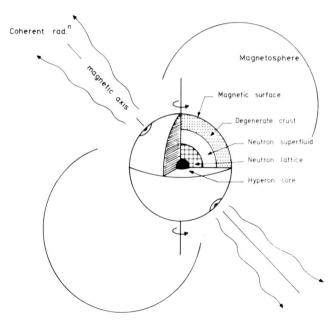

Fig. 5. Model of a neutron star.

At the surface of the star it is likely that there exists a shell of iron since ^{56}Fe is the most stable nucleus. The atoms would be normal if no magnetic field were present. In astrophysics it is unwise to ignore magnetic phenomena and gravitational collapse following a supernova explosion probably compresses the original stellar magnetic flux to produce surface field strengths of 10^8 T or more. In fields of this magnitude the radius of gyration of electrons in atomic energy levels becomes smaller than the Bohr radius and the electronic wave functions adopt a cylindrical shape. It is far harder to ionize distorted atoms of this kind and this is of importance when considering the generation of a magnetosphere surrounding the neutron star.

Beneath the iron skin the increasing compression forces electrons into higher energy states until they are entirely freed from the positive nuclei. The unscreened nuclei then settle into a rigid lattice having a melting temperature of about 10^9 K. At greater depths the electron energies become relativistic and they begin to combine with protons in the nuclei, thus adding to the neutron population. This is the process of inverse β decay. At a sufficient depth nearly all the electrons and protons have disappeared and the nuclei have been converted to a sea of neutrons.

The energy gap for neutron pairing is of the order of several MeV, corresponding to a superfluid transition temperature of 10^9—10^{10} K, and since young neutron stars cool rapidly to temperatures below 10^9 K, the neutron sea is expected to behave like a quantum superfluid. The few remaining protons will similarly pair and enter a superconducting state, while the residual electrons will behave normally. The bulk motion of the neutron superfluid must be irrotational, but an effective solid body rotation can be simulated with a distribution of quantised vortex lines containing a small fraction of normal fluid neutrons.

At yet deeper levels the neutron-neutron interaction may result in the creation of a solid neutron lattice, although this possibility is under debate, and finally there is the question of a material composed of stable hyperons.

Evidence that neutron stars do indeed have a structure similar to the predicted models has been obtained from extended timing observations of pulsars (13). These show that the systematic increase of period, corresponding to a steady loss of rotational energy from the spinning star, is sometimes interrupted by discontinuous changes. Most pulsars are observed to be slowing down on a typical timescale of 10^6—10^7 years, althouh the most rapid pulsars, in the Crab and Vela supernovae, have timescales of only 10^3 and 10^4 years respectively. The discontinuities often show an abrupt decrease of period, followed by a recovery to a slightly reduced value with a characteristic relaxation time.

For the Crab pulsar this effect can be explained by a rigid crust-liquid core model. Young neutron stars are likely to be spinning rapidly at birth, with angular velocities up to 10^4 radian s^{-1}, and they will therefore have a spheroidal shape. As a star slows down it will tend to become less spheroidal and the rigid crust will fracture at irregular intervals as the increasing strain overcomes rigidity. When this occurs the crust will momentarily spin more rapidly, but later the increased angular momentum will be coupled into the fluid interior, where the bulk of the mass resides. The observed time constant for coupling is in good agreement with the superfluid model, and would be far smaller in the case of a normal fluid interior. It is remarkable that a crust shrinkage of only 10 μm is sufficient to explain the period anomalies for the Crab pulsar. When similar reasoning is applied to the Vela pulsar, for which the anomalies are larger, it is found necessary to invoke a solid neutron lattice core in which strains imposed when the star was young are intermittently relaxed.

PLASMA PHYSICS OUTSIDE NEUTRON STARS

It is strange that there appears to be more understanding of the interior of neutron stars, than of their atmospheres wherein is generated the radiation which makes them detectable. Ginzburg and Zheleznyakov (14) have summarised the electrodynamic problems in detail. The model upon which theorists are concentrating most attention is that of an oblique magnetic rotator, in which the pulsar may be regarded as a dynamo, powered by the initial store of rotational kinetic energy, and converting this into radiation together with a flux of relativistic particles by means of the large magnetic field. The oblique rotator model was first considered by Pacini (15) before pulsars had been found, and it was Gold (8) who suggested that an extended corotating magnetosphere played a vital role.

Goldreich and Julian (16) showed that electrical forces arising from unipolar induction would be sufficient to drag charges from the stellar surface

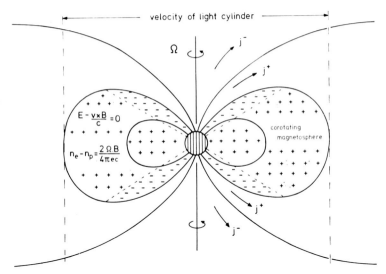

Fig. 6. The neutron star magnetosphere for an aligned magnetic rotator.

and then distribute them in a corotating magnetosphere. It is not yet known whether such a distribution is stable, and the plasma differs from laboratory plasmas in that almost complete charge separation occurs. Inertial forces must dominate when the corotation velocity approaches c, and beyond the velocity of light cylinder the plasma breaks away to create a stellar wind. In such models the polar regions are believed to play a crucial role since particles can escape along 'open' field lines.

Within such an overall framework exists the ordered motion of the charges which generate the beamed radio waves that we observe, and also those regions which emit light and X-rays for the youngest pulsar in the Crab. The fascinating richness of the phenomena involving polarisation, pulse shapes, radio spectra, intensity variations, and complex secondary periodicities, must eventually provide vital evidence to resolve our present uncertainties. There is good reason to believe that the general outline is correct. Simple dynamics shows that the surface magnetic field strength B_0 is proportional to $\left(P\dfrac{dP}{dt}\right)_{/2\tau}$ were P is the pulsar period, and observations of many pulsars give $B_0 \sim 10^8$ T when conventional neutron star models are assumed. Further evidence comes from pulsar ages which are aproximately $P\left(\dfrac{dP}{dt}\right)^{-1}$.

Typical ages are 10^6—10^7 years although 10^3 years is obtained for the Crab pulsar, in good agreement with the known age of the supernova.

Conclusion

In outlining the physics of neutron stars, and my good fortune in stumbling upon them, I hope I have given some idea of the interest and rewards of extending physics beyond the confines of laboratories. These are good times in which to be an astrophysicist. I am also deeply aware of my debt to all my colleagues in the Cavendish Laboratory. Firstly to Sir Martin Ryle for his unique flair in creating so congenial and stimulating a team in which to work. Secondly to Jocelyn Bell for the care, diligence and persistence that led to our discovery so early in the scintillation programme, and finally to my friends who contributed so generously in many aspects of the work.

REFERENCES

1. Hewish, A., Proc. Roy. Soc. (London), *214,* 494, (1952).
2. Hewish, A. and Wyndham, J. D., Mon. Not. R. astr. Soc., *126,* 469, (1963).
3. Clarke, M. E., Ph.D. Thesis. Cambridge (1964).
4. Hewish, A., Scott, P. F. and Wills, D., Nature, *203,* 1214, (1964).
5. Dennison, P. A. and Hewish, A., Nature, *213,* 343, (1967).
6. Hewish, A. and Okoye, S. E., Nature, *207,* 59, (1965).
7. Hewish, A., Bell, S. J., Pilkington, J. D. H., Scott, P. F. and Collins, R. A., Nature *217,* 709, (1968).
8. Gold, T., Nature, *218,* 731, (1968).
9. Staelin, D. H. and Reifenstein, E. C., Science, *162,* 1481, (1968).
10. Comella, J. M., Craft, H. D., Lovelace, R. V. E., Sutton, J. M. and Tyler, G. L., Nature, *221,* 453, (1969).
11. Baade, W., and Zwicky, F., Proc. Nat. Acad. Sci. *20,* 255, (1934).
12. Ruderman, M., Ann. Rev. Astron. Astrophys., *10,* 427, (1972).
13. Pines, D., Shaham, J., and Ruderman, M., I.Au.c Symposium No 53, (1973).
14. Ginzburg, V. L. and Zheleznyakov, V. V., Ann. Rev. Astron. Astrophys., *13.* (1975) in press.
15. Pacini, F., Nature, *219,* 145, (1968).
16. Goldreich, P. and Julian, W. H., Astrophys. J., *157,* 869, (1969).

Martin Ryle

MARTIN RYLE

I was born on September 27, 1918, the second of five children. My father John A. Ryle was a doctor who, after the war, was appointed to the first Chair of Social Medicine at Oxford University.

I was educated at Bradfield College and Oxford, where I graduated in 1939. During the war years I worked on the development of radar and other radio systems for the R.A.F. and, though gaining much in engineering experience and in understanding people, rapidly forgot most of the physics I had learned.

In 1945 J. A. Ratcliffe, who had been leading the ionospheric work in the Cavendish Laboratory, Cambridge before the war, suggested that I apply for a fellowship to join his group to start an investigation of the radio emission from the Sun, which had recently been discovered accidentally with radar equipment.

During these early months, and for many years afterwards both Ratcliffe and Sir Lawrence Bragg, then Cavendish Professor, gave enormous support and encouragement to me. Bragg's own work on X-ray crystallography involved techniques very similar to those we were developing for "aperture synthesis", and he always showed a delighted interest in the way our work progressed.

In 1948 I was appointed to a Lectureship in Physics and in 1949 elected to a Fellowship at Trinity College. At this time Tony Hewish joined me, and in fact four other members of our present team started their research during the period 1948—52.

In 1959 the University recognized our work by appointing me to a new Chair of Radio Astronomy.

During 1964—7 I was president of Commission 40 of the International Astronomical Union, and in 1972 was appointed Astronomer Royal.

In 1947 I married Rowena Palmer, and we have two daughters, Alison and Claire, and a son, John. We enjoy sailing small boats, two of which I have designed and built myself.

Awards

1952   Fellow of Royal Society of London.
1954   Hughes Medal, Royal Society of London.
1955   Halley Lecturer, University of Oxford.
1958   Bakerian Lecturer, Royal Society of London.

1963 Van der Pol Medal, U.R.S.I.

1964 Gold Medal, Royal Astronomical Society, London.

1965 Henry Draper Medal, U.S. National Academy of Sciences; Holweck Prize, Société Française de Physique.

1968 Elected Foreign Member of the Royal Danish Academy of Sciences and Letters.

1970 Elected Foreign Honorary Member of American Academy of Arts and Sciences.

1971 Elected Foreign Member of U.S.S.R. Academy of Sciences.

Morris N. Liebmann Award; Institution of Electrical & Electronic Engineers.

Faraday Medal, Institution of Electrical Engineers.

Popov Medal, USSR Academy of Sciences.

Michelson Medal, Franklin Institute, U.S.A.

1973 Royal Medal, Royal Society of London.

1974 Bruce Medal, Astronomical Society of the Pacific.

Foreign Member, Deutsche Akademie der Naturforscher, Leopoldina.

Honorary D.Sc. of the Universities of Strathclyde (1968), Oxford (1969) and Nicholas Copernicus University of Torun (1973).

RADIO TELESCOPES OF LARGE RESOLVING POWER

Nobel Lecture, December 12, 1974

by MARTIN RYLE
University of Cambridge, Cavendish Laboratory, Cambridge, England

I think that the event which, more than anything else, led me to the search for ways of making more powerful radio telescopes, was the recognition, in 1952, that the intense source in the constellation of Cygnus was a distant galaxy—1000 million light years away. This discovery showed that some galaxies were capable of producing radio emission about a million times more intense than that from our own Galaxy or the Andromeda nebula, and the mechanisms responsible were quite unknown. It seemed quite likely that some of the weaker sources already detected with the small radio telescopes then available might be similar in character; if so they would be at distances comparable with the limits of observation of the largest optical telescopes. It was therefore possible that more powerful radio telescopes might eventually provide the best way of distinguishing between different cosmological models. It was not until 1958 (1) that it could be shown with some certainty that most of the sources were indeed powerful extragalactic objects, but the possibilities were so exciting even in 1952 that my colleagues and I set about the task of designing instruments capable of extending the observations to weaker and weaker sources, and of exploring their internal structure.

The early observations were severely limited both by the poor angular resolution and by the limited sensitivity. It was usually impossible to obtain any information about the structure of a source, and adjacent sources could often not be properly separated, whilst attempts to relate the radio sources to optically visible objects were often prevented by the poor positional accuracy. The use of interferometers allowed better positions to be obtained, and sometimes made it possible to derive simple models for the source structure. Few of the sources were found to have an angular size greater than 2—3 minutes of arc.

The problem of making detailed maps of such sources arises simply from the fact that the wavelengths used are some million times greater than optical wavelengths—so that even to obtain a radio picture with the same resolution as that of the unaided human eye ($\sim 1'$ arc) we would need a telescope having a diameter of about 1 km operating at a wavelength of 50 cm. At the same time the instrument will be effective only if the surface accuracy is good enough to make a proper image, corresponding to errors of $\leqslant \lambda/20$ or a few cm; the engineering problems of building such an instrument are clearly enormous.

With the development, around 1960, of masers and parametric amplifiers capable of providing receiving systems of good sensitivity at wavelengths of a few cm, it became possible to build telescopes of diameter 10—100 m with

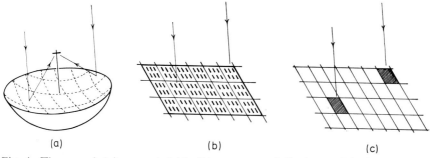

Fig. 1. The use of (a) a paraboloid, (b) an array of dipoles or (c) the sequential sampling of the wavefront by small aerial elements to achieve a high resolving power by combining the signals from a large part of the incident wavefront.

sufficient sensitivity and with angular resolutions of $\sim 1'$ arc; even with such instruments the engineering problems of constructing a rigid enough surface are considerable, and it is likely to be difficult to build a conventional paraboloid capable of angular resolutions much better than $1'$ arc.

I would like now to describe an entirely different approach to the problem in which small aerial elements are moved to occupy successively the whole of a much larger aperture plane. The development and use of "aperture synthesis" systems has occupied much of our team in Cambridge over the past 20 years.

The principle of the method is extremely simple. In all methods used to obtain a large resolving power, that is to distinguish the wavefront from a particular direction and ignore those from adjacent directions, we arrange to combine the field measured over as large an area as possible of the wavefront. In a paraboloid we do this by providing a suitably shaped reflecting surface, so that the fields incident on different parts of the sampled wavefront are combined at the focus (Fig. 1(a)); the voltage produced in the receiving dipole represents the sum of these fields. We can achieve the same result if we use an array of dipoles connected together through equal lengths of cable (Fig. 1(b)).

Suppose now that only a small part of the wavefront is sampled, but that different parts are sampled in turn (Fig. 1(c)); could we combine these signals to produce the same effect? Since in general, we do not know the phase of the incident field at different times this would not normally be possible but if we continue to measure *one* of the samples while we measure the others we can use the signal from this one as a phase reference to correct the values measured in other parts of the wavefront. In this way, by using two small aerial elements, we can again add the fields over the wavefront—the area of which is now determined by the range of relative positions taken by the two aerial elements.

It might be thought that this method would be extremely slow, for if we are to sample an area of side D using elements of side d, it is necessary to observe with $\dfrac{2D^2}{d^2}$ different relative positions of the two aerial elements. In practice, however, the method is not significantly slower than the use of the large equivalent instrument for although a large number of observations must be made, the results may be combined in a computer using additional phase differences, which correspond to many different wave directions (as in a phased array or dipoles), so that with the one set of observations an *area* of sky may be mapped which is limited only by the diffraction pattern of the small elements themselves; there are in fact some $\dfrac{D^2}{d^2}$ different directions which can be scanned in this way, and which would have had to be explored sequentially by a conventional instrument, so that the total observing time of the two methods is nearly the same.

It can also be seen that the sensitivity of the system is much better than would be associated with the small elements, for the signal from a particular point in the sky is contributing to that point on the map for the *whole* observing period; the resulting signal-to-noise is in fact equivalent to the use of an instrument having a collecting area $2d^2 \sqrt{\dfrac{2D^2}{d^2}}$

$\sim 3Dd$, a figure which may be much greater than that of the elements themselves, and although it is not as great as if the full instrument of area D^2 had been built, it may exceed that of any instrument which *can* be built.

Unlike a paraboloid or array, in which both the sensitivity and resolving power are fixed as soon as the wavelength is decided, the value of d may be chosen so that the sensitivity, for any particular wavelength and type of observation, is matched to the resolution.

The method of aperture synthesis avoids the severe structural problems of building very large and accurate paraboloids or arrays, and allows both high resolving power and large effective collecting area to be obtained with a minimum of engineering structure and therefore cost. Provision must be made for the relative movement of the small elements, and their relative positions and electrical connecting paths must be known with an accuracy equal to the surface accuracy of the equivalent instrument ($\leqslant \lambda/20$). Automatic computing is needed to carry out the Fourier inversion involved in combining the observations to provide a map of the sky.

Historically, the forerunners fo this type of instrument were realized in the early days when observations in both Australia and England with aerial elements having a range of separations were used to determine the distribution of radio brightness across the solar disc. In the earliest observations the Sun was assumed to show spherical symmetry, and no measurements of phase were necessary so that a precise knowledge of the relative positions of the elements, and of the electrical path lengths to the receiver were unnecessary. A similar technique was used to establish the profile of radio brightness across the plane of the Galaxy (2).

The first synthesis instrument capable of mapping an abritrary distribution of sources was built at Cambridge in 1954 by John Blythe (3); it consisted of a long thin element covering, in effect, a whole row of Fig. 1(c) used in con-

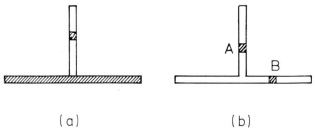

(a)   (b)

Fig. 2. (a) The arrangement used in the instrument built in 1954 by J. H. Bythe.
(b) The equivalent instrument using two small elements.

junction with a smaller element moved to 38 different positions along a perpendicular line (Fig. 2(a)) to synthesise a square instrument giving a resolution of 2°.2. This instrument provided the first detailed maps of the galactic emission at a long radio wavelength (7.9 m).

Larger instruments using this same configuration were built at Cambridge during the succeeding years, including an instrument of high sensitivity and 45′ arc resolution also at $\lambda = 7.9$ m (4) and a second operating at $\lambda = 1.7$ m with 25′ arc resolution which was used by Paul Scott and others to locate nearly 5000 sources in the northern sky (5, 6).

These instruments used a very cheap form of construction; for $\lambda > 1$ m an efficient reflecting surface may be provided by thin (~ 1 mm diameter) wires 5—10 cm apart. In the case of the $\lambda = 1.7$ m instrument, wires stretched across simple parabolic frames of welded steel tube provided a cylindrical paraboloid 450 m long and 20 m wide (Fig. 3) at a cost of about £2 per m².

Fig. 3. Photograph of the east—west arm of the $\lambda = 1.7$ m instrument built in 1957 with which nearly 5000 sources were located.

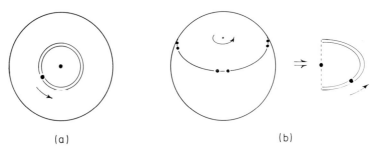

Fig. 4. (a) Two aerial elements mounted near the North Pole observing throughout the day are equivalent to one ring of a much larger instrument.
(b) The elements may be used at other latitudes if arranged on an east—west line and used to track the chosen point for 12^h.

With the need for still greater resolving power, we realized that physically larger systems operating at metre wavelengths would no longer prove successful, because of the limitation imposed by irregularities of electron density in the ionosphere. But at shorter wavelengths where these are unimportant it becomes difficult to make efficient reflectors by using stretched wires, both because of their deflection by the wind, and because with the closer spacing needed there is difficulty with them twisting together. For operating wavelengths of < 50 cm a much more rigid supporting structure must be used, and the engineering costs of building a long element become very great.

The obvious solution is to use the system illustrated in Fig. 1(c), in which the engineering structure is confined to two small elements—where much higher costs per m^2 are acceptable. The method for altering the relative positions of the two elements presents some practical problems; suppose that the elements are mounted on two railway tracks at right angles (Fig. 2(b)), so that for each position of A on the N—S track B is moved to every position along the E—W track. For values of $\dfrac{D}{d} \sim 50$, there are then 5000 different arrangements, and if B is moved each day, the observations will take 5000 days and although a map will then be available for the whole strip of sky, the period is too long for a graduate student's thesis!

Alternatively B could be moved rapidly—so that several positions could be fitted into the time during which the area of sky remains in the beam of the small elements. This will reduce the total time of the observations, at the expense of observing only parts of the strip of sky. We can clearly extend this period, and so allow more relative positions of A and B each day, if we arrange for the elements to track the chosen point in the sky for an extended period.

As soon as we do this, we realize that the rotation of the earth is itself providing us with a relative motion of A and B as seen from the source, without our having to move them on the surface of the earth at all. Suppose, for example, we have our two elements mounted near the North Pole and we use them to observe an area of sky centred on the Celestial Pole; in this case we do not even have to arrange for them to track. Over a 24^h period, one will have traced out a circular path about the other (Fig. 4(a)), and the signals recorded during this time can be combined to provide the same response as that of the equivalent ring aerial; by simply altering the separation along a line on say 50 successive days a complete aperture can then be synthesized. Miss Ann Neville and I set up an experimental system in 1960—61 to test the method and develop the computing; we used it to map a region 8° in diameter round the North Celestial Pole at a wavelength of 1.7 m (7). We connected up different 14 m sections of the long cylindrical paraboloid (Fig. 3) with some other small aerials to simulate the use of two 14 m diameter elements at different spacings. The effective diameter of the synthesized instrument was 1 km and it provided an angular resolution of 4'.5 arc.

As well as showing that the method really worked, it provided some interesting astronomical results—in particular by allowing the detection of sources some 8 times weaker than had been observed before; even though the area of sky covered was only some 50 square degrees the results were useful in our cosmological investigations.

In practice only 12^h observations are needed because of the symmetry of the system and observations need not be made *from* the North Pole or limited *to* the Celestial Pole, provided that the elements are situated on an East—West axis, and each is able to track the required region of sky for 12^h (Fig. 4(b)). At low declinations the synthesized instrument becomes elliptical with the north-south aperture reduced by sin δ. The engineering simplicity of moving the elements along a line, and the consequent great saving in the area of land needed are, however, such great advantages that we eventually built three large instruments in Cambridge with equivalent instrumental diameters of 0.8, 1.6 and nearly 5 km.

These instruments are known as the Half-Mile, the One-Mile and (because its construction coincided with the early negotiations for the entry of Britain into the European Community), the 5 km Telescopes! The One-Mile telescope was the first to be built, and this started observations in 1964.

It is interesting that as early as 1954 we had discussed the possibility of building a high resolution instrument on exactly these principles, and I have recently found two entries in an old note-book:—

"*8.6.1954 Possible research student and other projects.*
  ... 3(f). North Polar Survey on 81.5 Mc/s. Effective gain area $\sim 25 \times$ 1500 = 37,500 sq. ft. Effective resolving power area $\simeq 10^6$ sq. ft."
  (The entry included a diagram of the proposed aerial element)

"*29.6.1954*
  Do 3(f) in all directions where 180° rotation available? above about 20° might be possible by directing aerials in successively different directions— i.e. observation not on meridian."

A third entry on 22.7.1954 discusses the east—west rail track to be used for the latter programme with two 30 ft aerials mounted on it, the arrangement of cabling needed to compensate for the different path lengths to the two aerials when observing off the meridian, and the selection of directions of observation "to give uniform cover of Fourier terms".

Why then, with its obvious simplicity and economy, did we not build this instrument in 1954? The answer is that at this time there were no computers with sufficient speed and storage capacity to do the Fourier inversion of the data. EDSAC I, which was the first stored-programme computer, was built by Dr. M. V. Wilkes of the Cambridge University Mathematical Laboratory, and came into operation in 1949. It was used for reducing John Blythe's observations and took some 15^h of computing to do the 38-point transform for every 4^m of the 24^h scan of the sky. It would not have been practicable to use it for the 2-dimensional inversion needed for the earth-rotation synthesis. By 1958 the completion of the much faster EDSAC II, and the development by Dr. David Wheeler of the Mathematical Laboratory of the fast fourier transform (incidentally some six years before these methods came into general use) made possible the efficient reduction of the 7.9 m and 1.7 m surveys, and also enabled the trials of the 1.7 m earth-rotation synthesis to be made in 1961; even with EDSAC II, however, the reduction for the small area of sky covered in the latter survey took the whole night.

During the early stages in the design of the One-Mile telescope in 1961, I discussed with Maurice Wilkes the considerably greater problems of reducing the data from this instrument, but by then the replacement of EDSAC II was planned and the new TITAN computer, which came into operation in 1963, was easily capable of dealing with the output of the One-Mile telescope. The development of aperture synthesis has therefore been very closely linked to the development of more and more powerful computers, and it is interesting to speculate how our work in Cambridge would have proceeded if, for example, computer development had been five years behind its actual course.

The two programmes in my 1954 note-book subsequently formed the basis of two Ph.D. theses in 1964 and 1965.

Now I return to the design of the large instruments whose layout is shown in Fig. 5. The One-Mile telescope consists of three 18 m dishes, two fixed at 0.8 km spacing, the third mounted on a 0.8 km rail-track (Fig. 6); this ar-

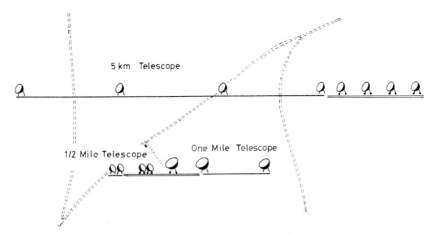

Fig. 5. Sketch map showing the arrangement of One-Mile, Half-Mile and 5 km telescopes.

Fig. 6. The One-Mile telescope, showing the west, railmounted, dish in the foreground, with the two fixed dishes behind.

rangement was cheaper than building the longer rail track and it also provided two spacings at a time. It was designed for two main programmes: (a) The detection of much fainter and therefore more distant sources (see Fig. 7) in order to explore the early history of the Universe, and so try and distinguish between different cosmological models, and (b) To make radio maps of individual sources in an attempt to understand the physical mechanisms within them; most of the sources studied have been powerful extragalactic objects, but the remnants of supernova explosions are perhaps physically as important.

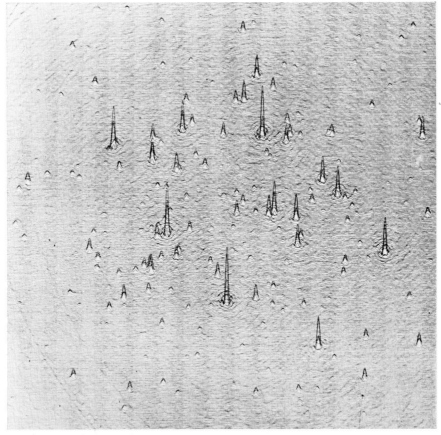

Fig. 7. Map obtained with the One-Mile telescope showing sources about 100 times fainter than had been observed before.

The problem of the physics of radio galaxies and quasars and the cosmological problem are strangely linked; we appear to be living in an evolving Universe, so that very distant sources which, due to the signal travel time, we observe as they were when the Universe was younger, may be systematically different from a sample of nearby sources. But the intrinsically most powerful sources are so rare that there *are* no nearby ones, whilst the weak sources cannot be detected at great distances. If we are to understand *how* the Universe is evolving, we may first have to solve the physical problem of the individual source—so that we can infer the differences in its evolution at earlier cosmological epochs.

The Half-Mile telescope was built later by John Shakeshaft and John Baldwin. It was actually built very cheaply because as can be seen from Fig. 5, it made use of the same rail track, and we were able to get the four 9 m dishes at scrap-metal prices from a discontinued radio link service, and only the mounts had to be built. It has been used mainly with a radio spectrometer covering the 21 cm wavelength band of neutral hydrogen to map the distribution of density and velocity of the hydrogen in a number of nearby galaxies,

91

Fig. 8. The 5 km telescope, with the movable dishes in the foreground.

and forms part of a programme concerning the formation and evolution of galaxies.

The 5 km telescope was completed in 1971, and because it represents a rather more advanced design I will describe it in more detail. It was designed solely for the purpose of mapping individual sources, and besides its larger overall size, the individual dishes are more accurate to allow operation at wavelengths as short as 2 cm. As a result the angular resolution is $\sim 1''$ arc, a figure comparable with the resolution attained by large optical telescopes on good mountain sites. It is at present being used on a wavelength of 6 cm, where the resolution is $2''$ arc.

In order to improve the speed of observation, four fixed and four movable elements mounted on a rail-track are used, as shown in Fig. 5; this arrangement provides 16 spacings simultaneously, and a single 12^h observation produces a $2''$ arc main response with circular grating responses separated by $42''$ arc. Sources of smaller extent than $42''$ arc can therefore be mapped with a single 12^h observation; more extensive fields of view require further observations with intermediate positions of the movable elements to suppress the grating responses.

For operation at these short wavelengths the positioning of the elements, and the electrical cable connections, must be stable and measured with an accuracy better than 1 mm. Conventional surveying methods allowed each element to be located to ± 10 mm, and the final alignment had to be based entirely on radio observations; the distance between the two outer fixed elements (on which the scale of declination is based) was found in this way to be 3430828.7 ± 0.25 mm, and no changes outside this error have been found over a 2-year period. The combination of azimuth and longitude, on which the measurement of right-ascension depends, was established by observing the bright fundamental star Algol, which is a weak and variable radio source.

The telescope is controlled by an on-line computer which continually updates the position of the selected map-centre for precession, aberration etc., and uses this to compute the path differences (corrected for atmospheric refraction) to each pair of elements; these values are then used to control electrical delays in the signals from each element before they are combined in the receivers. The outputs of the receivers are sampled by the computer and stored on a magnetic disc, so that at the completion of the observation they may be combined to form a map of the area observed. The map is then drawn on a curve-plotter controlled by the computer.

This instrument has been used in a wide range of astronomical programmes from the study of ionized hydrogen clouds in our Galaxy to distant quasars. Following the accurate calibration survey it became evident that as an astrometric instrument—to establish a coordinate system across the sky—its measuring accuracy was comparable with the best optical methods, whilst overcoming some of the difficulties in optical work such as the measurement of large angles. Bruce Elsmore is involved in a collaborative programme with optical observers to relate the positions of quasars—(some of which are compact sources at both optical and radio wavelengths)—as measured by radio means, to those derived from the fundamental stars, in order to determine any large-scale non-uniformities which may exist in the present astrometric systems. He also showed how this type of instrument may be used for the direct measurement of astronomical time—without the need for collaborative observations at different longitudes to correct for polar motion—again with an accuracy comparable with optical methods (~ 5 mS in a 12^h observation).

Another programme is concerned with a study of the birth of stars; when a cloud of gas condenses to form a star, the dust which it contains provides such an effective screen that newly-formed stars, with their surrounding regions of ionized hydrogen, can never be seen optically; only after this dust cloud has dispersed does the star appear. The dust introduces no appreciable absorption at radio wavelengths, so that radio observations allow these regions to be studied at the earliest stages.

NGC 7538 is an example of such a region, and the upper part of Fig. 9 shows the radio emission as mapped with the One-Mile telescope. The large diffuse component corresponds almost exactly with the optical nebulosity, and represents the cloud of gas ionized by one or more O-stars formed about a million years ago, with the dust sufficiently dispersed to allow the light to be seen. The compact lower component corresponds to gas ionized by much younger stars, which are still embedded in dust too dense for any optical emission to escape, and it is invisible on the photograph. When this southern component was mapped with the higher resolution of the 5 km telescope, the

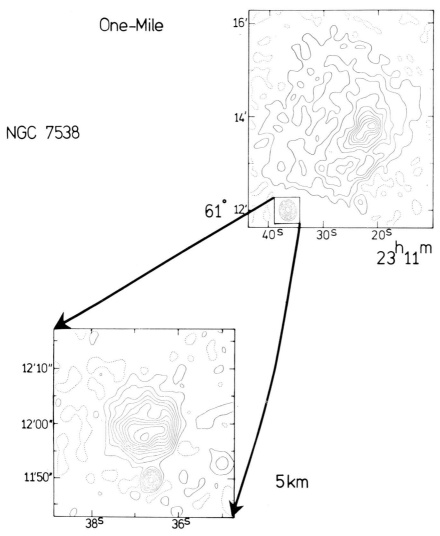

Fig. 9. The ionized hydrogen cloud NGC 7538. The upper radio map shows the large cloud associated with the optical emission, and another, compact, component to the south. This compact component is shown with greater resolution below.

lower map was obtained, showing that there is an ionized cloud some 10″ arc in diameter, probably produced by the radiation from a star of spectral type O8, and an even more compact cloud to the south of this, produced by a still younger star, only a few thousand years old. The dust surrounding these two compact regions is heated by the young stars they contain, and both have been detected by their infra-red emission (8).

But the most extensive programme has been the mapping of extragalactic sources—the radio galaxies and quasars; galaxies which, during a brief fraction of their lives, produce some 10^{60} ergs of energy, equivalent to the total annihilation of the matter in about a million suns, by a mechanism which is not understood.

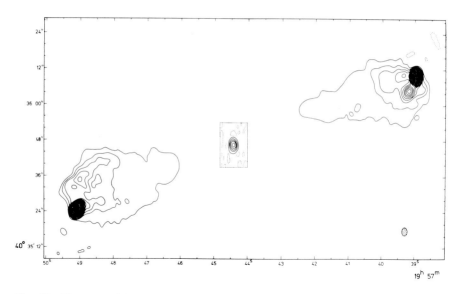

Fig. 10. The powerful radio galaxy in the constellation of Cygnus mapped with the 5 km telescope. The compact outer components are exceedingly bright—(31 and 41 contours). The central component—which corresponds to the nucleus of the optical galaxy is very weak and is drawn with contours spaced at 1/5 the interval.

Fig. 10 shows the new radio map of the source in the constellation of Cygnus—the first powerful radio galaxy to be recognized. The distribution of polarized emission from the north component is shown in Fig. 11, giving in-

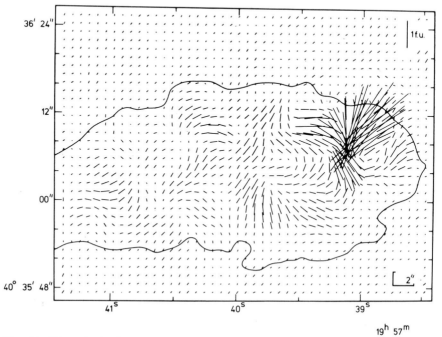

Fig. 11. The polarization of the emission from the north component of the Cygnus source which shows the magnetic field to be turbulent on a scale $\sim 10^4$ light-years.

95

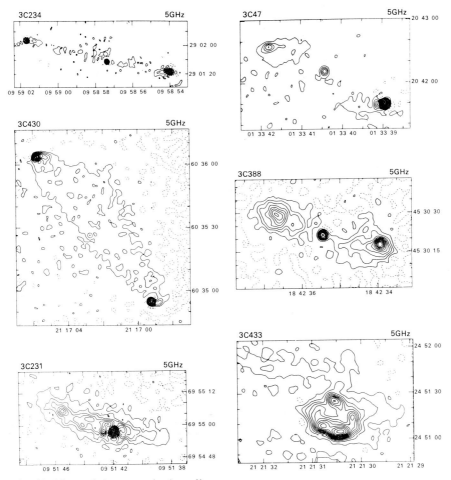

Fig. 12. Maps of six extragalactic radio sources.

formation on the magnetic field. Maps of a number of other sources made with the 5 km telescope are shown in Fig. 12.

In most cases the radio emission originates mainly in two huge regions disposed far outside the associated galaxy—although weak emission may also be detectable from a very compact central source coincident with the nucleus of the galaxy. In some cases much more extensive components or a bridge linking the components occur.

The finer detail provided by the 5 km telescope has already enabled some important conclusions to be drawn; the energy is probably being produced more or less continuously over a period of 10^7—10^8 years in a very compact nucleus and not, as was originally thought, in some single explosive event. The source of this energy may be associated with the gravitational collapse of large numbers of stars, in the manner which Tony Hewish describes in his lecture, or by material falling into a much more massive collapsed object at the nucleus of the galaxy. The mechanism for transmitting this energy to the compact heads of the main components (e.g. Fig. 10) is not understood, but

96

may involve a narrow beam of low frequency electromagnetic waves or relativistic particles (9, 10). The interaction of this beam with the surrounding intergalactic medium might then accelerate the electrons responsible for the radio emission from the compact heads, and their subsequent diffusion into the region behind the heads can probably explain the general shape of the extensive components.

While much remains unanswered, the present conclusions were only reached when detailed maps became available; the physical processes relating the nucleus, the compact heads, and the extensive tails or bridges can clearly only be investigated when the relationship between these structural components is known.

What can we expect in the future? In 1954, the first aperture synthesis telescope provided maps with a resolution of $2°.2$; today we have maps with a resolution of $2''$ arc. Can we foresee a continuing development with radio pictures having much *better* resolution than the optical ones? The technical problems of increasing the aperture or decreasing the operating wavelength are severe, but they do not appear to be as serious as the limitations imposed by the earth's atmosphere; in optical observations atmospheric turbulence on a scale of ~ 10 cm in the lower atmosphere introduces irregularities in the incident wavefront which normally limits the resolution to $\sim 1''$ arc. At radio wavelengths the contribution of these small-scale irregularities is not important, but there are also irregularities of refractive index on a much larger scale in the troposphere. Two distinct types have been found in a series of observations with the One-Mile and 5 km telescopes; neither can be attributed to variations of air density, and both are probably due to non-uniformity in the partial pressure of water-vapour, which makes an important contribution to the refractive index at radio wavelengths. One class has a typical scale size of ~ 0.7 km and is attributed to turbulence in the troposphere due to solar heating of the ground in the same way that fair-weather cumulus clouds develop. These irregularities, however, are often detected in clear air conditions without the formation of cumulus clouds; they only occur during day-time and are more severe during summer months. The second class,—which shows only slight diurnal or annual variation, has a much larger scale size, typically 10—20 km, and there may be still larger scales which have not yet been recognized. The origin of these disturbances is not known, and it is therefore not possible to predict how they might depend on geographical position.

Under very good conditions—representing about 1 % of the total time, the atmospheric irregularities are extremely small and correspond to a distortion of the incident wavefront by < 0.2 mm over 5 km; under these conditions, operation at a wavelength of 4 mm or less would be possible and should provide maps with a resolution better than $0''.2$ arc. These excellent observing conditions have only been encountered during periods of widespread winter fog when the atmosphere is extremely stable, a result which illustrates the differing requirements in seeking good sites for optical and radio observatories!

97

For most of the time the atmospheric irregularities are considerably worse, and although there is insufficient information on scale sizes > 20 km, the use of instruments much larger than this will introduce difficulties associated with the curvature of the atmosphere. One might guess that it should be possible to build instruments which would give a resolution better than $0''.5$ arc for perhaps 50 % of the winter months.

To reach a greater resolution new techniques capable of correcting for the atmospheric effects will be necessary. One simple, though expensive, solution would be to build a second dish alongside each element, so that observations of a reference point source close to the area to be mapped, could be made simultaneously at every spacing; the observed phase errors for this reference source could then be used to provide a continuous correction for the signals from the area being mapped.

Such techniques can clearly be extended to the interferometers having baselines of many thousands of km (VLBI) which have been made possible by the development of atomic frequency standards. These instruments have shown the existence of very small components, $\sim 0''.001$ arc in some sources. The use of a comparison source for eliminating both atmospheric and in-strumental phase was first used at Jodrell Bank in the special case of sources of the OH maser line at $\lambda = 18$ cm, where different components within the primary beam can be distinguished by their frequency; if one is used as a phase reference the relative positions of the others can be found (11).

For continuum sources a reference outside the primary beam of the in-strument must, in general, be used and two elements at each location are needed. This technique has been used in the U.S.A. to reduce both in-strumental and atmospheric phase variations in measurements of the gravi-tational deflection of radio waves by the sun (12); one pair of elements was used to observe a source close to the Sun, while the other pair observed a reference source about $10°$ away.

The accuracy of the correction, and hence the shortest wavelength at which mapping could be achieved, would depend on the angular separation between the area to be mapped and a reference source sufficiently intense and of suf-ficiently small angular size. But even if adequate phase stability can be at-tained in this way, there is a serious practical difficulty in making maps with resolution $\sim 0''.001$ arc, due to the inevitable poor sampling of the aperture plane. Even with 5 or 6 stations distributed across one hemisphere of the world, and using every possible combination of the signals from them, with observing periods lasting several hours, the fraction of the aperture plane which can be filled is still very small, so that the field of view which can be mapped without ambiguity from secondary responses is unlikely to exceed $\sim 0''.02$ arc. Whilst there seems little hope of deriving complete maps of most sources with this resolution, there are certainly some central components where such a map could provide very important information.

But I think it may also be important for our understanding of the mechanisms operating in the main components of radio sources, to obtain complete maps with intermediate resolution; for this work extensions of the present synthesis techniques, while retaining good filling of the aperture plane, are needed.

The last 25 years have seen a remarkable improvement in the performance of radio telescopes, which has in turn led to a much greater understanding of the strange sources of "high-energy astrophysics" and of the nature of the Universe as a whole.

I feel very fortunate to have started my research at a time which allowed me and my colleagues to play a part in these exciting developments.

REFERENCES

1. Ryle, M. (1958) Proc. Roy. Soc. A., *248*, 289.
2. Scheuer, P. A. G. & Ryle, M. (1953) Mon. Not. R. astr. Soc., *113*, 3.
3. Blythe, J. H. (1957) Mon. Not. R. astr. Soc., *117*, 644.
4. Costain, C. H. & Smith, F. G. (1960) Mon. Not. R. astr. Soc., *121*, 405.
5. Pilkington, J. D. H. & Scott, P. F. (1965) Mem. R. astr. Soc., *69*, 183.
6. Gower, J. F. R., Scott, P. F. & Wills, D. (1967) Mem. R. astr. Soc., *71*, 49
7. Ryle, M. & Neville, A. C. (1962) Mon. Not. R. astr. Soc., *125*, 39.
8. Wynn-Williams, C. G., Becklin, E. E. & Neugebauer, G. (1974) Ap. J., *187*, 473.
9. Rees, M. (1971) Nature, *229*, 312.
10. Scheuer, P. A. G. (1974) Mon. Not. R. astr. Soc., *166*, 513.
11. Cooper, A. J., Davies, R. D. & Booth, R. S. (1971) Mon. Not. R. astr. Soc., *152*, 383
12. Counselmann, C. C., Kent, S. M., Knight, C. A., Shapiro, I. I., Clarke, T. A., Hinteregger, H. F., Rogers, A. E. E. & Whitney, A. R. (1974) Phys. Rev. Lett., *33*, 1621.

Paul J. Flory

PAUL J. FLORY

I was born on 19 June, 1910, in Sterling, Illinois, of Huguenot-German parentage, mine being the sixth generation native to America. My father was Ezra Flory, a clergyman-educator; my mother, nee Martha Brumbaugh, had been a schoolteacher. Both were descended from generations of farmers in the New World. They were the first of their families of record to have attended college.

My interest in science, and in chemistry in particular, was kindled by a remarkable teacher, Carl W. Holl, Professor of Chemistry at Manchester College, a liberal arts college in Indiana, where I graduated in 1931. With his encouragement, I entered the Graduate School of The Ohio State University where my interests turned to physical chemistry. Research for my dissertation was in the field of photochemistry and spectroscopy. It was carried out under the guidance of the late Professor Herrick L. Johnston whose boundless zeal for scientific research made a lasting impression on his students.

Upon completion of my Ph.D. in 1934, I joined the Central Research Department of the DuPont Company. There it was my good fortune to be assigned to the small group headed by Dr. Wallace H. Carothers, inventor of nylon and neoprene, and a scientist of extraordinary breadth and originality. It was through the association with him that I first became interested in exploration of the fundamentals of polymerization and polymeric substances. His conviction that polymers are valid objects of scientific inquiry proved contagious. The time was propitious, for the hypothesis that polymers are in fact covalently linked macromolecules had been established by the works of Staudinger and of Carothers only a few years earlier.

A year after the untimely death of Carothers, in 1937, I joined the Basic Science Research Laboratory of the University of Cincinnati for a period of two years. With the outbreak of World War II and the urgency of research and development on synthetic rubber, supply of which was imperiled, I returned to industry, first at the Esso (now Exxon) Laboratories of the Standard Oil Development Company (1940—43) and later at the Research Laboratory of the Goodyear Tire and Rubber Company (1943—48). Provision of opportunities for continuation of basic research by these two industrial laboratories to the limit that the severe pressures of the times would allow, and their liberal policies on publication, permitted continuation of the beginnings of a scientific career which might otherwise have been stifled by the exigencies of those difficult years.

In the Spring of 1948 it was my privilege to hold the George Fisher Baker Non-Resident Lectureship in Chemistry at Cornell University. The invitation on behalf of the Department of Chemistry had been tendered by the late Professor Peter J. W. Debye, then Chairman of that Department. The experience of this lectureship and the stimulating asociations with the Cornell faculty led me to accept, without hesitation, their offer of a professorship commencing in the Autumn of 1948. There followed a most productive and satisfying period of research and teaching. "Principles of Polymer Chemistry," published by the Cornell University Press in 1953, was an outgrowth of the Baker Lectures.

It was during the Baker Lectureship that I perceived a way to treat the effect of excluded volume on the configuration of polymer chains. I had long suspected that the effect would be non-asymptotic with the length of the chain; that is, that the perturbation of the configuration by the exclusion of one segment of the chain from the space occupied by another would increase without limit as the chain is lengthened. The treatment of the effect by resort to a relatively simple "smoothed density" model confirmed this expectation and provided an expression relating the perturbation of the configuration to the chain length and the effective volume of a chain segment. It became apparent that the physical properties of dilute solutions of macromolecules could not be properly treated and comprehended without taking account of the perturbation of the macromolecule by these intramolecular interactions. The hydrodynamic theories of dilute polymer solutions developed a year or two earlier by Kirkwood and by Debye were therefore reinterpreted in light of the excluded volume effect. Agreement with a broad range of experimental information on viscosities, diffusion coefficients and sedimentation velocities was demonstrated soon thereafter.

Out of these developments came the formulation of the hydrodynamic constant called Φ, and the recognition of the Theta point at which excluded volume interactions are neutralized. Criteria for experimental identification of the Theta point are easily applied. Ideal behavior of polymers, natural and synthetic, under Theta conditions has subsequently received abundant confirmation in many laboratories. These findings are most gratifying. More importantly, they provide the essential basis for rational interpretation of physical measurements on dilute polymer solutions, and hence for the quantitative characterization of macromolecules.

In 1957 my family and I moved to Pittsburgh where I undertook to establish a broad program of basic research at the Mellon Institute. The opportunity to achieve this objective having been subsequently withdrawn, I accepted a professorship in the Department of Chemistry at Stanford University in 1961. In 1966, I was appointed to the J. G. Jackson—C. J. Wood Professorship in Chemistry at Stanford.

The change in situation upon moving to Stanford afforded the opportunity to recast my research efforts in new directions. Two areas have dominated the interests of my coworkers and myself since 1961. The one concerns the spatial configuration of chain molecules and the treatment of their configuration-dependent properties by rigorous mathematical methods; the other constitutes a new approach to an old subject, namely, the thermodynamics of solutions.

102

Our investigations in the former area have proceeded from foundations laid by Professor M. V. Volkenstein and his collaborators in the Soviet Union, and were supplemented by major contributions of the late Professor Kazuo Nagai in Japan. Theory and methods in their present state of development permit realistic, quantitative correlations of the properties of chain molecules with their chemical constitution and structure. They have been applied to a wide variety of macromolecules, both natural and synthetic, including polypeptides and polynucleotides in the former category. The success of these efforts has been due in no small measure to the outstanding students and research fellows who have collaborated with me at Stanford during the past thirteen years. A book entitled "Statistical Mechanics of Chain Molecules," published in 1969, summarizes the development of the theory and its applications up to that date.

Mrs. Flory, the former Emily Catherine Tabor, and I were married in 1936. We have three children: Susan, wife of Professor George S. Springer of the Department of Mechanical Engineering at the University of Michigan; Melinda, wife of Professor Donald E. Groom of the Department of Physics at the University of Utah; and Dr. Paul John Flory, Jr., currently a post-doctoral Research Associate at the Medical Nobel Institute in Stockholm. We have four grandchildren: Elizabeth Springer, Mary Springer, Susanna Groom and Jeremy Groom.

Honors and Awards

Joseph Sullivant Medal, The Ohio State University, 1945.
Baekeland Award, New Jersey Section, American Chemical Society, 1947.
Sc.D. (Honorary), Manchester College (Indiana), 1950.
Colwyn Medal, Institution of Rubber Industry, Great Britain, 1954
Nichols Medal, New York Section, American Chemical Society, 1962.
High-Polymer Physics Prize, American Physical Society, 1962.
Laurea Honoris Causa, Politecnico di Milano, 1964.
International Award in Plastics Science and Engineering, 25th Anniversary, Society of Plastics Engineers, 1967.
Charles Goodyear Medal, American Chemical Society, 1968.
Peter Debye Award in Physical Chemistry, American Chemical Society, 1969.
D.Sc., Honoris Causa, University of Manchester, England, 1969.
Sc.D. (Honorary), The Ohio State University, 1970.
Charles Frederick Chandler Medal, Columbia University, 1970.
First Award for Excellence-Chemistry, The Carborundum Company, 1971.
Cresson Medal, The Franklin Institute, 1971.
John G. Kirkwood Medal, Yale University, 1971.
J. Willard Gibbs Medal, Chicago Section, American Chemical Society, 1973.
Priestley Medal, American Chemical Society, 1974.
Nobel Prize in Chemistry, 1974.

SPATIAL CONFIGURATION OF MACROMOLE-CULAR CHAINS

Nobel Lecture, December 11, 1974

by

PAUL J. FLORY

Department of Chemistry

Stanford University, Stanford, California

The science of macromolecules has developed from primitive beginnings to a flourishing field of investigative activities within the comparatively brief span of some forty years. A wealth of knowledge has been acquired and new points of view have illumined various branches of the subject. These advances are the fruits of efforts of many dedicated investigators working in laboratories spread around the world. In a very real sense, I am before you on this occasion as their representative.

In these circumstances, the presentation of a lecture of a scope commensurate with the supreme honor the Royal Swedish Academy of Sciences has bestowed in granting me the Nobel Prize for Chemistry is an insuperable task. Rather than attempt to cover the field comprehensively in keeping with the generous citation by the Royal Academy of Sciences, I have chosen to dwell on a single theme. This theme is central to the growth of ideas and concepts concerning macromolecules and their properties. Implemented by methods that have emerged in recent years, researches along lines I shall attempt to highlight in this lecture give promise of far-reaching advances in our understanding of macromolecular substances—materials that are invaluable to mankind.

These polymeric substances are distinguished at the molecular level from other materials by the concatenation of atoms or groups to form chains, often of great length. That chemical structures of this design should occur is implicit in the multivalency manifested by certain atoms, notably carbon, silicon, oxygen, nitrogen, sulfur and phosphorus, and in the capacity of these atoms to enter into sequential combinations. The concept of a chain molecule consisting of atoms covalently linked is as old as modern chemistry. It dates from the origins of the graphic formula introduced by Couper in 1858 and advanced by Kekulé, Loschmidt and others shortly thereafter. Nothing in chemical theory, either then apparent or later revealed, sets a limit on the number of atoms that may be thus joined together. The rules of chemical valency, even in their most primitive form, anticipate the occurrence of macromolecular structures.

The importance of macromolecular substances, or polymers, is matched by their ubiquity. Examples too numerous to mention abound in biological systems. They comprise the structural materials of both plants and animals. Macromolecules elaborated through processes of evolution perform intricate regulatory and reproductive functions in living cells. Synthetic polymers in great variety are familiar in articles of commerce. The prevailing structural motif is the linear chain of serially connected atoms, groups or structural units. Departures from strict linearity may sometimes occur through the agency of occasional branched units that impart a ramified pattern to the over-all structure. Linearity is predominant in most macromolecular substances, however.

It is noteworthy that the chemical bonds in macromolecules differ in no discernible respect from those in "monomeric" compounds of low molecular weight. The same rules of valency apply; the lengths of the bonds, e.g., C—C, C—H, C—O, etc., are the same as the corresponding bonds in monomeric molecules within limits of experimental measurement. This seemingly trivial observation has two important implications: first, the chemistry of macromolecules is coextensive with that of low molecular substances; second, the chemical basis for the special properties of polymers that equip them for so many applications and functions, both in nature and in the artifacts of man, is not therefore to be sought in peculiarities of chemical bonding but rather in their macromolecular constitution, specifically, in the attributes of long molecular chains.

Comprehension of the spatial relationships between the atoms of a molecule is a universal prerequisite for bridging the connection between the graphic formula and the properties of the substance so constituted. Structural chemistry has provided a wealth of information on bond lengths and bond angles. By means of this information the graphic formula, primarily a topological device, has been superseded by the structural formula and by the space model that affords a quantitative representation of the molecule in three dimensions. The stage was thus set for the consideration of rotations about chemical bonds, i.e., for conformational analysis of conventional organic compounds, especially cyclic ones. A proper account of bond rotations obviously is essential for a definitive analysis of the spatial geometry of a molecule whose structure permits such rotations.

The configuration of a linear macromolecule in space involves circumstances of much greater complexity. A portion of such a molecule is shown schematically in Figure 1. Consecutive bonds comprising the chain skeleton are joined at angles θ fixed within narrow limits. Rotations φ may occur about these skeletal bonds. Each such rotation is subject, however, to a potential determined by the character of the bond itself and by hindrances imposed by steric interactions between pendant atoms and groups. The number and variety of configurations (or conformations in the language of organic chemistry) that may be generated by execution of rotations about each of the skeletal bonds of a long chain, comprising thousands of bonds in a typical polymer, is prodigious beyond comprehension. When the macromolecule is free of constraints, e.g., when in dilute solution, all of these configurations are accessible. Analysis of the manner in which such a molecule may arrange itself in space finds close analogies elsewhere in science, e.g., in the familiar problem of random walk, in diffusion, in the mathematical treatment of systems in one dimension, and in the behavior of real gases.

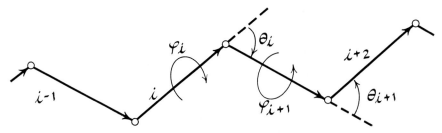

Fig. 1. Representation of the skeletal bonds of a section of a chain molecule showing supplements θ of bond angles, and torsional rotations φ for bonds i, i+1, etc.

Inquiry into the spatial configuration of these long-chain molecules, fascinating in itself, derives compelling motivation from its close relevancy to the properties imparted by such molecules to the materials comprising them. Indeed, most of the properties that distinguish polymers from other substances are intimately related to the spatial configurations of their molecules, these configurations being available in profusion as noted. The phenomenon of rubber-like elasticity, the hydrodynamic and thermodynamic properties of polymer solutions, and various optical properties are but a few that reflect the spatial character of the random macromolecule. The subject is the nexus between chemical constitution and physical and chemical properties of polymeric substances, both biological and synthetic.

The importance of gaining a grasp of the spatial character of polymeric chains became evident immediately upon the establishment, *ca.* 1930, of the hypothesis that they are covalently linked molecules rather than aggregates of smaller molecules, an achievement due in large measure to the compelling evidence adduced and forcefully presented by H. Staudinger, Nobelist for 1953. In 1932 K. H. Meyer[1] adumbrated the theory of rubber-like elasticity by calling attention to the capacity of randomly coiled polymer chains to accommodate large deformations owing to the variety of configurations accessible to them.

W. Kuhn[2] and E. Guth and H. Mark[3] made the first attempts at mathematical description of the spatial configurations of random chains. The complexities of bond geometry and of bond rotations, poorly understood at the time, were circumvented by taking refuge in the analogy to unrestricted random flights, the theory of which had been fully developed by Lord Rayleigh. The skeletal bonds of the molecular chain were thus likened to the steps in a random walk in three dimensions, the steps being uncorrelated one to another. Restrictions imposed by bond angles and hindrances to rotation were dismissed on the grounds that they should not affect the form of the results.

For a random flight chain consisting of n bonds each of length l, the mean-square of the distance r between the ends of the chain is given by the familiar relation

$$\langle r^2 \rangle = nl^2 \tag{1}$$

The angle brackets denote the average taken over all configurations. Kuhn[4] argued that the consequences of fixed bond angles and hindrances to rotation could be accommodated by letting several bonds of the chain molecule be represented by one longer "equivalent" bond, or step, of the random flight. This would require n to be diminished and l to be increased in Eq. 1. Equivalently, one may preserve the identification of n and l with the actual molecular quantities and replace Eq. (1) with

$$\langle r^2 \rangle = C\, nl^2, \tag{2}$$

where C is a constant for polymers of a given homologous series, i.e., for polymers differing in length but composed of identical monomeric units. The proportionality between $\langle r^2 \rangle$ and chain length expressed in Eq. (2) may be shown to hold for any random chain of finite flexibility, regardless of the structure, provided that the chain is of sufficient length and that it is unperturbed by external forces or by *effects due to excluded volume (cf. seq.)*.

The result expressed in Eq. (2) is of the utmost importance. Closely associated with it is the assertion that the density distribution $W(\mathbf{r})$ of values of the end-to-end vector $\mathbf{r}$ must be Gaussian for chains of sufficient length, irrespective of their chemical structure, provided only that the structure admits of some degree of flexibility. Hence, for large n the distribution of values of r is determined by the single parameter $\langle r^2 \rangle$ that defines the Gaussian distribution.

Much of polymer theory has been propounded on the basis of the Kuhn "equivalent" random flight chain, with adjustment of n and l, or of C, as required to match experimental determination of $\langle r^2 \rangle$ or of other configuration-dependent quantities. The validity of this model therefore invites critical examination. Its *intrinsic artificiality* is its foremost deficiency. Actual bond lengths, bond angles and rotational hindrances cannot be incorporated in this model. Hence, contact is broken at the outset with the features of chemical constitution that distinguish macromolecular chains of one kind from those of another. The model is therefore incapable of accounting for the vast differences in properties exhibited by the great variety of polymeric substances.

The random flight chain is patently unsuited for the treatment of constitutive properties that are configuration-dependent, e.g., dipole moments, optical polarizabilities and dichroism. Inasmuch as the contribution to one of these properties from a structural unit of the chain is a vector or tensor, it cannot be referenced to an equivalent bond that is a mere line. Moreover, the equivalent bond cannot be embedded unambiguously in the real structure.

Methods have recently been devised for treating macromolecular chains in a realistic manner. They take full account of the structural geometry of the given chain and, in excellent approximation, of the potentials affecting bond rotations as well. Before discussing these method, however, I must direct your attention to another aspect of the subject. I refer to the notorious effect of volume exclusion in a polymer chain.

At the hazard of seeming trite, I should begin by pointing out that the chain molecule is forbidden to adopt a configuration in which two of its parts, or segments, occupy the same space. The fact is indisputable; its consequences are less obvious. It will be apparent, however, that volume exclusion vitiates

107

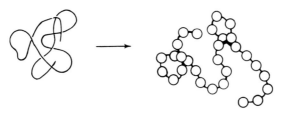

Fig. 2. The effect of excluded volume. The configuration on the left represents the random coil in absence of volume exclusion, the chain being equivalent to a line in space. In the sketch on the right, the units of the chain occupy finite domains from which other units are excluded, with the result that the average size of the configuration is increased.

the analogy between the trajectory of a particle executing a random flight and the molecular chain, a material body. The particle may cross its own path at will, but self intersections of the polymer chain are forbidden.

The effect of excluded volume must be dealt with regardless of the model chosen for representation of the chain. In practice, elimination of the effect of volume exclusion is a prerequisite to the analysis of experimental results, as I will explain in more detail later.

The closely related problems of random flights with disallowance of self intersections and of volume exclusion within long-chain molecules have attracted the attention of many theorists. A variety of mathematical techniques have been applied to the treatment of these problems, and a profusion of theories have been put forward, some with a high order of sophistication. Extensive numerical computations of random walks on lattices of various sorts also have been carried out. Convergence of results obtained by the many investigators captivated by the subject over the past quarter century seems at last to be discernible. I shall confine myself to a brief sketch of an early, comparatively simple approach to the solution of this problem.[5] The results it yields contrast with its simplicity.

Returning to the analogy of the trajectory traced by a particle undergoing a sequence of finite displacements, we consider only those trajectories that are free of intersections as being acceptable for the chain molecule. Directions of successive steps may or may not be correlated, i.e., restrictions on bond angles and rotational hindrances may or may not be operative; this is immaterial with respect to the matter immediately at hand. Obviously, the set of eligible configurations will occupy a larger domain, on the average, than those having one or more self intersections. Hence, volume exclusion must cause $\langle r^2 \rangle$ to increase. The associated expansion of the spatial configuration is illustrated in Fig. 2. Other configuration-dependent quantities may be affected as well.

This much is readily evident. Assessment of the magnitude of the perturbation of the configuration and its dependence on chain length require a more penetrating examination.

The problem has two interrelated parts: (i) the mutual exclusion of the space occupied by segments comprising the chain tends to disperse them over a larger volume, and (ii) the concomitant alteration of the chain configuration opposes expansion of the chain. Volume exclusion (i) is commonplace. It is prevalent in conventional dilute solutions and in real gases, molecules of which mutually exclude one another. In the polymer chain the same rules of exclusion apply, but treatment of the problem is complicated by its association with (ii).

Pursuing the analogies to dilute solutions and gases, we adopt a "smoothed density" or "mean field" model. The segments of the chain, x in number, are considered to pervade a volume V, the connections between them being ignored insofar as part (i) is concerned. The segment need not be defined explicitly; it may be identified with a repeating unit or some other approximately isometric portion of the chain. In any case, x will be proportional to the number n of bonds; in general $x \neq n$, however. For simplicity, we may consider the segment density ϱ to be uniform throughout the volume V; that is, $\varrho = x/V$ within V and $\varrho = 0$ outside of V. This volume should be proportional to $\langle r^2 \rangle^{3/2}$, where $\langle r^2 \rangle$ is the mean-square separation of the ends of the chain averaged over those configurations *not disallowed by excluded volume interactions*. Accordingly, we let

$$V = A \langle r^2 \rangle^{3/2}, \tag{3}$$

where A is a numerical factor expected to be of the order of magnitude of unity.

It is necessary to digress at this point for the purpose of drawing a distinction between $\langle r^2 \rangle$ for the chain perturbed by the effects of excluded volume and $\langle r^2 \rangle_0$ for the unperturbed chain in the absence of such effects. If a denotes the factor by which a linear dimension of the configuration is altered, then

$$\langle r^2 \rangle = a^2 \langle r^2 \rangle_0 \tag{4}$$

Equation (2), having been derived without regard for excluded volume interactions, should be replaced by

$$\langle r^2 \rangle_0 = C \, nl^2, \tag{2'}$$

where C reaches a constant value with increase in n for any series of finitely flexible chains.

The smoothed density within the domain of a linear macromolecule having a molecular weight of 100,000 or greater (i.e., n > 1000) is low, only on the order of one percent or less of the space being occupied by chain segments. For a random dispersion of the segments over the volume V, encounters in which segments overlap are rare in the sense that few of them are thus involved. However, the expectation that such a dispersion is entirely free of overlaps between any pair of segments is very small for a long chain. The attrition of configurations due to excluded volume is therefore severe.

In light of the low segment density, it suffices to consider only binary encounters. Hence, if β is the volume excluded by a segment, the probability that an arbitrary distribution of their centers within the volume V is free of conflicts between any pair of segments is

109

$$P_{(i)} \approx \prod_{i=1}^{x} (1-i\beta/V) \approx \exp(-\beta x^2/2V). \tag{5}$$

Introduction of Eq. (3) and (4) gives

$$P_{(i)} = \exp(-\beta x^2/2A\langle r^2\rangle_0^{3/2}a^3) \tag{6}$$

or, in terms of the conventional parameter z defined by

$$z = (3/2\pi)^{3/2} (\langle r^2\rangle_0/x)^{-3/2}x^{1/2}\beta, \tag{7}$$

$$P_{(i)} = \exp[-2^{1/2}(\pi/3)^{3/2}A^{-1}za^{-3}]. \tag{8}$$

Since $\langle r^2\rangle_0$ is proportional to x for long chains (see Eq. (2′)), z depends on the square-root of the chain length for a given series of polymer homologs.

We require also the possibility $P_{(ii)}$ of a set of configurations having the average density corresponding to the dilation a^3 relative to the probability of a set of configurations for which the density of segments corresponds to $a^3 = 1$. For the former, the mean-squared separation of the ends of the chain is $\langle r^2\rangle$; for the latter it is $\langle r^2\rangle_0$. The distribution of chain vectors **r** for the unperturbed chain is approximately Gaussian as noted above. That is to say, the probability that **r** falls in the range **r** to **r**+d**r** is

$$W(\mathbf{r})d\mathbf{r} = \text{Const} \exp(-3r^2/2\langle r^2\rangle_0)d\mathbf{r}, \tag{9}$$

where d**r** denotes the element of volume. The required factor is the ratio of the probabilities for the dilated and the undilated sets of configurations. These probabilities, obtained by taking the products of $W(\mathbf{r})d\mathbf{r}$ over the respective sets of configurations, are expressed by $W(\mathbf{r})$ according to Eq. (9) with r^2 therein replaced by the respective mean values, $\langle r^2\rangle$ and $\langle r^2\rangle_0$, for the perturbed and unperturbed sets. Bearing in mind that the volume element d**r** is dilated as well, we thus obtain

$$\begin{aligned}P_{(ii)} &= [(d\mathbf{r})/(d\mathbf{r})_0]\exp[-3(\langle r^2\rangle-\langle r^2\rangle_0)/2\langle r^2\rangle_0] \\ &= a^3\exp[-(3/2) (a^2-1)]. \end{aligned} \tag{10}$$

The combined probability of the state defined by the dilation a^3 is

$$P_{(i)}P_{(ii)} = a^3\exp[-2^{1/2}(\pi/3)^{3/2}A^{-1}za^{-3}-(3/2) (a^2-1)]. \tag{11}$$

Solution for the value of a that maximizes this expression gives

$$a^5-a^3 = 2^{1/2}(\pi/3)^{3/2}A^{-1}z. \tag{12}$$

Recalling that z is proportional to $x^{1/2}\beta$ according to Eq. (7), one may express this result alternatively as follows

$$a^5-a^3 = Bx^{1/2}\beta, \tag{12′}$$

where $B = (\langle r^2\rangle_0/x)^{-3/2}(2A)^{-1}$ is a constant for a given series of polymer homologs.

In the full treatment[5,6] of the problem along the lines sketched briefly above, the continuous variation of the mean segment density with distance from the center of the molecule is taken into account, and the appropriate sums are executed over all configurations of the chain. The squared radius of gyration s^2, i.e., the mean-square of the distances of the segments from their center of gravity, is preferable to r^2 as a parameter with which to characterize the spatial distribution.[7] Treatments carried out with these refinements affirm the essential validity of the result expressed by Eq. (12) or (12′). They show conclusively[7,8] that the form of the result should hold in the limit of large values of $\beta x^{1/2}$, i.e., for large excluded volume and/or high chain length, and hence for $\alpha \gg 1$. In this limit, $(\alpha^5 - \alpha^3)/z = 1.67$ according to H. Fujita and T. Norisuye.[8] For $\alpha < \sim 1.4$, however, this ratio decreases, reaching a value of 1.276 at $\alpha = 1$.[8,9]

The general utility of the foregoing result derived from the most elementary considerations is thus substantiated by elaboration and refinement of the analysis, the quantitative inaccuracy of Eqs. (12) and (12′) in the range $1.0 < \alpha \leqslant 1.4$ notwithstanding. The relationship between α and the parameter z prescribed by these equations, especially as refined by Fujita and Norisuye,[8] appears to be well supported by experiment.[10,11]

The principal conclusions to be drawn from the foregoing results are the following: the expansion of the configuration due to volume exclusion increases with chain length *without limit* for $\beta > 0$; for very large values of $\beta x^{1/2}$ relative to $(\langle r^2 \rangle_0/x)^{3/2}$ it should increase as the 1/10 power of the chain length. The sustained increase of the perturbation with chain length reflects the fact that interactions between segments that are remote in sequence along the chain are dominant in affecting the dimensions of the chain. It is on this account that the excluded volume effect is often referred to as a long-range interaction.[9-12]

The problem has been treated by a variety of other procedures.[9-12] Notable amongst these treatments is the self-consistent field theory of S. F. Edwards.[12] The asymptotic dependence of α on the one-tenth power of the chain length, and hence the dependence of $\langle r^2 \rangle$ on $n^{6/5}$ for large values of the parameter z, has been confirmed.[12]

The dilute solution is the milieu chosen for most physicochemical experiments conducted for the purpose of characterizing polymers. The effect of excluded volume is reflected in the properties of the polymer molecule thus determined, and must be taken into account if the measurements are to be properly interpreted. The viscosity of a dilute polymer solution is illustrative. Its usefulness for the characterization of polymers gained recognition largely through the work of Staudinger and his collaborators.

Results are usually expressed as the intrinsic viscosity $[\eta]$ defined as the ratio of the increase in the relative viscosity η_{rel} by the polymeric solute to its concentration c in the limit of infinite dilution. That is,

$$[\eta] = \lim_{c \to 0} [(\eta_{rel} - 1)/c]$$

the concentration c being expressed in weight per unit volume. The increment in viscosity due to a polymer molecule is proportional to its hydrodynamic volume, which in turn should be proportional to $\langle r^2 \rangle^{3/2}$ for a typical polymer chain. Hence, $\eta_{rel}-1$ should be proportional to the product of $\langle r^2\rangle^{3/2}$ and the number density of solute molecules given by c/M where M is the molecular weight. It follows that

$$[\eta] = \Phi\langle r^2\rangle^{3/2}/M, \tag{13}$$

where Φ is a constant of proportionality.[6,13] Substitution from Eq. (4) and rearrangement of the result gives

$$[\eta] = \Phi(\langle r^2\rangle_0/M)^{3/2}M^{1/2}a^3 \tag{13'}$$

The ratio $\langle r^2\rangle_0/M$ should be constant for a series of homologs of varying molecular weight, provided of course that the molecular weight, and hence the chain length, is sufficiently large.

If the excluded volume effect could be ignored, the intrinsic viscosity should vary proportionally to $M^{1/2}$. Since, however, a increases with M, a stronger dependence on M generally is observed. Often the dependence of $[\eta]$ on molecular weight can be represented in satisfactory approximation by the empirical relation

$$[\eta] = KM^a \tag{14}$$

where $0.5 \leqslant a \leqslant 0.8$. Typical results are shown by the upper sets of data in Figs. 3 and 4 for polystyrene dissolved in benzene[14] and for poly(methyl methacrylate) in methyl ethyl ketone,[15] respectively. Values of a^3 are in the range 1.4 to 5. At the asymptote for chains of great length and large excluded volume β, the exponent a should reach 0.80 according to the treatment given above. Although this limit is seldom reached within the accessible range of molecular weights, the effects of excluded volume can be substantial. They must be taken into account in the interpretation of hydrodynamic measurements.[13,16] Otherwise, the dependences of the intrinsic viscosity and the translational friction coefficient on molecular chain length are quite incomprehensible.

Measurement of light scattering as a function of angle, a method introduced by the late P. Debye, affords a convenient means for determining the mean-square radius of gyration. Small-angle scattering of x-rays (and lately of neutrons) offers an alternative for securing the same information. From the radius of gyration one may obtain the parameter $\langle r^2\rangle$ upon which attention is focused here. The results are affected, of course, by the perturbation due to excluded volume. Inasmuch as the perturbation is dependent on the solvent and temperature, the results directly obtained by these methods are not intrinsically characteristic of the macromolecule. Values obtained for $\langle r^2\rangle$ from the intrinsic viscosity by use of Eq. (13), or by other methods, must also be construed to be jointly dependent on the macromolecule and its environment.

If the factor a were known, the necessary correction could be introduced readily to obtain the more substantive quantities, such as $\langle r^2\rangle_0$ and $\langle s^2\rangle_0$ that characterize the macromolecule itself and are generally quite independent of the solvent. Evaluation of a according to Eq. (11) and (12) would require the excluded volume β. This parameter depends on the solvent in a manner that eludes prediction. Fairly extensive experimental measurements are required for its estimation, or for otherwise making correction for the expansion a.

All these difficulties are circumvented if measurements on the polymer solution are conducted under conditions such that the effects of excluded volume are suppressed. The resistance of atoms to superposition cannot, of course, be set aside. But the consequences thereof can be neutralized. We have only to recall that the effects of excluded volume in a gas comprising real molecules of finite size are exactly compensated by intermolecular attractions at the Boyle temperature (up to moderately high gas densities). At this temperature the real gas masquerades as an ideal one.

For the macromolecule in solution, realization of the analogous condition requires a relatively poor solvent in which the polymer segments prefer self-contacts over contacts with the solvent. The incidence of self-contacts may then be adjusted by manipulating the temperature and/or the solvent composition until the required balance is established. Carrying the analogy to a real gas a step further, we require the excluded volume integral for the interaction between a pair of segments to vanish; that is, we require that $\beta=0$. This is the necessary and sufficient condition.[5,6,13]

As already noted, estimation of the value of β is difficult; the prediction of conditions under which β shall precisely vanish would be even more precarious. However, the "Theta point," so-called, at which this condition is met is readily identified with high accuracy by any of several experimental procedures. An excluded volume of zero connotes a second virial coefficient of zero, and hence conformance of the osmotic pressure to the celebrated law of J. H. van't Hoff. The Theta point may be located directly from osmotic pressure determinations, from light scattering measured as a function of concentration, or from determination of the precipitation point as a function of molecular weight.[6,13]

The efficacy of this procedure, validated a number of years ago with the collaboration of T. G. Fox, W. R. Krigbaum, and others,[13,17,18] is illustrated in Figs. 3 and 4 by the lower plots of data representing intrinsic viscosities measured under ideal, or Theta conditions.[6] The slopes of the lines drawn through the lower sets of points are exactly $1/2$, as required by Eq. (13') when $\beta = 0$ and hence $a=1$. The excellent agreement here illustrated has been abundantly confirmed for linear macromolecules of the widest variety, ranging from polyisobutylene and polyethylene to polyribonucleotides.[19] At the Theta point the mean-square chain vector $\langle r^2 \rangle_0$ and the mean-square radius of gyration $\langle s^2 \rangle_0$ invariably are found to be proportional to chain length.

A highly effective strategy for characterization of macromolecules emerges from these findings. By conducting experiments at the Theta point, the disconcerting (albeit interesting!) effects of excluded volume on experimentally measured quantities may be eliminated. Parameters (e.g., $\langle r^2 \rangle_0$ and $\langle s^2 \rangle_0$) are thus obtained that are characteristic of the molecular chain. They are found to be virtually independent of the nature of the "Theta solvent" selected. Having eliminated the effects of long range interactions, one may turn

113

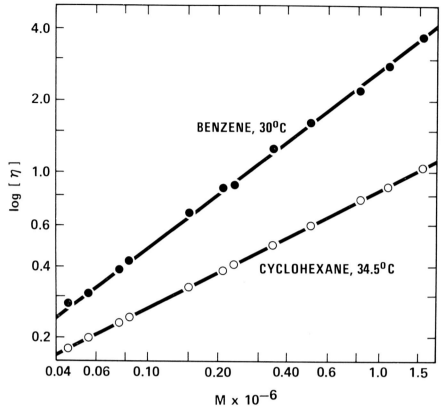

Fig. 3. Intrinsic viscosities of polystyrene fractions plotted against their molecular weights on logarithmic scales in accordance with Eq. (14). The upper set of data was determined in benzene, a good solvent for this polymer. The lower set of data was determined in cyclohexane at the Theta point. The slopes of the lines are $a = 0.75$ and 0.50, respectively. From the results of Altares, Wyman and Allen.[14]

attention to the role of short range features: structural geometry, bond rotation potentials, and steric interactions between near-neighboring groups. It is here that the influences of chemical architecture are laid bare. If the marked differences in properties that distinguish the great variety of polymeric substances, both natural and synthetic, are to be rationally understood in fundamental, molecular terms, this must be the focus of future research.

Rigorous theoretical methods have recently become available for dealing realistically with short-range features peculiar to a given structure. Most of the remainder of this lecture is devoted to a brief overview of these methods. Although the field is comparatively new and its exploration has only begun, space will not permit a digest of the results already obtained.

The broad objective of the methods to which we now turn attention is to treat the structure and conformations accessible to the chain molecule in such a manner as will enable one to calculate configuration-dependent quantities and to average them over all conformations, or spatial configurations, of the unperturbed chain. The properties under consideration are constitutive; they

114

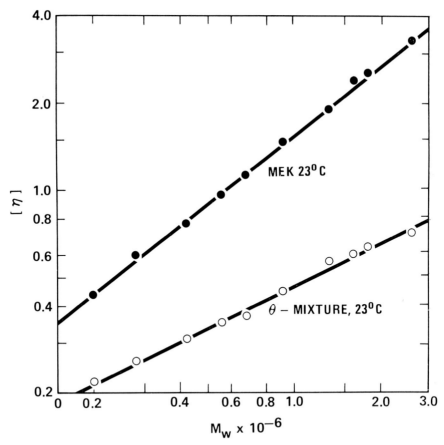

Fig. 4. Intrinsic viscosities of fractions of poly(methyl methacrylate) according to Chinai and Samuels[15] plotted as in Fig. 3. The upper set of points was measured in methyl ethyl ketone, a good solvent. The lower set was determined in a mixture of methyl ethyl ketone and isopropanol at the Theta point. Slopes are $a = 0.79$ and 0.50, respectively.

represent sums of contributions from the individual units, or chemical groupings, comprising the chain. In addition to $\langle r^2 \rangle_0$ and $\langle s^2 \rangle_0$, they include: mean-square dipole moments; the optical anisotropies underlying strain birefringence, depolarized light scattering and electric birefringence; dichroism; and the higher moments, both scalar and tensor, of the chain vector **r**. Classical statistical mechanics provides the basis for evaluating the configurational averages of these quantities. Since bond lengths and bond angles ordinarily may be regarded as fixed, the bond rotations φ are the variables over which averaging must be carried out. The procedure rests on the *rotational isomeric state scheme*, the foundations for which were set forth in large measure by M. V. Volkenstein[20] and his colleagues[21] in Leningrad in the late 1950's and early 1960's. It is best explained by examples.

Consider rotation about an internal bond of an n-alkane chain. As is now well established,[22,23] the three staggered conformations, trans(t), gauche-plus(g⁺) and its mirror image, gauche-minus(g⁻), are of lower energy than

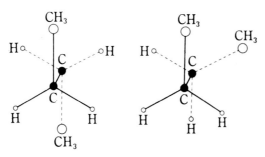

Fig. 5. Two of the staggered conformations for n-butane: trans on the left and gauche-minus on the right.

the eclipsed forms. The t and g⁻ conformations of n–butane are shown in Fig. 5. The energies of the eclipsed conformations separating t from g⁺ and t from g⁻ are about 3.5 kcal. mol⁻¹ above the energy of the trans conformation. Hence, in good approximation, it is justified to consider each bond to occur in one of three *rotational isomeric states* centered near (but not necessarily precisely at) the energy minima associated with the three staggered conformations.[20–24] The gauche minima lie at an energy of about 500 cal. mol⁻¹ above trans. Each of the former is therefore disfavored compared to the latter by a "statistical weight" factor we choose to call $\sigma \approx \exp(-E_g/RT)$, where E_g is about 500 cal. mol⁻¹; thus, $\sigma \approx 0.5$ at $T = 400$ K.

A complication arises from the fact that the potentials affecting bond rotations usually are neighbor dependent; i.e., the potential affecting φ_i depends on the rotations φ_{i-1} and φ_{i+1}. Bond rotations cannot, therefore, be treated independently.[20,21,24,25] The source of this interdependence in the case of an n-alkane chain is illustrated in Fig. 6 showing a pair of consecutive bonds in three of their nine conformations. In the conformations tt, tg⁺, g⁺t, tg⁻ and g⁻t, the two methylene groups pendant to this pair of bonds are well separated. For gauche rotations g⁺g⁺ and g⁻g⁻ of the same hand (Fig. 6b), these groups are proximate but not appreciably overlapped. Semi-empirical calculations[21,24,26,27] show the intramolecular energy for these two equivalent conformations to be very nearly equal to the sum (*ca.* 1000 cal. mol⁻¹) for two well-separated gauche bonds; i.e., the interdependence of the pair of rotations is negligible. In the remaining conformations, g⁺g⁻ and g⁻g⁺, the steric overlap is severe (Fig. 6c). It may be alleviated somewhat by compromising rotations, but the excess energy associated therewith is nevertheless about 2.0 kcal. mol⁻¹. Hence, a statistical weight factor $\omega \approx \exp(-2000/RT)$ is required for each such pair.[24,26,28] Inspection of models in detail shows that interactions dependent upon rotations about three, four of five consecutive bonds are disallowed by interferences of shorter range and hence may be ignored.[24] It suffices therefore to consider first neighbors only.

The occurrence of interactions that depend on pairs of skeletal bonds is the rule in chain molecules. In some of them, notably in vinyl polymers, such interactions may affect most of the conformations. Hence, interdependence of rotations usually plays a major role in determining the spatial configuration

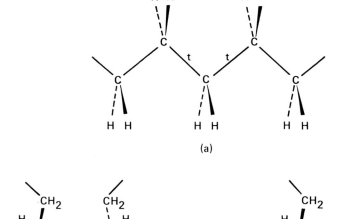

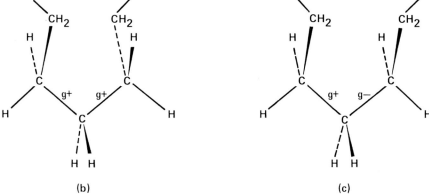

Fig. 6. Conformations for a pair of consecutive bonds in an n-alkane chain: (a), tt, (b), g^+g^+; (c), g^+g^-. Wedged bonds project forward from the plane of the central bonds, dashed bonds project behind this plane.

of the chain. The rotational isometric state approximation, whereby the continuous variation of each φ is replaced by discrete states, provides the key to mathematical solution of the problem posed by rotational interdependence.[20,21,24,25]

It is necessary therefore to consider the bonds pairwise consecutively, and to formulate a set of statistical weights for bond i that take account of the state of bond i—1. These statistical weights are conveniently presented in the form of an array, or matrix, as follows:

$$\mathbf{U}_i = \begin{bmatrix} u^{tt} & u^{tg^+} & u^{tg^-} \\ u^{g^+t} & u^{g^+g^+} & u^{g^+g^-} \\ u^{g^-t} & u^{g^-g^+} & u^{g^-g^-} \end{bmatrix}_i , \tag{15}$$

where the rows are indexed in the order t, g^+, g^- to the state of bond i—1, and the columns are indexed to the state of bond i in the same order. According to the analysis of the alkane chain conformations presented briefly above, $\mathbf{U}_i$ takes the form[24,26,28]

117

$$\mathbf{U_i} = \begin{bmatrix} 1 & \sigma & \sigma \\ 1 & \sigma & \sigma\omega \\ 1 & \sigma\omega & \sigma \end{bmatrix}_i \tag{16}$$

for any bond $1 < i < n$.

A conformation of the chain is specified in the rotational isometric state approximation by stipulation of the states for all internal bonds 2 to $n-1$ inclusive; e.g., by $g^+ttg^-g^-$, etc. Owing to the three-fold symmetry of the terminal methyl groups of the alkane chain, rotations about the terminal bonds are inconsequential and hence are ignored. The statistical weight for the specified conformation of the chain is obtained by selecting the appropriate factor for each bond from the array (15) according to the state of this bond and of its predecessor, and taking the product of such factors for all bonds 2 to $n-1$. In the example above this product is $u^{g^+} u^{g^+t} u^{tt} u^{tg^-} u^{g^-g^-}$, etc. It will be obvious that the first superscripted index in one of the factors u must repeat the second index of its predecessor since these indices refer to the same bond.

The configuration partition function, representing the sum of all such factors, one for each conformation of the chain as represented by the scheme of rotational isomeric states, is

$$Z = \sum_{\text{all states}} u_2 u_3 \ldots u_1 \ldots u_{n-1}, \tag{17}$$

where the subscripts are serial indexes. Each u_i must be assigned as specified above. The sum, which extends over all ordered combinations of rotational states, may be generated identically as the product of the arrays $\mathbf{U_i}$ treated as matrices. That is, according to the rules of matrix multiplication

$$Z = \prod_{i=1}^{n} \mathbf{U_i}, \tag{18}$$

where $\mathbf{U_1} = $ row $(1, 0, 0)$ and $\mathbf{U_n} = $ column $(1, 1, 1)$. Matrix multiplication generates products precisely of the character to which attention is directed at the close of the preceding paragraph. Serial multiplication of the statistical weight matrices generates this product for each and every conformation of the chain, and Eq. (18) with the operators $\mathbf{U_1}$ and $\mathbf{U_n}$ appended gives their sum.

The foregoing procedure for evaluation of Z is a minor variant of the method of H. A. Kramers and G. H. Wannier [29] for treating a hypothetical one-dimensional ferromagnet or lattice. A number of interesting characteristics of the chain molecule can be deduced from the partition function by application of familiar techniques of statistical mechanics. I shall resist the temptation to elaborate these beyond mentioning two properties of the molecule that may be derived directly from the partition function, namely, the incidences of the various rotational states and combinations thereof, and the equilibrium constants between isomeric structures of the chain in the presence of catalysts effectuating their inter-conversion. Vinyl polymers having the structure depicted in Fig. 7 with $R' \neq R$ afford examples wherein the study of equilibria

118

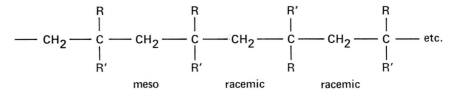

Fig. 7. A vinyl polymer chain shown in projection in its planar (fully extended) conformation. If the substituents R and R′ differ (e.g., if R = C₆H₅ and R′ = H as in polystyrene), diastereomeric dyads must be distinguished as indicated for the stereochemical structure shown.

between various diastereomeric forms arising from the local chirality of individual skeletal bonds has been especially fruitful.[30]

Consider the evaluation of a configuration-dependent property for a given configuration, or conformation, of the chain. Since the configuration is seldom "given", the problem as stated is artificial. Its solution, however, is a necessary precursor to the ultimate goal, which is to obtain the average of the property over all configurations. A property or characteristic of the chain that will serve for illustration is the end-to-end vector $\mathbf{r}$. Suppose we wish to express this vector with reference to the first two bonds of the chain. For definiteness, let a Cartesian coordinate system be affixed to these two bonds with its X_1-axis along the first bond and its Y_1-axis in the plane of bonds 1 and 2, as shown in Fig. 8.

The vector $\mathbf{r}$ is just the sum $\sum\limits_{i=1}^{n} \mathbf{l}_i$ of all of the bond vectors $\mathbf{l}_i$, each expressed in this reference frame.

In order to facilitate the task of transforming every bond vector to the reference frame affiliated with the first bond, it is helpful to define a reference frame for each skeletal bond of the chain. For example, one may place the axis X_i along bond i, the Y_i-axis in the plane of bonds $i-1$ and i, and choose the Z_i-axis to complete a right-handed Cartesian system. Let $\mathbf{T}_i$ symbolize the transformation that, by premultiplication, converts the representation of a vector in reference frame $i+1$ to its representation in the preceding reference frame i. Then bond i referred to the initial reference frame is given by

$$\mathbf{T}_1\mathbf{T}_2\ldots\mathbf{T}_{i-1}\mathbf{l}_i,$$

where $\mathbf{l}_i$ is presented in reference frame i. The required sum is just

$$\mathbf{r} = \sum_{i=1}^{n} \mathbf{T}_1\ldots\mathbf{T}_{i-1}\mathbf{l}_i. \tag{19}$$

This sum of products can be generated according to a simple algorithm. We first define a "generator" matrix $\mathbf{A}_i$ as follows[31,32]

$$\mathbf{A}_i = \begin{bmatrix} \mathbf{T}_i & \mathbf{l}_i \\ 0 & 1 \end{bmatrix}, \qquad 1 < i < n, \tag{20}$$

119

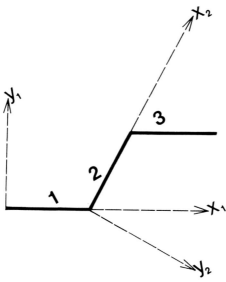

Fig. 8. Specification of the coordinate axes affixed to each of the first two bonds of the chain: X_1Y_1 for bond 1 and X_2Y_2 for bond 2.

together with the two terminal matrices

$$\mathbf{A}_1 = [\mathbf{T}_1 \quad \mathbf{1}_1], \tag{21}$$

$$\mathbf{A}_n = \begin{bmatrix} \mathbf{1}_n \\ 1 \end{bmatrix}. \tag{22}$$

In these equations $\mathbf{T}_i$ is the matrix representation of the transformation specified above and $\mathbf{0}$ is the null matrix of order 1×3. The desired vector $\mathbf{r}$ is generated identically by taking the serial product of the $\mathbf{A}$'s; i.e.,

$$\mathbf{r} = \prod_{i=1}^{n} \mathbf{A}_i, \tag{23}$$

as may easily be verified from the elementary rules of matrix multiplication. Each generator matrix $\mathbf{A}_i$ depends on the length of bond i and, through $\mathbf{T}_i$, on both the angle θ_i between bonds i and i+1 and on the angle of rotation φ_i about bond i (see Fig. 1).

In order to obtain the average of $\mathbf{r}$ over all configurations of the chain, it is necessary to evaluate the sum over all products of the kind given in Eq. (23) with each of them multiplied by the appropriate statistical weight for the specified configuration of the chain; see Eq. (17). That is,

$$\langle \mathbf{r} \rangle_0 = Z^{-1} \Sigma u_2 u_3 \ldots u_{n-1} \mathbf{A}_1 \mathbf{A}_2 \ldots \mathbf{A}_n, \tag{24}$$

where the sum includes all configurations. This sum can be generated by serial multiplication of matrices defined as follows:

120

$$a_i = \begin{bmatrix} u^{tt}\mathbf{A}^t & u^{tg^+}\mathbf{A}^{g^+} & u^{tg^-}\mathbf{A}^{g^-} \\ u^{g^+t}\mathbf{A}^t & u^{g^+g^+}\mathbf{A}^{g^+} & u^{g^+g^-}\mathbf{A}^{g^-} \\ u^{g^-t}\mathbf{A}^t & u^{g^-g^+}\mathbf{A}^{g^+} & u^{g^-g^-}\mathbf{A}^{g^-} \end{bmatrix}_i, \qquad 1 < i < n, \tag{25}$$

$$a_1 = [\mathbf{A}_1 \quad 0 \quad 0], \tag{26}$$

$$a_n = \text{column } (\mathbf{A}_n, \mathbf{A}_n, \mathbf{A}_n). \tag{27}$$

Then[31]

$$\langle \mathbf{r} \rangle_0 = Z^{-1} \prod_{i=1}^{n} a_i. \tag{28}$$

The matrix a_i comprises the elements of $\mathbf{U}_i$ (see Eq. (15)) joined with the $\mathbf{A}$ matrix for the rotational state of bond i as prescribed by the column index. It will be apparent that serial multiplication of the a_i according to Eq. (28) generates the statistical weight factor $u_2 u_3 \ldots u_{n-1}$ for every configuration of the chain in the same way that these factors are generated by serial multiplication of the statistical weight matrices $\mathbf{U}_i$ in Eq. (18). Simultaneously, Eq. (28) generates the product of $\mathbf{A}$'s (see Eq. (23)) that produces the vector $\mathbf{r}$ for each configuration thus weighted. The resulting products of statistical weights and of $\mathbf{A}$'s are precisely the terms required by Eq. (24). The terminal factors in Eq. (28) yield their sum.

With greater mathematical concision[31,32]

$$a_i = (\mathbf{U}_i \otimes \mathbf{E}_3)\|\mathbf{A}_i\|, \qquad 1 < i < n, \tag{29}$$

$$a_1 = \mathbf{U}_1 \otimes \mathbf{A}_1, \tag{30}$$

$$a_n = \mathbf{U}_n \otimes \mathbf{A}_n, \tag{31}$$

where $\mathbf{E}_3$ is the identity matrix of order three, $\otimes$ signifies the direct product, and $\|\mathbf{A}_i\|$ denotes the diagonal array of the matrices $\mathbf{A}_i^t$, $\mathbf{A}_i^{g^+}$ and $\mathbf{A}_i^{g^-}$.

A characteristic of the chain commanding greater interest is the quantity $\langle r^2 \rangle_0$ introduced in earlier discussion. For a given configuration of the chain, r^2 is just the scalar product of $\mathbf{r}$ with itself, i.e.,

$$r^2 = \mathbf{r} \cdot \mathbf{r} = \sum_{i=1}^{n} l^2_i + 2 \sum \sum_{i<j} \mathbf{l}_i \cdot \mathbf{l}_j \tag{32}$$

If each bond vector $\mathbf{l}_i$ is expressed in its own reference frame i, then

$$r^2 = \sum_{1}^{n} l_i^2 + 2 \sum \sum_{i<j} \mathbf{l}_i^T \mathbf{T}_i \mathbf{T}_{i+1} \ldots \mathbf{T}_{j-1} \mathbf{l}_j, \tag{33}$$

where $\mathbf{l}_i^T$ is the transposed, or row form of vector $\mathbf{l}_i$. These sums can be evaluated by serial multiplication of the generator matrices[24,33]

$$\mathbf{G}_i = \begin{bmatrix} 1 & 2l^T\mathbf{T} & l^2 \\ 0 & \mathbf{T} & 1 \\ 0 & 0 & 1 \end{bmatrix}_i, \qquad 1 < i < n. \tag{34}$$

121

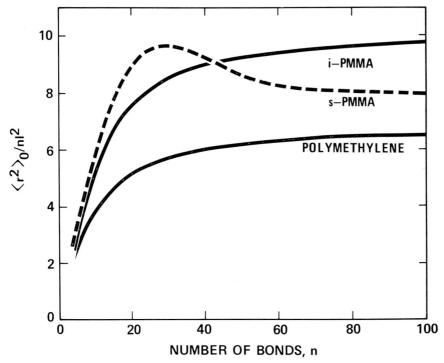

Fig. 9. Characteristic ratios $\langle r^2 \rangle_0 / nl^2$ plotted against the number of bonds n in the chain for polymethylene, and for isotactic and syndiotactic poly(methyl metacrylate)'s. From the calculations of Abe, Jernigan and Flory[26] and of Yoon.[34]

That is,

$$r^2 = \prod_{1}^{n} G_i \tag{35}$$

where G_1 has the form of the first row, and G_n that of final column of Eq. (34). Evaluation of $\langle r^2 \rangle_0$ proceeds exactly as set forth above for $\langle \mathbf{r} \rangle_0$.[32,33]

The foregoing method enjoys great versatility. The chain may be of any specified length and structure. If it comprises a variety of skeletal bonds and repeat units, the factors entering into the serial products have merely to be fashioned to introduce the characteristics of the bond represented by each of the successive factors. The mathematical methods are exact; the procedure is free of approximations beyond that involved in adoption of the rotational isomeric state scheme. With judicious choice of rotational states, the error here involved is generally within the limits of accuracy of basic information on bond rotations, nonbonded interactions, etc.

Other molecular properties that may be computed by straightforward adaptation of these methods[24,32] include the higher scalar moments $\langle r^4 \rangle_0$, $\langle r^6 \rangle_0$, etc; the moment tensors formed from $\mathbf{r}$; the radius of gyration $\langle s^2 \rangle_0 = (n+1)^{-2}$ $\sum_i \sum_j \langle r^2_{ij} \rangle$; the optical polarizability and its invariants that govern the optical anistropy as manifested in depolarized light scattering, in strain bire-

122

fringence and in electric birefringence; x-ray scattering at small angles; and NMR chemical shifts.

For illustration, characteristic ratios $\langle r^2 \rangle_0 / nl^2$ are plotted in Fig. 9 against the numbers n of bonds for n-alkanes and for isotactic and syndiotactic poly-(methyl methacrylate), or PMMA. Isotactic PMMA is represented by the formula in Fig. 7 with R = COOCH$_3$ and R' = CH$_3$ and with all dyads of the meso form, i.e., with R occurring consistently above (or below) the axis of the chain. In the syndiotactic stereoisomer, the substituents R and R' alternate from one side to the other, all dyads being racemic.

For the alkane and the isotactic PMMA chains the characteristic ratios increase monotonically with chain length, approaching asymptotic values for n $\approx$ 100 bonds. This behavior is typical. For syndiotactic PMMA, however, the characteristic ratio passes through a maximum at intermediate values of n, according to these computations by D. Y. Yoon.[34] This behavior can be traced[34] to the inequality of the skeletal bond angles in PMMA in conjunction with the preference for tt conformations in the syndiotactic chain.[35] The maximum exhibited in Fig. 9 for this polymer is thus a direct consequence of its constitution. This peculiarity manifests itself in the small angle scattering of x-rays and neutrons by predominantly syndiotactic PMMA of high molecular weight.[36] Scattering intensities are enhanced at angles corresponding, roughly, to distances approximating $\langle r^2 \rangle_0^{1/2}$ at the maximum in Fig. 9. This enhancement, heretofore considered anomalous, is in fact a direct consequence of the structure and configuration of syndiotactic PMMA.

It is thus apparent that subtle features of the chemical architecture of polymeric chains are manifested in their molecular properties. Treatment in terms of the artificial models much in use at present may therefore be quite misleading.

The analysis of the spatial configurations of macromolecular chains presented above is addressed primarily to an isolated molecule as it exists, for example, in a dilute solution. On theoretical grounds, the results obtained should be equally applicable to the molecules as they occur in an amorphous polymer, even in total absence of a diluent. This assertion follows unambiguously from the statistical thermodynamics of mixing of polymer chains,[5,6,37] including their mixtures with low molecular diluents. It has evoked much skepticism, however, and opinions to the contrary have been widespread. These opposing views stem primarily from qualitative arguments to the effect that difficulties inherent in the packing of long chains of consecutively connected segments to space-filling density can only be resolved either by alignment of the chains in bundle arrays, or by segregation of individual molecules in the form of compact globules. In either circumstance, the chain configuration would be altered drastically.

Whereas dense packing of polymer chains may appear to be a distressing task, a thorough examination of the problem leads to the firm conclusion that macromolecular chains whose structures offer sufficient flexibility are capable of meeting the challenge without departure or deviation from their intrinsic proclivities. In brief, the number of configurations the chains may assume is sufficiently great to guarantee numerous combinations of arrangements in which the condition of mutual exclusion of space is met throughout the system as a whole. Moreover, the task of packing chain molecules is not made easier by partial ordering of the chains or by segregating them.[6,37] Any state of organization short of complete abandonment of disorder in favor of creation of a crystalline phase offers no advantage, in a statistical-thermodynamic sense.

Theoretical arguments aside, experimental evidence is compelling in showing the chains to occur in random configurations in amorphous polymers, and further that these configurations correspond quantitatively with those of the unperturbed state discussed above.[38] The evidence comes from a variety of sources: from investigations on rubber elasticity, chemical cyclization equilibria, thermodynamics of solutions, and, most recently, from neutron scattering studies on protonated polymers in deuterated hosts (or *vice versa*).[39] The investigations last mentioned go further. They confirm the prediction made twenty-five years ago that the excluded volume perturbation should be annulled in the bulk amorphous state.[5] The excluded volume effect is therefore an aberration of the dilute solution, which, unfortunately, is the medium preferred for physicochemical characterization of macromolecules.

Knowledge gained through investigations, theoretical and experimental, on the spatial configuration and associated properties of random macromolecular chains acquires added significance and importance from its direct, quantitative applicability to the amorphous state. In a somewhat less quantitative sense, this knowledge applies to the intercrystalline regions of semicrystalline polymers as well. It is the special properties of polymeric materials in amorphous phases that render them uniquely suited to many of the functions they perform both in biological systems and in technological applications. These properties are intimately related to the nature of the spatial configurations of the constituent molecules.

Investigation of the conformations and spatial configurations of macromolecular chains is motivated therefore by considerations that go much beyond its appeal as a stimulating intellectual exercise. Acquisition of a thorough understanding of the subject must be regarded as indispensable to the comprehension of rational connections between chemical constitution and those properties that render polymers essential to living organisms and to the needs of man.

REFERENCES

1. Meyer, K. H., von Susich, G., and Valkó, F., Kolloid-Z, *59*, 208 (1932).
2. Kuhn, W., Kolloid-Z, *68*, 2 (1934).
3. Guth, E., and Mark, H., Monatsch., *65*, 93 (1934).
4. Kuhn, W., Kolloid-Z., *76*, 258 (1936); *87*, 3 (1939).
5. Flory, P. J., J. Chem. Phys., *17*, 303 (1949).
6. Flory, P. J., *Principles of Polymer Chemistry,* Cornell University Press, Ithaca, N.Y., 1953.
7. Flory, P. J., and Fisk, S., J. Chem. Phys., *44*, 2243 (1966).
8. Fujita, H., and Norisuye, T., J. Chem. Phys., *52*, 115 (1971).
9. Fixman, M., J. Chem. Phys., *23*, 1656 (1955).

10. Yamakawa, H., *Modern Theory of Polymer Solutions,* Harper and Row, New York, 1971.
11. Yamakawa, H., Pure and Appl. Chem., *31,* 179 (1972).
12. Edwards, S. F., Proc. Phys. Soc., (London), *85,* 613 (1965).
13. Fox, T. G., Jr., and Flory, P. J., J. Phys. and Coll. Chem., *53,* 197 (1949). Flory, P. J., and Fox, T. G., Jr., J. Polymer Sci., *5,* 745 (1950); J. Amer. Chem. Soc., *73,* 1904 (1951).
14. Altares, T., Wyman, D. P. and Allen, V. R., J. Polymer Sci., A, *2,* 4533 (1964).
15. Chinai, S. N., and Samuels, R. J., J. Polymer Sci., *19,* 463 (1956).
16. Mandelkern, L., and Flory, P. J., J. Chem. Phys., *20,* 212 (1952), Mandelkern, L., Krigbaum, W. R. and Flory, P. J., ibid., *20,* 1392 (1952).
17. Fox, T. G., Jr., and Flory, P. J., J. Amer. Chem. Soc., *73,* 1909, 1915 (1951).
18. Krigbaum, W. R., Mandelkern, L., and Flory, P. J., J. Polymer Sci., *9,* 381 (1952). Krigbaum, W. R. and Flory, P. J., ibid, *11,* 37 (1953).
19. Eisenberg, H., and Felsenfeld, G., J. Mol. Biol., *30,* 17 (1967). Inners, L. D., and Felsenfeld, G., ibid., *50,* 373 (1970).
20. Volkenstein, M. V., *Configurational Statistics of Polymeric Chains,* translated from the Russian ed., 1959, by S. N. and M. J. Timasheff, Interscience, New York, 1963.
21. Birshtein, T. M. and Ptitsyn, O. B., *Conformations of Macromolecules,* translated from the Russian ed., 1964, by S. N. and M. J. Timasheff, Interscience, New York, 1966.
22. Pitzer, K. S., Discussions Faraday Soc., *10,* 66 (1951).
23. Mizushima, S., Structure of Molecules and Internal Rotation, Academic Press, New York, 1954.
24. Flory, P. J., *Statistical Mechanics of Chain Molecules,* Interscience Publishers, New York, 1969.
25. Gotlib, Yu. Ya., Zh. Fiz Tekhn, *29,* 523 (1959). Birshtein, T. M., and Ptitsyn, O. B., ibid., *29,* 1048 (1959). Lifson, S., J. Chem. Phys., *30,* 964 (1959). Nagai, K., ibid., *31,* 1169 (1959), Hoeve, C. A. J., ibid., *32,* 888 (1960).
26. Abe, A., Jernigan, R. L., and Flory, P. J., J. Amer. Chem. Soc., *88,* 631 (1966).
27. Scott, R. A., and Scheraga, H. A., J. Chem. Phys., *44,* 3054 (1966).
28. Hoeve, C. A. J., J. Chem. Phys., *35,* 1266 (1961).
29. Kramers, H. A., and Wannier, G. H., Phys. Rev., *60,* 252 (1941).
30. Williams, A. D., and Flory, P. J., J. Amer. Chem. Soc., *91,* 3111, 3118 (1969). Flory, P. J., and Pickles, C. J., J. Chem. Soc., Faraday Trans. II, *69,* 632 (1973). Suter, U. W., Pucci, S., and Pino, P., J. Amer. Chem. Soc., *97* 1018 (1975).
31. Flory, P. J., Proc. Nat. Acad. Sci., *70,* 1819 (1973).
32. Flory, P. J., Macromolecules, *7,* 381 (1974).
33. Flory, P. J., and Abe, Y., J. Chem. Phys. *54,* 1351 (1971).
34. Yoon, D. Y., unpublished results, Laboratory of Macromolecular Chemistry, Stanford University.
35. Sundararajan, P. R., and Flory, P. J., J. Amer. Chem. Soc., *96,* 5025 (1974).
36. Kirste, R. G., and Kratky, O., Z. Physik, Chem. Neue Folge, *31,* 363 (1962). Kirste, R. G., Makromol. Chem., *101,* 91 (1967). Kirste, R. G., Kruse, W. A., and Ibel, K., Polymer, *16,* 120 (1975).
37. Flory, P. J., Proc. Royal Soc., A, *234,* 60 (1956). Flory, P. J., J. Polym. Sci., *49,* 105 (1961).
38. Flory, P. J., Pure & Appl. Chem., Macromolecular Chem., *8,* 1—15 (1972).
39. Kirste, R. G., Kruse, W. A., and Schelten, J., Makromol. Chem., *162,* 299 (1972). Benoit, H., Decker, D., Higgins, J. S., Picot, C., Cotton, J. P., Farnoux, B., Jannink, G., and Ober, R., Nature, Physical Sciences, *245,* 13 (1973). Ballard, D. G. H., Wignall, G. D., and Schelten, J., Eur. Polymer J., *9,* 965 (1973); ibid, *10,* 861 (1974). Fischer, E. W., Leiser, G., and Ibel, K. Polymer Letters, *13,* 39 (1975).

125

ALBERT CLAUDE

I was born in Belgium, in 1899. Longlier, my birthplace, is located in a high point of the Belgian Ardennes, atop the rising spur of an eroded remnant of the foot of the Alps, next to a deep valley. In the Middle Ages, it had been a fortified place, of the Francs and Carolegian dynasties. Pepin le Bref, crowned King of the Francs in 751 spent in Longlier two winters, from October to Easter, in the years 750 and 763. His son Charlemagne who by then had become Emperor of the Occident called a High Court of Justice of the Empire to meet in Longlier: the diploma, still preserved, was signed by him there in 771. In the year 1050, the Charlemagne Villa became a Monastery, and renamed later "Ferme Charlemagne". In the 17th—18th century, it was adorned with a high sloping roof "à la mansarde", whereas the round towers, standing high at the wall corners, matched the roof with elegant, bell-shaped tops, a situation which remained unchanged until 1914.

The landscape of the Longlier region is covered with remnants of the primeval forest of oak trees, progressively invaded by evergreens. The blue-green color of the pines, which blends with the blue-grey color of the massif of slate rocks emerging through a meager soil gives the countryside an aspect, severe, but also of serene beauty, and even more, when the pure coat of the snow covers it during the long and cold winters.

The population was sparse, at least at the time I was a boy. Our agglomeration was made of scattered small farms, regrouped into hamlets which, with the village, amounted to about 800 inhabitants in all. Rarely, because the people were few, a funeral procession was climbing slowly from the valley, back of our house, and to the old church next to the Charlemagne farm, with the cemetery between them.

The unique school of the Longlier region was built at the outskirt, a kilometer from my home, and about equal distances from the surrounding hamlets, so that the children could leave their home, and reach the school at about the same time. Actually, this school was just a single room with high windows, and a central stove, fed with coal and wood, by the teacher himself. As I remember, there was a set of 5 benches at either side of the stove, with a common sitting board which could accomodate 5 children, in all 50 seats, for an average population, from year to year, of 40 pupils, at the most. The sexes and grades were mixed, and the ages, from 6 to 11 years old. All the courses were taught at the same time, in the same room, by the same and unique teacher. Under this highly pluralistic system, the school was running smoothly, and the results, remembering over the years, turned out to be, in every respect, excellent.

As usual for the time, the roads were not lighted at night, and no water distribution was available, nor in prospect. Due to the elevation of the site, we had to rely on rainwater, collected from the roofs, and on the clear water, filtering and running from the bare rocks, to the river and the streams below.

In the Ardennes, the washed soil is poor, and the configuration rugged. When the spring and summer came, the heat of the sun brought life and beauty to the land. The farmers, however, rose early and worked late, each on their farm, relatively far apart, without the occasion, or the need, to communicate between themselves. Even more than in the cold of the winter, there was a strange stillness, in the heat of the afternoon.

After supper, and when the daily work was over, we did not light the kerosene lamp, nor the makeshift carbide lamp we used, when the war came upon us, but sat outdoors, in the silence and the darkness of the night. As many have done before us, since the early rise of mankind, I reclined on the sloping back of a chair, and gazed intensely, and for hours, at the quivering milky way, and watched the coming of falling stars.

When I became old enough, I took my turn in getting up early, and ringing the church bells (there were two of them) calling for the daily mass, at six o'clock in the morning. The ropes of the bells were hanging freely down the hollow shaft of the church tower, so that we could seize them and pull them from the ground, with the bells seen overhead. When the bells were in full swing, we used to grasp the rope firmly and let ourselves be lifted, just when the hammer hit the roaring bronze. This little familiarity had created an affectionate and reciprocal understanding between us and the Bells. One night, during a heavy storm, we were awaken by a crash. The Pepin le Bref tower, as it was called, which had stood there for many centuries had collapsed, bringing down, with it, the church bells. A few years later, in 1914, the madness of war reached our peaceful shores; the Charlemagne Villa, and part of the village, next to our home, was burnt. I was 15 years old, and starting to become an adult. For us, and for the dying Europe, and the thousands years of its past, it was a new World, and the end of an Era.

My grandfather was born in 1830, just the year the Flemish and French speaking Catholics decided to secede from the Lutheran Dutch people of the low lands, governed by the House of Orange. His place of birth was not Longlier. For a number of generations tracing back to the 17th century, his ancestors had been active in maintaining a Relay, or Stagecoach stop, providing horses, food and lodging for travellers, and wagons for the conveyance of goods. The site of this undertaking was a small plateau, about the locality of Offaing, rising from the opposite side of the Longlier valley, away and higher up from the Charlemagne Villa. From this rather ancient time, I have a witness helping me to imagine and recreate the past. It is a chest of heavy oak with a secret lock, and a slit with a receptacle underneath, in which the hostess, my great-grandmother, would drop the coins she received from the customers, in payment for their expenditure at the inn. This chest, for the past twenty years, has been in my bedroom, next to my bed, supporting a lamp and a clock.

My great-grandfather, Godfroid, born on the heights of Offaing in 1800, or about, had five or six sons, including my grandfather, and a similar number of daughters, most of them promised to live well over ninety. In this healthy, no doubt dynamic, but crowded environment, my grandfather may have felt the pressure of competition, but most likely happened to the most adventurous and most farsighted: he decided to move and settle on his own.

Following the Belgian revolution of 1830 the new nation decided to give itself a King, the choice being Léopold, Prince of Saxe-Cobourg and recent widower of the heir of the throne of England, with the crowning in 1831. Léopold the First was a man of high character and wisdom. It is to his knowledge of the industry of England and to his own initiative that Belgium owed to have had the first railroad lines on the Continent, the first one connecting Bruxelles with Antwerp and its harbor. The next undertaking was much more ambitious. This second line was to be transcontinental, starting from Brussels, through Namur, Luxembourg, Vienna, and further on.

The Longlier valley gap, however, which happened to stand exactly across the projected direction of the new railroad line, would have to be bridged. In addition to this technical difficulty, it was found that the Devonian synclinal, which is the geologic substructure of the region was disturbed by a tectonic anomaly in the form of a narrow band, less than one kilometer in width, which had become deflected in front of the Longlier valley, passing just under the terminal point where the construction of the railroad had stopped. The problems were such that the construction of the line was postponed, for an undetermined length of time. My grandfather saw the opportunity and moved to Longlier. Apparently, he was not without means. Within a relatively short time he built a hotel, next to the freight depot of the railroad terminus. From the commissioned Agency handling the freight traffic for the line, the "Messageries Van Gent", he obtained some agreement whereby he would be responsible of the freight that landed at the Terminal, for its distribution outside the railroad areas. Very soon, he had horses and wagons distributing goods and wares in various directions, as far as the north of France, especially Sedan and Bazeilles, where we had some relatives. His business prospered rapidly, and he became relatively wealthy.

For me, this story of railroads and of a diligent grandfather, which I have recalled, has been more meaningful than the effect of a tectonic anomaly on a Devonian synclinal. Without the decision of my grandfather to move to Longlier, my mother would have been someone else, and there would have been no tales of ringing bells in a medieval church tower, and no ailing uncle to take care of. It was a question of being, or not being. Once the first step taken, what remains to deal with are the important but universal problems of the individual, versus his environment. My mother, Glaudice Watriquant, was 45 years old when I was born, and my father 43. I was the youngest of four, two brothers and one sister, with a gap of 9 years with the oldest. As it happened, most of my early years were spent in the company of old, or very old people, each having their problems and ailments, but never com-

129

plaining. This created a pervading feeling of tolerance, kindness, and stoic strength which made me happy and feel secure..

For a while, my father worked for my grandfather. As a child eight years old he was already accompanying the driver, not much older than himself, returning by night bringing back fresh vegetables and labile goods from the renowned French market-garden of Fonds-de-Givonne. They took turn to rest, although the traffic was rare at night, especially in the long forest roads; moreover, the horses knew the way and kept on driving even if both drivers fell asleep, as ocurred more than once. It was pleasant for youngsters to wake up at the songs of the birds, in a mellow summer night. I would have enjoyed it as they did. My father was gentle, and romantic, in tune with his century. He liked to memorize poetry, from Lamartine, and especially Victor Hugo, who he admired the most. When he returned from his work and we were very young, we asked him to recite verses to us or sing a lieder, quite well, of the same vein. When he came of age, my father chose to become a baker and pastry maker, perhaps as a complement to the hotel, and for which he spent three years of training in Paris. He was there the year the poet Hugo died. On the Champs Elysées early, he found his way on the top of a gas lamp-post from where he watched pass the funeral procession of hundreds of thousands, for hours. It was in 1885, and my father was 29. It was also his last year of training. His first residence when married, two years later, was in the right wing of the Charlemagne Farm, next to the round tower, and my eldest brother was born there. The second residence, with the bakery and a store, where my second brother and my sister were born, was next to the railroad station. By the time of my birth, my father had taken over a former property of my grandfather, remodeled it and added a large building to serve as a kind of general store. During my time, the local work was already done by hired bakers, my father being away all day, taking care of orders and deliveries.

Two or 3 years after I was born, my mother developed a carcinoma of the breast which appeared shortly after she hurt herself in a fall. She died when I was 7. Too young to go to school, and my elder brothers away in the high school in the town nearby, I was with her most of the time. She suffered, but calmly. I was careful not to make demands on her, and tried to help her when I could. Neighbours and acquaintances came to visit her, sometimes two or three at a time. They didn't pay attention to me; on their way out I followed them to the door, and heard them describe, in their own way, the future course of the disease. I was sad but kept it to myself. Not to leave me alone at home, she took me with her when visiting some healer that had been recommended to her. For one of them, in Marbehan, we had to take the train. Living close to her and partaking her pain, I felt more and more being as a little nurse at her side. But like the grown-ups of that time, I could not help.

The death of our mother made a big change in the family. After a few years of increasing difficulties (there was a pre-war depression going-on), the decision was made to move to Athus, a prosperous steel mills region bordering both France and the Grand Duchy of Luxembourg. A couple of years before we left, my eldest brother Léon, student at the high school was sitting, one day, at the kitchen table with a book flat beside him. Cautiously, I approached him and said, pointing the right hand page to him: what is this? I remember that, in order to see the page, I had to stand on the tip of my toes, and stretch my head forward. What I saw was the simple outline of a retord, drawn in a square, marginal indentation of the text. My brother did not turn me but began to explain, molding his words with his hands. I did not remember what he said, and could not understand their technical meaning, but as he was speaking I felt my chest, my heart, and the roots of my soul expand. It was a revelation, never to be forgotten. How beautiful this world within the book. I intensely wished to see and know more. In the innocence of my age, I did not doubt that I could. I was 8 ½ years old. The kitchen table of our youth followed in Athus, an is now in Brussels, in the kitchen of our home.

My attendance at the Longlier primary school was curtailed more than a year before the moving. When we arrived in Athus, we found ourselves in an essentially German speaking community. In the church, the hymns and prayers were said in German, and German was spoken in the school where I was received. Every day at 4 PM, each pupil in turn had to read aloud a chapter of the bible. The bible in use, and of which I had a copy, was printed in gothic characters of the oldest type. I may have practiced the sound of them at home, orduring the long, idle hours in the school: when my turn came, I succeeded in reading my part aloud without knowing the words. Again, as before in the world of the aged people I had lived in, I was made to observe my environment from without, in an abstract way, as visitors in an aquarium.

After a year or two, I was asked to return to Longlier to help in the care of an uncle who had suffered a major cerebral hemorrhage. His right side was paralyzed and he had lost the use of his speech. He was tall and heavy, and my aunt was in her 60th year, and ailing. Soon, I took over all the care of my uncle, day and night, and later, progressively the responsability of the management and the routine work of the household. I was about 13 years old, and more duties and problems of other sorts were added when the war came. My only outside contacts then were the frequent visits of the doctor, who came regularly, or when we called for him in case of emergencies. He came driving himself his horse and cab which he used also when making the rounds of his patients in the country. To me, he looked old, but must have been less than 60. He had experience and common sense, and never seemed in a hurry. I reported to him about my uncle, and listened to his comments and advices. Finally, we conversed about other subjects and the news of the day. This familiarity with a respected physician and my appreciation of his work, or the tragedy I experienced with the long, tormented agony and death of my mother might have influenced me in wanting to study medicine. It was not the case. As far as I remember, even younger than eight, I have always been guided by reason. Not cold reason, but that which leads to the truth, to the real, and to sane Justice. When I went to the University, the medical school was the only place where one could hope to find the means to study life, its nature, its origins, and its ills.

Summarized Civic and Academic Status

Albert Claude was born in Longlier, Belgium, August 23, 1899, and obtained his medical degree from the Université de Liège, Belgium, in 1928.

He spent the winter of 1928—29 in Berlin, first at the Institute für Krebsforschung, and then at the Kaiser Wilhelm Institute, Dahlem, in the laboratory of tissues culture of Prof. Albert Fischer.

He joined the Rockefeller Institute (now the Rockefeller University), in the summer of 1929, and has been connected with this Institution, in different degrees, ever since.

He is Director emeritus of the Jules Bordet Institute for Cancer Researche and treatment, and Professor emeritus, the Faculty of Medicine, at the University of Brussels, Belgium.

He is now Professor, at the Rockefeller University, New York, N.Y., and Professor, at the Université Catholique de Louvain, Louvain, Belgium.

He is Director of the "Laboratoire de Biologie Cellulaire et Cancérologie", at the Université Catholique de Louvain, Louvain-la-Neuve, Belgium.

THE COMING OF AGE OF THE CELL

Inventory of living mechanisms by cell fractionation, biochemistry and electron microscopy, and a view of the impact of the findings on our status and thinking.

Nobel Lecture, December 12, 1974

by

ALBERT CLAUDE

The Rockefeller University, New York, N.Y., USA., and the Université Catholique de Louvain, Louvain, Belgium.

Fifty years of cell research can hardly be summarized in the twenty to thirty minutes of a lecture; to expose only part of it might be unrepresentative, unfair, and altogether unnecessary, since by now you have already been informed of the essential facts and discoveries that have accumulated in the course of these years.

What I would like to do instead, is to discuss with you the impact of these discoveries on our daily life, and their significance for the present and the future. At the same time I will try to recall, first hand, what has been my own experience in this century's endeavor to uncover what were, not so long ago, the mysteries of life itself.

Until 1930 or thereabout biologists, in the situation of Astronomers and Astrophysicists, were permitted to see the objects of their interest, but not to touch them; the cell was as distant from us, as the stars and galaxies were from them. More dramatic and frustrating was that we knew that the instrument at our disposal, the microscope,—so efficient in the 19th century—had ceased to be of any use, having reached, irremediably, the theoretical limits of its resolving power.

I remember vividly my student days, spending hours at the light microscope, turning endlessly the micrometric screw, and gazing at the blurred boundary which concealed the mysterious ground substance where the secret mechanisms of cell life might be found. Until I remembered an old saying, inherited from the Greeks—that the same causes, always produce the same effects. And I realized that I should stop that futile game, and should try something else. In the meantime, I had fallen in love with the shape and the color og the eosinophilic granules of leucocytes and attempted to isolate them. I failed—and consoled myself later on in thinking that this attempt was technically premature, especially for a pre-medical student, and that the eosinophilic granules were not pink, anyway. It was only postponed. That Friday, the 13th of September 1929, when I sailed from Antwerp on the fast liner "Arabic" for an eleven-day voyage to the United States, I knew exactly what I was going to do. I had mailed beforehand to Dr. Simon Flexner, Director of the Rockefeller Institute, my own research program, handwritten, in poor English, and it had been accepted. My proposition had been

133

to isolate, and determine by chemical and biochemical means the constitution of the Rous, chicken Tumor I "Agent", at that time still controversial in its nature and not yet recognized as a bonafide Virus. This task occupied me for about five years. Two short years later the microsomes, basophilic components of the cell ground substance, had settled in one of my test tubes, still a structureless jelly, but now captive in our hands.

In the following ten years, the general method of cell fractionation by differential centrifugation was tested and improved, and the basic principles codified in two papers in 1946. This attempt to isolate cell constituents might have been a failure if they had been destroyed by the relative brutality of the technique employed. But this did not happen. The subcellular fragments obtained by rubbing cells in a mortar, and further subjected to the multiple cycles of sedimentations, washings and resuspensions in an appropriate fluid medium, continued to function in our test tubes, as they would in their original, cellular environment. The strict application of the balance sheet-quantitative analysis method permitted to trace their respective distribution among the various cellular compartments and thus, determine the specific role they performed in the life of the Cell.

Small bodies, about half a micron in diameter, and referred to later under the name of "mitochondria" were detected under the light microscope as early as 1894. Although they continued to be extensively investigated by microscopy in the course of the following 50 years, leaving behind an enormous and controversial litterature, no progress was achieved, and the chemical constitution and biochemical functions of mitochondria remained unknown, to the end of that period.

In the early 1940's, I began to make plans for an investigation on the distribution of respiratory pigments in cells. Considering the complexity of the problem, I realized that it should be a collaborative undertaking. A year or so before, I had collaborated with Dean Burk and Winsler in providing them a material of interest to them, Chicken Tumor No 10, which they used in their studies of the respiratory function in tumor cells. We started experimenting, although they were but mildly impressed by the scientific value of my project, as they told me years later. Their laboratory was conveniently located at the corner of York and 68th, at street level with the Cornell University Department of Vincent du Vignaud. I remember tunning across the street, handing them, through the window, each fractions as they were isolated, my share being the determination of the chemical constitution of the fractions, and their respective distribution within the Cell. One day, Rollin D. Hotchkiss appeared, returning from a one-yar fellowship spent in Cambridge, England, who was delighted to find on arrival, quote, "the golden fruits on my doorstep". We were soon rejoined by Hogeboom, and later by W. C. Schneider as regards the distribution of cytochrome c in the Cell, and its participation in respiratory processes. Together, the observations provided conclusive evidence to support the view that most, if not all, of cytochrome oxidase, succinoxidase and cytochrome c, three important members of the respiratory system responsible for most of the oxygen uptake, were segregated in mitochondria. In parallel with these biochemical studies, evidence was also obtained, by tests carried out with characteristic dyes, both under the microscope and in vitro, showing that the respiratory organelles and the mitochondria seen under the microscope were one and the same, a morphological information which would have remained meaningless, however, if we had not secured beforehand, the knowledge of their biochemical functions.

Altogether, these observations demonstrated that the power of respiration exists in a discrete state in the cytoplasm, a fact which led me to suggest, in my Harvey Lecture, that the mitochondria may be considered "as the real power plants of the Cell". At about the same time, with the help of electron microscopy, the microsomes became the endoplasmic reticulum.

Looking back 25 years later, what I may say is that the facts have been far better than the dreams. In the long course of cell life on this earth it remained for our age, for our generation, to receive the full ownership of our inheritance. We have entered the cell, the Mansion of our birth, and started the inventory of our acquired wealth.

For over two billion years, through the apparent fancy of her endless differentiations and metamorphosis the Cell, as regards its basic physiological mechanisms, has remained one and the same. It is life itself, and our true and distant ancestor.

It is hardly more than a century since we first learned of the existence of the cell: this autonomous and all-contained unit of living matter, which has acquired the knowledge and the power to reproduce; the capacity to store, transform and utilize energy, and the capacity to accomplish physical works and to manufacture practically unlimited kinds of products. We know that the cell has possessed these attributes and biological devices and has continued to use them for billions of cell generations and years.

In the course of the past 30 or 40 years, we have learned to appreciate the complexity and perfection of the cellular mechanisms, miniaturized to the utmost at the molecular level, which reveal within the cell an unparalleled knowledge of the laws of physics and chemistry. If we examine the accomplishments of man in his most advanced endeavors, in theory and in practice, we find that the cell has done all this long before him, with greater resourcefulness and much greater efficiency.

In addition, we know also that the cell has a memory of its past, certainly in the case of the egg cell, and foresight of the future, together with precise and detailed patterns for differentiations and growth, a knowledge which is materialized in the process of reproduction and the development of all beings from bacteria to plants, beasts, or men. It is this cell which plans and composes all organisms, and which transmits to them its defects and potentialities. Man, like other organisms, is so perfectly coordinated that he may easily forget, whether awake or asleep, that he is a colony of cells in action, and that it is the cells which achieve, through him, what he has the illusion of accomplishing himself. It is the cells which create and maintain in us, during the span of our lives, our will to live and survive, to search and experiment, and to struggle.

The cell, over the billions of years of her life, has covered the earth many times with her substance, found ways to control herself and her environment, and insure her survival. Man has now become an adjunct to perfect and carry forward these conquests. Is it absurd to imagine that our social behavior, from gregarious amoeba to man, is also planned and dictated, from stored information, by the cells? And that the time has come for men to be entrusted with the task, through heroic efforts, of bringing life to other worlds?

I am afraid that in this description of the cell, based on experimental facts, I may be accused of reintroducing a vitalistic and teleological concept which the rationalism and the scientific materialism of the 19th and early 20th centuries had banished from our literature and from our scientific thinking.

Of course, we know the laws of trial and error, of large numbers and probabilities. We know that these laws are part of the mathematical and mechanical fabric of the universe, and that they are also at play in biological processes. But, in the name of the experimental method and out of our poor knowledge, are we really entitled to claim that everything happens by chance, to the exclusion of all other possibilities?

About a year ago, I was invited to an official party by the Governor of a State. As the guests were beginning to leave, the Governor took me aside in a room nearby. He looked concerned and somewhat embarrassed. "Dr. Claude," he asked, "you seem to know much about life. Please tell me: what do you think about the existence of God." The question was unexpected, but I was not unprepared. I told him that for a modern scientist, practicing experimental research, the least that could be said, is that we do not know. But I felt that such a negative answer was only part of the truth. I told him that in this universe in which we live, unbounded in space, infinite in stored energy and, who knows, unlimited in time, the adequate and positive answer, according to my belief, is that this universe may, also, possess infinite potentialities. The wife of the Governor had joined us in the meantime. Hearing this, she seized her husband by the arm and said, "You see, I always told you so."

Life, this anti-entropy, ceaselessly reloaded with energy, is a climbing force, toward order amidst chaos, toward light, among the darkness of the indefinite, toward the mystic dream of Love, between the fire which devours itself and the silence of the Cold. Such a Nature does not accept abdication, nor skepticism.

No doubt, man will continue to weigh and to measure, watch himself grow, and his Universe around him and with him, according to the ever growing powers of his tools. For the resolving powers of our scientific instruments decide, at a given moment, of the size and the vision of our Universe, and of the image we then make of ourselves. Once Ptolemy and Plato, yesterday Newton, today Einstein, and tomorrow new faiths, new beliefs, and new dimensions.

As a result of the scientific revolution of the present century we are finding ourselves living in a magic world, unbelievable less than hundred years ago—magic our telephone, radio, television by multichannel satellites, magic our conversations with the moon, with Mars and Venus, with Jupiter—magic these means which transform our former solitude into a permanent simultaneity of presence, among the members of the Solar System.

And here, at home, thanks to these new media, and the ever increasing speed of transports, we are witnessing a vast mutation taking place, no longer local, but at the dimensions of the Globe: the birth of a new biological organism, in which all Continents, and all the human races participate.

For this equilibrium now in sight, let us trust that mankind, as it has occurred in the greatest periods of its past, will find for itself a new code of ethics, common to all, made of tolerance, of courage, and of faith in the Spirit of men.

CHRISTIAN DE DUVE

I was born on October 2nd 1917, in Thames-Ditton, near London. My parents, of Belgian-German extraction, were Belgian nationals who had taken refuge in England during the war. They returned to Belgium in 1920, and I grew up in the cosmopolitan harbour city of Antwerp, at a time when education in the Flemish part of the country was still half French and half Flemish. Due to these various circumstances, when I entered the Catholic University of Louvain in 1934, I had already travelled in a number of European countries and spoke four languages fairly fluently. This turned out to be a valuable asset in my subsequent career as a scientist.

That I would embrace such a career was, however, very far from my mind. My education, according to the tradition of the jesuit school which I attended, had been centered on the "ancient humanities", and I was strongly attracted to the more literary branches. I nevertheless decided to study medicine, largely because of the appeal of medical practice as an occupation. Medical studies left a fair amount of free time in those days, and there was a tradition at the university that the better students joined a research laboratory. So it was that I entered the physiology laboratory of Professor J. P. Bouckaert, whose rigorous analytical mind exerted a strong influence on my intellectual development. I was attached to a group investigating the effect of insulin on glucose uptake. By the time when I graduated as an MD in 1941, I had abandoned all thought of a medical career, and had only one ambition: to elucidate the mechanism of action of insulin.

In the meantime, war had broken out. After a brief interval in the army and a temporary stay in a prisoners' camp, from which I promptly escaped thanks to the general confusion which followed the disastrous defeat of the allies, I had returned to Louvain to complete my studies. I had become convinced that the problem of insulin action needed to be approached by means of biochemical methods. Since research activities were almost paralysed due to lack of essential supplies, I embarked an another four-year curriculum, to gain the degree of "Licencié en Sciences Chimiques". I combined these studies with a clinical internship in the Cancer Institute, with as much experimental work as war circumstances allowed, and with extensive reading of the earlier literature on insulin.

As a medical student, I had been rather relaxed, but I worked really hard during those four years. Still I could not have achieved what I did without the support of my clinical chief, Professor Joseph Maisin, who enthusiastically approved of my plans and gave me a great deal of free time. By 1945, I had presented a thesis on the mechanism of action of insulin, which earned me the degree of "Agrégé de l'Enseignement Supérieur", written a 400-page book entitled "Glucose, Insuline et Diabète", and prepared a number of research articles for publication.

By that time, the war had ended and I felt a great need of further training in biochemistry. In 1946—1947, I had the good fortune of spending 18 months at the Medical Nobel Institute in Stockholm, in the laboratory of Hugo Theorell, who was awarded the Nobel Prize in 1955. I then spent 6 months as a Rockefeller Foundation fellow at Washington University, under Carl and Gerty Cori who jointly received the Nobel Prize while I was there. In St. Louis, I collaborated with Earl Sutherland, Nobel laureate in 1971. Indeed, I have been very fortunate in the choice of my mentors, all sticklers for technical excellence and intellectual rigour, those prerequisites of good scientific work.

I returned to Louvain in March 1947 to take over the teaching of physiological chemistry at the medical faculty, becoming full professor in 1951. I started a small research laboratory, where I was joined by a young physician, Géry Hers, who had already worked with me during the war, and by an increasing number of first class students, including Jacques Berthet, Henri Beaufay, Robert Wattiaux, Pierre Jacques and Pierre Baudhuin. All have since carved distinguished careers for themselves.

Insulin, together with glucagon which I had helped rediscover, was still my main focus of interest, and our first investigations were accordingly directed on certain enzymatic aspects of carbohydrate metabolism in liver, which were expected to throw light on the broader problem of insulin action. But fate had a surprise in store for me, in the form of a chance observation, the so-called "latency" of acid phosphatase. It was essentially irrelevant to the object of our research but it was most intriguing. My curiosity got the better of me, and as a result I never elucidated the mechanism of action of insulin. I pursued my accidental finding instead, drawing most of my collaborators along with me.

Our investigations were very fruitful. They led to the discovery of a new cell part, the lysosome, which received its name in 1955, and later of yet another organelle, the peroxisome. At the same time, we were prompted to develop progressively improved instrumental, technical and conceptual tools in relation to the separation and analysis of cell components, and to apply them to an increasing variety of problems of biological and also medical interest.

In 1962, I was appointed a professor at the Rockefeller Institute in New York, now the Rockefeller University, the institution where Albert Claude had made his pioneering studies between 1929 and 1949, and where George Palade had been working since 1946. I retained my position in Louvain and have since shared my time more or less equally between the two universities. In New York, I was able to develop a second flourishing group, which follows the same general lines of research as the Belgian group, but with a program of its own. The two laboratories work closely together and complement each other in many respects.

Recently, with a number of colleagues, I have created a new institute, the International Institute of Cellular and Molecular Pathology, or ICP, located on the new site of the Louvain Medical School in Brussels. The aim of the ICP is to accelerate the translation of basic knowledge in cellular and molecular biology into useful practical applications.

In September 1943, I married the former Janine Herman, the daughter of a physician. We have four children, three of whom are married, and two grandchildren.

EXPLORING CELLS WITH A CENTRIFUGE

Nobel Lecture, December 12, 1974

by

Christian de Duve

Université Catholique de Louvain, Belgium and The Rockefeller University, New York, N.Y., USA

Introduction

In one of her masterpieces, Nobel Laureate Selma Lagerlöf tells how the little boy Nils Holgersson visited the whole of Sweden, from Skåne to Lappland, on the wings of a friendly white gander.

I too have made a wonderful journey, using like Nils Holgersson an unconventional mode of travel. For the last 25 years, I have roamed through living cells, but with the help of a centrifuge rather than of a microscope.

On these trips I was never alone. I want to mention this at the onset, since I owe much to my travelling companions. Some of their names will come up as my tale unfolds; but there are so many of them that I will be quite unable to mention them all. My debt goes also to my early mentors in science: Joseph Bouckaert, Joseph Maisin, Hugo Theorell, Carl and Gerty Cori, Earl Sutherland. Four of them have preceded me on this podium. Three, unfortunately, are not with us any more.

The Development of Analytical Cell Fractionation

Thirty years ago, much of the living cell still remained virtually unexplored. The reasons for this are simple. Morphological examination was limited downward in the scale of dimensions by the resolving power of the light microscope, whereas chemical analysis stopped upward at the size of the smaller macromolecules. In between, covering almost two orders of magnitude, lay a vast "terra incognita", impenetrable with the means of the day. Invasion of this territory started almost simultaneously on its two frontiers, after electron microscopy became available to morphology and centrifugal fractionation to biochemistry.

When, in 1949, I decided to join the little band of early explorers who had followed Albert Claude in his pioneering expeditions, electron microscopy was still in its infancy. But centrifugal fractionation, the technique I wanted to use, was already well codified. It had been described in detail by Claude himself (1), and had been further refined by Hogeboom, Schneider and Palade (2) and by Schneider (3). According to the scheme developed by these workers, a tissue, generally rat or mouse liver, was first ground with a Potter-Elvehjem homogenizer, in the presence of either 0.88 M (2) or 0.25 M (3) sucrose. The homogenate was then fractionated quantitatively by means of three successive centrifugations and washings, under increasing centrifugal

142

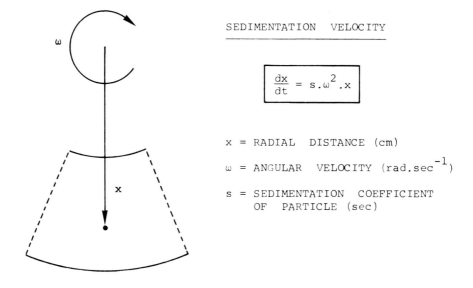

$$\frac{dx}{dt} = s.\omega^2.x$$

x = RADIAL   DISTANCE   (cm)

ω = ANGULAR   VELOCITY $(rad.sec^{-1})$

s = SEDIMENTATION   COEFFICIENT
   OF   PARTICLE   (sec)

FOR   SPHERICAL   PARTICLE   OF   RADIUS   r   (cm)   AND
OF   DENSITY ρ_p $(g.cm^{-3})$

IN   MEDIUM   OF   DENSITY ρ_m $(g.cm^{-3})$ AND   OF
VISCOSITY η (poises)

$$s = \frac{2\ r^2\ (\rho_p - \rho_m)}{9\ \eta}$$

Fig. 1. The Svedberg equation and its application to a spherical particle.

force x time integrals, to yield "nuclei", "mitochondria", "microsomes" and a final supernatant. The fractions, as well as the original homogenate, could then be analyzed for their chemical composition, enzyme content, and other properties.

All these details were available in the literature, and there seemed little more for us to do than to acquire the necessary equipment and follow instructions carefully, especially since our interest in cell fractionation itself was rather peripheral at that time. All we wanted was to know something about the localization of the enzyme glucose 6-phosphatase, which we thought might provide a possible clue to the mechanism of action, or lack of action, of insulin on the liver cell.

Fortunately, this is not exactly how things happened. Working with me on this project was Jacques Berthet, still a medical student at that time, but with an unusually mature and rigorous mind. He went about the job of setting up the technique in a careful and systematic fashion, paying special attention to all physical parameters. A few practical tips from Claude, who had just returned to Belgium, were also helpful.

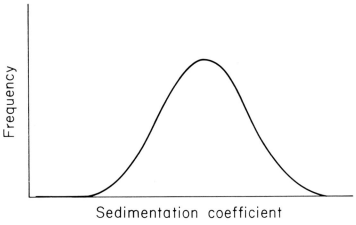

Fig. 2. Image of a polydisperse population of particles. Owing to individual differences in size and/or density, different members of the population do not have the same sedimentation coefficient. The centrifugal properties of the population as a whole are depicted by a *frequency distribution curve* of sedimentation coefficients. Size and/or density distribution can be similarly represented. Frequency is usually defined as $\dfrac{dn}{Ndx}$ (or in the case of histograms $\dfrac{\varDelta n}{N\varDelta x}$), in which $\dfrac{dn}{N}$ is the fraction of total particles having an abscissa value comprised between x and $x + dx$. Similar diagrams may be drawn in terms of relative mass, relative enzyme activity, etc . . ., instead of relative number.

Particularly important, I now realize in retrospect, was the fact that we took some time to study the theory of centrifugation, as beautifully exposed in the classical book by Svedberg and Pedersen (4).

Although separating mitochondria and microsomes might appear worlds apart from the determination of the molecular weight of macromolecules, certain concepts were common to the two operations and could be usefully transposed from the latter to the former.

One was that of *sedimentation coefficient* (Fig. 1), which obviously was applicable to any particle, irrespective of its size.

Another was that of *polydispersity* which, owing to biological variability, was likely to be a property of the populations made up by subcellular organelles. This meant that the centrifugal behavior of such populations could be described only by a frequency distribution curve of sedimentation coefficients (Fig. 2), not by a single *s* value as for most molecular populations.

A third important point related to the *resolving power* of differential sedimentation, which some elementary calculations revealed to be surprisingly low (Fig. 3).

There was much insistance in those days on the various artifacts that complicate centrifugal fractionation, such as, for instance, breakage or agglutination of particles, adsorption or leakage of soluble constituents. But these were only accidents, no doubt serious, but amenable to experimental correction. The problem, as it appeared to us, was a more fundamental one.

144

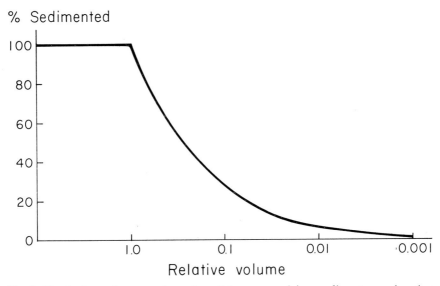

% Sedimented

Relative volume

Fig. 3. Graph shows the percentage of particles recovered in a sediment as a function of relative particle volume. Particle density is assumed to be the same for all particles. The meniscus of fluid in the rotating centrifuge is assumed to be half-way between the axis and the bottom of the tube or cell.

What we were doing was trying to separate populations which, owing to overlapping polydispersities, might at best be only partly separable from each other. In addition, we were using a poorly discriminating method for this purpose.

I cannot claim that all this was immediately clear to us. But considerations of this sort undoubtedly colored our approach from the start (5). We fully expected centrifugally isolated fractions to be impure, while suspecting that populations of cell organelles might be difficult, if not impossible, to resolve quantitatively. Conscious also of the severe limitations of light microscopic examination of the fractions, we tried to extend the biochemical interpretation as far as possible. Instead of looking at each fraction separately and focusing on its enzyme content, as was usually done, we looked rather at each individual enzyme and contemplated its distribution between all the fractions.

In order to permit a comprehensive view of enzyme distribution patterns, I introduced a histogram form of representation, illustrated in Fig. 4. In this figure are shown the distribution patterns of three of the first enzymes we studied, on the left as determined by the classical 4-fraction scheme, and on the right as determined by the modified 5-fraction scheme that we worked out in an effort to elucidate the significance of the small difference in distribution observed between acid phosphatase and cytochrome oxidase (6). This difference, as can be seen, is very much magnified by the modification in fractionation scheme.

These histograms turned out to be very revealing, by more or less automatically conveying the notion of polydispersity, illustrated in Fig. 2. In fact,

145

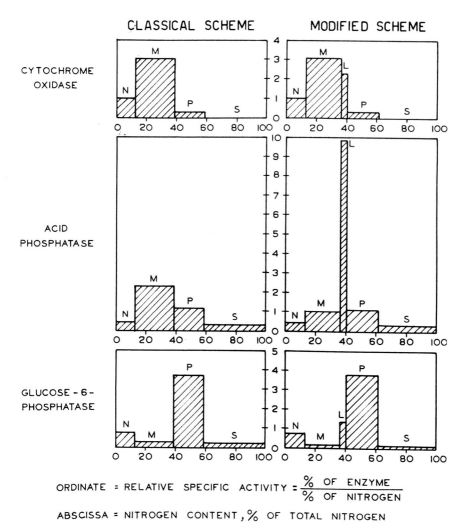

CLASSICAL SCHEME   MODIFIED SCHEME

ORDINATE = RELATIVE SPECIFIC ACTIVITY = $\dfrac{\% \ \text{OF} \ \text{ENZYME}}{\% \ \text{OF} \ \text{NITROGEN}}$

ABSCISSA = NITROGEN CONTENT, % OF TOTAL NITROGEN

Fig. 4. Enzyme distributions represented in histogram form. The relative specific enzyme content (% activity/% protein) of the fractions is plotted against their relative protein content, inscribed cumulatively from left to right in their order of isolation (decreasing sedimentation coefficient): nuclear N, mitochondrial M, microsomal P, and super-natant S, in classical 4-fraction scheme; and nuclear N, heavy-mitochondrial M, light-mitochondrial L, microsomal P and supernatant S, in modified 5-fraction scheme (6). Although very crude, similarity with frequency distribution curves of polydisperse populations can be recognized. Distinction between three populations, now known to consist of mitochondria (cytochrome oxidase), lysosomes (acid phosphatase) and endoplasmic reticulum fragments (glucose 6-phosphatase), is enhanced by use of 5-fraction scheme. From reference 7.

since the fractions are aligned along the abscissa in order of decreasing sedi-mentation coefficient, one may, in a very crude fashion, look at the abscissa as a deformed scale of sedimentation coefficients, and at the histograms as correspondingly deformed frequency distribution histograms of sedimentation coefficients. The logical next step in this line of reasoning was to assimilate enzyme distributions to particle distributions, and therefore to interpret, at least tentatively, significant differences in the distribution patterns of two enzymes as reflecting association of the enzymes with distinct particle populations.

Extrapolation from enzymes to particles could, however, not be made without some sort of assumption concerning the relationship between relative enzyme activity, the numerator in the ordinate of Fig. 4, and relative particle number, the numerator in the ordinate of Fig. 2. The simplest, and at the same time most plausible, such assumption was that members of a given particle population have essentially the same biochemical composition, larger particles simply having more of everything than smaller particles. Within the limits of validity of this assumption, which I have called the *postulate of biochemical homogeneity*, the histograms of Fig. 4 could now be likened to distribution diagrams of total particle mass or protein (not of actual particle numbers, it should be noted, although further conversion to numerical distributions can be made with some additional information). We had to assume, of course, that the enzyme distributions were not grossly distorted by translocation artifacts, or to correct for such artifacts as much as possible.

Another postulate we made was that each enzyme is restricted to a single intracellular site. This *postulate of single location* is less essential than that of biochemical homogeneity, since bimodal or multimodal distributions are amenable to the same kind of interpretation. In practice, however, single location made a useful addition to biochemical homogeneity, supporting the use of enzymes as *markers* of their host-particles.

First used empirically as pure working hypotheses, the above considerations were progressively validated, as more enzymes were studied and a limited number of typical distribution patterns began to emerge. Actually, as shown by the results of Fig. 5, things were not quite as simple, and a number of complications of various sorts tended to blur the picture. But most of these could be dealt with satisfactorily by ancillary experiments (8).

In these studies, a second line of evidence proved very useful, based on *enzyme latency*. Owing to impermeability of particle membranes to one or more of the substrates used in the assay of enzymes, many particle-bound enzymes fail to display activity "in vitro" as long as the membrane surrounding them is intact. Various means, mechanical, physical or chemical, can be used to disrupt the membrane and to release the enzymes, as we first showed for rat-liver acid phosphatase (Fig. 6). If two or more enzymes are present together in the same particles, they will be released together in this kind of experiment; if in different particles, they may come out separately (Fig. 7). In our hands, such studies have been very useful, providing an independent verification of the significance of the similarities and differences revealed by centrifugation experiments.

By 1955, our results were sufficiently advanced to allow us to propose with a certain measure of assurance the existence of a new group of particles with lytic properties, the lysosomes, and to hint at the existence of another group of particles, the future peroxisomes (8). At the same time, we had, from the

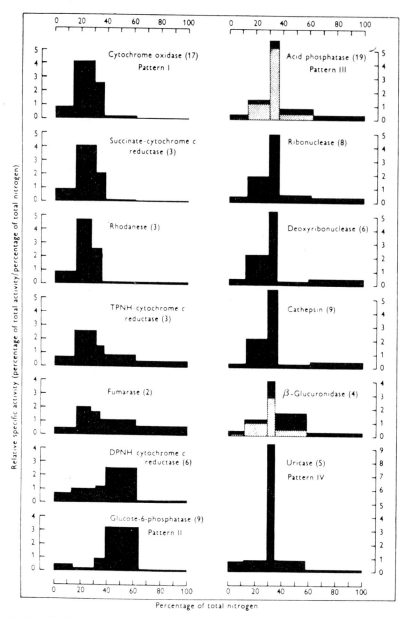

Fig. 5. Distribution patterns of enzymes in rat-liver fractions separated by 5-fraction procedure (see: Fig. 4). Pattern I, shared by 3 enzymes, represents the distribution of mitochondria; pattern II (glucose 6-phosphatase) that of microsomes. In between, in left-hand column, are complex combinations of patterns I and II. Pattern III is shared by 5 lysosomal acid hydrolases, except for β-glucuronidase which has an additional microsomal component. Pattern IV belongs to the peroxisomal urate oxidase. Details are given in original paper (8).

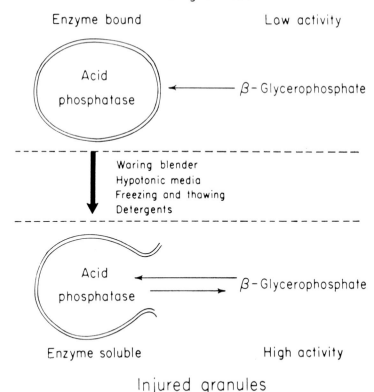

Intact granules

Enzyme bound   Low activity

Acid
phosphatase   ←———————— β-Glycerophosphate

- -
                    Waring blender
                    Hypotonic media
                    Freezing and thawing
                    Detergents
- -

Acid   ←—————————
phosphatase   —————————→   β-Glycerophosphate

Enzyme soluble   High activity

Injured granules

Fig. 6. Model of latency of rat-liver acid phosphatase, as proposed in 1951 (9). From reference 10.

mixture of theoretical considerations and experimental results that I have just briefly recalled, derived a certain "philosophy" of centrifugal fractionation, which I subsequently elaborated in greater detail in several publications (11). The key word here was *"analytical"*. Basically, we felt that our approach was no more than an extension of the classical Svedberg technique from the molecular to the submicroscopic and microscopic level.

A major difficulty at this stage, however, was that available techniques did not measure up to the kind of information we were hoping to extract. The answer to this problem was provided by density gradient centrifugation, which was introduced in the early 1950's. This new technique offered prospects of improved resolution; it allowed the use of density, as well as of sedimentation coefficient, as separation parameter; and, finally, its analytical character was unmistakable (Fig. 8). In fact, as shown as early as 1954 by Hogeboom and Kuff (13), it could even be used successfully for the determination of molecular weights.

Here again, we devoted some time to theoretical studies (12). In this, Berthet and I were joined by another young co-worker, Henri Beaufay, whose skills as a self-taught engineer proved particularly valuable for the design of

149

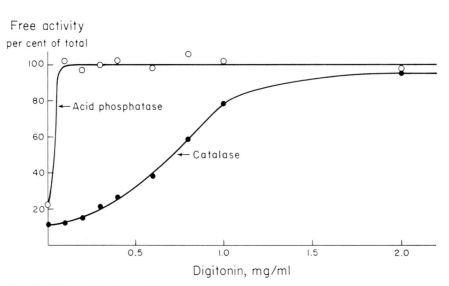

Free activity
per cent of total

Fig. 7. Differential release of the lysosomal acid phosphatase and of the peroxisomal catalase by increasing concentrations of digitonin. From reference 10.

various accessories, culminating in the construction of a completely automatic rotor (14), different in principle from the zonal rotors built by Norman Anderson (15), and particularly adapted to rapid isopycnic separation at minimum hydrostatic pressure. The importance of the latter advantage has been emphasized by my former collaborator Robert Wattiaux (16).

Particles sedimenting through a density gradient are apt to undergo a progressive increase in density, due to inflow of solute or outflow of water or both, depending on the number and permeability properties of their membranes and on the nature of the solute(s) and solvent used to make the gradient. These factors we tried to incorporate in a theoretical model of particle behavior (12, 17), and at the same time to take into account in the design of our experiments. It appeared from our theoretical considerations that the sucrose concentration of the medium might be a particularly important variable, and that different types of particles might respond differently to changes in sucrose concentration. We therefore subfractionated large granule fractions from rat liver in iso-osmotic glycogen gradients prepared with sucrose solutions of different concentrations as solvent, as well as in sucrose gradients prepared with either H_2O or D_2O (18).

The results of these experiments confirmed and extended our earlier findings, establishing the existence of three distinct groups of enzymes, as defined by their centrifugal behavior. There was little doubt in our minds that these observations reflected the occurrence of three distinct populations of particles in the large granule fraction. By fitting our results to the theoretical equation, we were even able to evaluate a number of physical parameters for each putative particle population, and to construct, from purely biochemical data, a sort of "robot picture" of the particles themselves. This is shown in Table I. Due to heterogeneity within the population, the data given in this table for the

Table I. *Typical Physical Properties of Rat-Liver Particles*

From reference 10

Parameter	Mito-chondria	Lysosomes		Peroxisomes		
Reference enzyme:	Cyto-chrome oxidase	Acid phospha-tase	Acid DNase	Urate oxidase	Catalase	D-Amino acid oxidase
Dry weight (μg)	10^{-7}	2.7×10^{-8}	3.6×10^{-8}	2.4×10^{-8}	—	—
Dry density	1.315	1.300	1.331	1.322	1.319	1.315
Osmotically active solutes (milliosmoles/g dry weight)	0.157	0.128	0.334	0	0	0
Water compartments (cm³/g dry weight)						
Hydration	0.430	0.256	0.212	0.214	0.295	0.296
Sucrose space	0.905	1.075	0.330	2.51	2.68	2.54
Osmotic space in 0.25 M sucrose	0.595	0.485	1.265	0	0	0
Total in 0.25 M sucrose	1.930	1.816	1.807	2.724	2.975	2.836
Sedimentation coefficient in 0.25 M sucrose (Svedberg units)	10^4	4.4×10^3	5×10^3	4.4×10^3	—	—
Diameter in 0.25 M sucrose (μm)	0.8	0.51	0.56	0.54	—	—
Density in 0.25 M sucrose	1.099	1.103	1.100	1.095	1.088	1.090

lysosomes are of questionable significance. On the other hand, those listed for mitochondria and peroxisomes agree very well with measurements made by other techniques.

Though analytically satisfactory, the results described so far still fell short from definitive proof, since they had unfortunately confirmed our fear that distinct populations of subcellular particles might prove intrinsically inseparable quantitatively due to overlapping of size and/or density distributions. It was possible to obtain pure samples by cutting off non-overlapping parts of the populations; but this introduced the danger of biased sampling. A means of almost complete separation, although under somewhat artificial conditions, was provided in 1962 by Wattiaux, Wibo and Baudhuin (19), when they discovered that pretreatment of the animals with Triton WR-1339 causes a selective decrease in the density of lysosomes, due to accumulation of the Triton within these particles (Fig. 9). Thanks to this finding and to the Beaufay rotor, large-scale separation of the three populations has now become possible, allowing a variety of biochemical and functional studies that were not feasible before (20).

While the biochemical approach I have outlined was being developed in our laboratory, electron microscopy was making great strides of its own, soon becoming available for the examination of subcellular fractions. For obvious

151

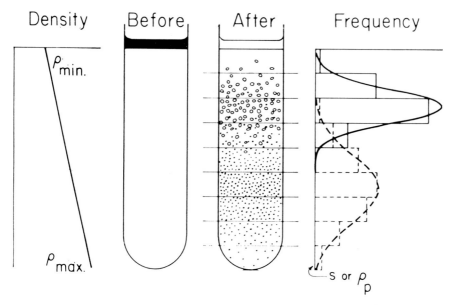

Density Before After Frequency

$\rho_{min.}$

$\rho_{max.}$

S or ρ_p

1. Differential sedimentation

   Gradient: *Shallow stabilizing,* $\rho_{max.} < \rho_{p\,min.}$

   Centrifugation: → *Incomplete sedimentation*

   Abscissa of frequency distribution: *Sedimentation coefficient*

2. Density equilibration

   Gradient: *Steep,* $\rho_{max.} > \rho_{p\,max.}$

   Centrifugation: *Prolonged, high speed*

   Abscissa of frequency distribution: *Equilibrium density*

Fig. 8. Schematic representation of density gradient centrifugation, with initial top-layering of the sample. Two forms, based on differences in sedimentation coefficient and density respectively, are shown. Diagram at the right pictures frequency distribution of particles or markers as a function of tube height. Conversion to frequency distributions of sedimentation coefficients or densities generally requires readjustment of ordinate and abscissa values, leaving surface area of each block (% content in fraction) unchanged. For details of calculations, see reference 12. From reference 10.

reasons we were very anxious to take a look at our purest fractions, in order to test our conclusions and eventually identify our hypothetical particles. Already in 1955, thanks to the expert collaboration of Alex Novikoff and to the facilities of Albert Claude in Brussels and of Wilhelm Bernhardt in Paris, we were able to do this for lysosome-rich fractions, which were found to contain dense bodies, surrounded by a membrane and of about the size predicted for lysosomes (21). Later, we were able to acquire an instrument of our own, and Henri Beaufay taught himself another skill, which he later perfected under

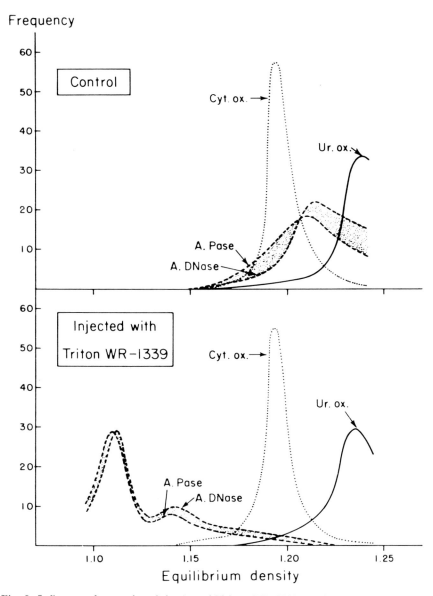

Fig. 9. Influence of a previous injection of Triton WR-1339 on the equilibrium density of rat-liver particles equilibrated in an aqueous sucrose gradient. Upper graph shows overlapping of lysosomes. (A.Pase = acid phosphatase; A.DNase = acid deoxyribonuclease) with mitochondria (Cyt.ox. = cytochrome oxidase) and peroxisomes (Ur.ox. = urate oxidase). Four days after intravenous injection of 170 mg of Triton WR-1339 to the animals, the density of the lysosomes has decreased drastically, that of mitochondria and of peroxisomes remains unchanged. Graph constructed from results of Wattiaux *et al.* (19), reproduced from reference 10.

the guidance of George Palade. With Pierre Baudhuin, he confirmed the identification of lysosomes as "pericanalicular dense bodies" and showed that the peroxisomes correspond to the particles known as "microbodies" (22).

Thus the gap between biochemistry and morphology was finally bridged, after some 15 years of research.

More recently, Baudhuin has adapted quantitative morphometric methods to the examination of subcellular fractions, making it possible to compare measurements derived from biochemical data with those obtained by direct mensuration (23). In several instances, excellent agreement has been found between the two sets of data (20, 23, 24, 25).

APPLICATIONS TO BIOLOGY

I have chosen to dwell at some length on our theoretical and technical studies, because they were, I believe, the key to whatever achievements were made by our group. I know that others have accomplished important advances by the alternative process of first purifying a subcellular component and then analyzing it. For example, nuclei, secretion granules, plasma membranes and Golgi elements have been largely characterized in this fashion. But purification is generally a laborious procedure, it is difficult to control, and it is rarely quantitative. The advantage of the analytical approach is that it is widely applicable, and it can provide a considerable amount of quantitative information, even with a relatively poor resolving power. The important point is that with this kind of methodology, we derive the information, not from the properties of specific fractions believed to approximate a given intracellular component, but from the manner in which properties are distributed over a large number of fractions, which together represent the whole tissue.

In our laboratories, this general approach has been applied to a variety of biological materials and for the study of many different problems. In continuation of the work on liver, already described, it has supported a number of studies concerned with the functions of lysosomes, including those of Robert Wattiaux on intralysosomal storage (26), of Pierre Jacques on pinocytosis (27), of Russell Deter on autophagy (28), of Jack Coffey, Nick Aronson and Stanley Fowler on lysosomal digestion (29), and of André Trouet and Paul Tulkens on the effects of anti-lysosome antibodies (30). It has also allowed Brian Poole, Federico Leighton, Tokuhiko Higashi and Paul Lazarow to make a searching analysis of the biogenesis and turnover of peroxisomes (24, 31). In recent years, a large team grouped around Henri Beaufay and Jacques Berthet, and including Alain Amar-Costesec, Ernest Feytmans, Mariette Robbi, Denise Thinès-Sempoux and Maurice Wibo, has launched a major attack on microsomal and other membrane fractions, with the aim of characterizing physically, chemically, enzymically and immunologically the various types of cytomembranes occurring in these fractions (32).

In its applications to other mammalian tissues and cell types, analytical cell fractionation has allowed Pierre Baudhuin and Brian Poole to recognize peroxisomes in kidney (33); Gilbert Vaes to carry out a thorough study of bone lysosomes, leading to very revealing observations on the role of these particles in bone resorption (34); Bill Bowers to make a comprehensive biochemical dissection of lymphoid tissues and lymphocytes, as a preliminary to an analysis of cell-mediated immune cytotoxicity (35); Marco Baggiolini to characterize the two types of granules present in neutrophil polymorphonuclear leucocytes (36); Richard Schultz and Pierre Jacques to unravel some of the complexities of placental tissue (37); Tim Peters to fractionate aortic smooth muscle cells (38) and enterocytes (39); and Paul Tulkens to do the same for cultured fibroblasts (40), a system also used by Brian Poole and Maurice Wibo for investigations of protein turnover (41).

Under the leadership of Miklós Müller, a series of fascinating studies have been performed in New York on a number of different protozoa. In *Tetrahymena pyriformis*, Müller was able to identify two types of lysosomes, which discharge their enzymes, one in phagocytic vacuoles and the other in the outside medium (42). In collaboration with Pierre Baudhuin and later with Jim Hogg, he has shown the existence in the same organism of peroxisomes which, like plant glyoxysomes, contain enzymes of the glyoxylate cycle (33, 43). More recently, with Don Lindmark, he has characterized in *Trichomonads* a completely new type of cytoplasmic particle, with the capacity of converting pyruvate to acetate, CO_2 and molecular hydrogen, the hydrogenosome (44).

Other studies have dealt with the role of lysosomes in tissue regression, notably those of Denise Scheib-Pfleger and Robert Wattiaux on Müllerian ducts in chick embryos (45), and those of Yves Eeckhout on the tail of metamorphosing tadpoles (46).

It has been my good fortune to participate in most of these investigations, sometimes actively and sometimes simply in an advisory capacity, and to watch at the same time the growing interest of other laboratories in similar problems. After trying, with increasing difficulty, to review the field of lysosomes at regular intervals (7, 47), I welcomed with some relief the appearance in 1969, under the editorship of Professor John Dingle and Dame Honor Fell, of the multi-author treatise "Lysosomes in Biology and Pathology", of which volume 4 is now in press (48). The literature on peroxisomes and related particles has grown more slowly, but has now also reached an appreciable size (49).

It must be pointed out that many of these advances have been made by means of morphological rather than by biochemical methods, or by a combination of both. In this respect, the development of cytochemical staining reactions for enzymes previously identified biochemically as specific particle markers has been an invaluable aid, thanks to the pioneering work of Alex Novikoff, Stanley Holt, Werner Straus, Fritz Miller, Sidney Goldfischer, Marilyn Farquhar and many others.

APPLICATIONS TO PATHOLOGY AND THERAPEUTICS

In recent years, we have become increasingly concerned with the possible medical applications of our findings. The possibility that lysosomes might accidentally become ruptured under certain conditions, and kill or injure their host-cells as a result, was considered right after we got our first clues to the existence of these particles. We even made a number of attempts to test this hypothesis in ischemic tissue and in the livers of animals subjected to hepatotoxic treatments or to carcinogenic diets (50). But we became discouraged by problems of interpretation (47). Even today, clear-cut demonstration of the so-called "suicide bag" hypothesis remains very difficult, although there seem to be at least a few authenticated cases involving this mechanism of cell death. Much more clearly documented is the mechanism of tissue injury through extracellular release of lysosomal enzymes, a field which has been pioneered by Honor Fell and her co-workers.

The two mechanisms mentioned above rely on the very plausible instance of lysosomal enzymes exerting their lytic effect at abnormal sites. What we did not suspect in the beginning was that the failure of lysosomal enzymes to act at their normal site could also cause serious diseases. This fact was brought home to us in a rather surprising fashion through the work of my colleague Géry Hers, who in 1962 diagnosed glycogen storage disease type II as being due to a severe deficiency of a lysosomal enzyme (51). This finding initiated a series of fruitful investigations on other storage diseases, in which François Van Hoof played a major part (52). It also provided useful guidelines to the chemists and pathologists who, in various parts of the world, were trying to unravel the pathogeny of hereditary lipidoses and mucopolysaccharidoses. Today, with more than twenty distinct congenital lysosomal enzyme deficiencies identified, this mysterious chapter of pathology has been largely elucidated (53).

According to some results obtained over the last few years by Tim Peters, Miklós Müller, Tatsuya Takano, Bill Black and Helen Shio, with the collaboration of Marilyn Farquhar, lipid accumulation in arterial cells during the development of atherosclerosis could well be due to a mechanism similar to that involved in congenital lipidoses. At least in cholesterol-fed rabbits, there is strong evidence, both biochemical and morphological, that the lysosomes of the aortic smooth muscle cells are the main site of intracellular cholesterol ester accumulation, and there are indications that a relative deficiency of the lysosomal cholesteryl esterase may be responsible for this phenomenon (38, 54). Fig. 10 shows some of the biochemical evidence: after cholesterol feeding, lysosomes become considerably less dense due to lipid accumulation. This figure also illustrates the sensitivity of our present techniques. These fractionations were performed on a total of about 1 mg of cell protein. Similar experiments can be, and have been successfully, carried out on a needle biopsy.

Other interesting applications of the lysosome concept are in pharmacology and therapeutics. In line with the "suicide bag" hypothesis, early investigations in this area focused on "labilizers" and "stabilizers" of the lysosomal membrane (55). One outcome of this work has been the suggestion that certain anti-inflammatory agents, such as cortisone and hydrocortisone, might owe at least part of their pharmacological properties to their effect on the lysosomal membrane.

More recently, we have extended our interest to the various substances that are taken up selectively into lysosomes and owe some of their main pharma-

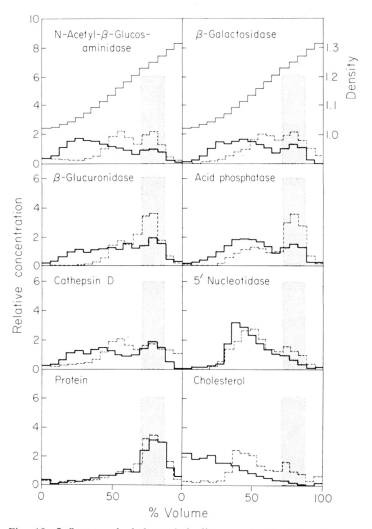

Fig. 10. Influence of cholesterol feeding on density of aortic smooth muscle cell lysosomes. Graphs show distribution patterns of enzymes after density equilibration (see: Fig. 8) in sucrose density gradient depicted by "staircase" on top. Starting material was a postnuclear supernatant of rabbit aortic cells brought to a density of 1.26 and layered initially at outer edge of gradient (dotted area). Broken lines give distributions in normal preparations, solid lines in preparation from a rabbit showing grade IV atheroma as a result of cholesterol feeding. Note extensive shift to the left of 5 acid hydrolases, indicating lowered density of lysosomes due to lipid accumulation. Distribution of protein, 5'-nucleotidase (plasma membranes) and mitochondrial cytochrome oxidase (not shown) was unchanged. From Peters and de Duve (54).

cological properties to this phenomenon. These "lysosomotropic" agents are surprisingly numerous, including such variegated compounds as neutral red, chloroquine, streptomycin, dextran, polyvinylpyrrolidone, Triton WR-1339 and trypan blue (56). Particularly interesting is the use of certain lysosomotropic agents as carriers for drugs. In Louvain, André Trouet has applied this principle to leukemia and cancer chemotherapy, by using DNA as carrier for the drugs daunorubicin and adriamycin. Experimentally, these DNA complexes proved less toxic and more effective on L1210 leukemia than the free drugs (57). Clinical trials under way over the last two years in several hospitals have given very encouraging results (58).

Conclusion

In the conclusion of his Nobel lecture delivered in 1955, Hugo Theorell asks the question: "What is the final goal of enzyme research?"

"The first stage", he answers, "is to investigate the entire steric constitution of all enzymes..."

"In the second stage," he continues, "it is a matter of deciding how the enzymes are arranged in the cell-structures. This implies, as a matter of fact, the filling of the yawning gulf between biochemistry and morphology".

The gulf still yawns toway. But it is a particular pleasure for me to be able to tell my old friend Theo that it yawns a little less. In our efforts to narrow it, my co-workers and I have been privileged to contemplate many marvelous aspects of the structural and functional organization of living cells. In addition, we have the deep satisfaction of seeing that our findings do not simply enrich knowledge, but may also help to conquer disease.

References

1. Claude, A., *J. Exp. Med.* **84**, 51, 61 (1946).
2. Hogeboom, G. H., Schneider, W. C., and Palade, G. E., *J. Biol. Chem.* **172**, 619 (1948).
3. Schneider, W. C., *ibid.* **176**, 259 (1948).
4. Svedberg, T., and Pedersen, K. O., *The Ultracentrifuge* (Clarendon Press, Oxford, 1940).
5. de Duve, C., and Berthet, J., *Intern. Rev. Cytol.* **3**, 225 (1954).
6. Appelmans, F., Wattiaux, R., and de Duve, C., *Biochem. J.* **59**, 438 (1955).
7. de Duve, C., in *Subcellular Particles* (Ronald Press, New York, 1959), pp. 128—159.
8. —, Pressman, B. C., Gianetto, R., Wattiaux, R., and Appelmans, F., *Biochem. J.* **60**, 604 (1955).
9. Berthet, J., and de Duve, C., *Biochem. J.* **50**, 174 (1951); —, Berthet, L., Appelmans, F., and de Duve, C., *ibid.* p. 182.
10. de Duve, C., *The Harvey Lectures* **59**, 49 (1965).
11. —, *J. Theoret. Biol.* **6**, 33 (1964); —, in *Enzyme Cytology*, Roodyn, D. B., Ed. (Academic Press, New York, 1967), pp. 1—26; —, *J. Cell Biol.* **50**, 20D (1971).
12. —, Berthet, J., and Beaufay, H., in *Progr. Biophys. Biophys. Chem.* **9**, 325 (1959).
13. Hogeboom, G. H., and Kuff, E. L., *J. Biol. Chem.* **210**, 733 (1954).
14. Beaufay, H., *La Centrifugation en Gradient de Densité* (Ceuterick, Louvain, 1966), 132 pp.
15. Anderson, N. G., editor. *The Development of Zonal Centrifuges and Ancillary Systems for Tissue Fractionation and Analysis*, Nat. Cancer Inst. Monogr. 21 (1966).
16. Wattiaux, R., *Mol. Cell. Biochem.* **4**, 21 (1974).
17. Beaufay, H., and Berthet, J., *Biochem. Soc. Symp.* **23**, 66 (1963).
18. —, Jacques, P., Baudhuin, P., Sellinger, O. Z., Berthet, J., and de Duve, C., *Biochem. J.* **92**, 184 (1964).

19. Wattiaux, R., Wibo, M., and Baudhuin, P., in *Ciba Foundation Symposium on Lysosomes* (Churchill, London, 1963), pp. 176—196.

20. Leighton, F., Poole, B., Beaufay, H., Baudhuin, P., Coffey, J. W., Fowler, S., and de Duve, C., *J. Cell Biol.* **37**, 482 (1968).

21. Novikoff, A. B., Beaufay, H., and de Duve, C., *J. Biophys. Biochem. Cytol.* **2**, 179 (1956).

22. Baudhuin, P., Beaufay, H., and de Duve, C., *J. Cell Biol.* **26**, 219 (1965).

23. Baudhuin, P., *L'Analyse Morphologique Quantitative de Fractions Subcellulaires* (Ceuterick, Louvain, 1968) 183 pp.

24. Poole, B., Higashi, T., and de Duve, C., *J. Cell Biol.* **45**, 408 (1970).

25. Wibo, M., Amar-Costesec, A., Berthet, J., and Beaufay, H., *ibid,* **51**, 52 (1971).

26. Wattiaux, R., *Etude Expérimentale de la Surcharge des Lysosomes* (Imprimerie J. Duculot, Gembloux, 1966) 129 pp.

27. Jacques, P., *Épuration Plasmatique de Protéines Étrangères, Leur Capture et Leur Destinée dans l'Appareil Vacuolaire du Foie* (Librairie Universitaire, Louvain, 1968), 150 pp.

28. Deter, R. L., and de Duve, C., *J. Cell Biol.* **33**, 437 (1967); —, Baudhuin, P., and de Duve, C., *ibid.* **35**, C11 (1967).

29. Coffey, J. W., and de Duve C., *J. Biol. Chem.* **243**, 3255 (1968); Aronson, N. N. Jr and de Duve, C., *ibid.* p. 4564; Fowler, S., and de Duve, C., *ibid.* **244**, 471 (1969); —, *Biochim. Biophys. Acta* **191**, 481 (1969).

30. Trouet, A., *Caractéristiques et Propriétés Antigéniques des Lysosomes du Foie* (Vander, Louvain, 1969), 185 pp.; Tulkens, P., Trouet, A., and Van Hoof, F., *Nature* **228**, 1282 (1970).

31. Leighton, F., Poole, B., Lazarow, P. B., and de Duve, C., *J. Cell Biol.* **41**, 521 (1969); Poole, B., Leighton, F., and de Duve, C., *ibid.* p. 536; Lazarow, P. B., and de Duve, C., *Biochem. Biophys. Res. Commun.* **45**, 1198 (1971); — and de Duve, C., *J. Cell Biol.* **59** 491 (1973); — and de Duve, C., *ibid.* p. 507.

32. Thinès-Sempoux, D., Amar-Costesec, A., Beaufay, H., and Berthet, J., *J. Cell Biol.* **43**, 189 (1969); Beaufay, H., Amar-Costesec, A., Feytmans, E. Thinès-Sempoux, D., Wibo, M., Robbi, M., and Berthet, J., *ibid.* **61**, 188 (1974); Amar-Costesec, A., Beaufay, H., Wibo, M., Thinès-Sempoux, D., Feytmans, E., Robbi, M., and Berthet, J., *ibid.* p. 201; Beaufay, H., Amar-Costesec, A., Thinès-Sempoux, D., Wibo, M., Robbi, M., and Berthet, J., *ibid.* p. 213; Amar-Costesec, A., Wibo, M., Thinès-Sempoux, D., Beaufay, H., and Berthet, J., *ibid.* **62**, 717 (1974).

33. Baudhuin, P., Müller, M., Poole, B., and de Duve, C., *Biochem. Biophys. Res. Commun.* **20**, 53 (1965).

34. Vaes, G., and Jacques, P., *Biochem. J.* **97**, 380 (1965); —, and Jacques, P., *ibid.* p. 389; —, *ibid.* p. 393; —, *Exptl. Cell Res.* **39**, 470 (1965); —, *La Résorption Osseuse et l'Hormone Parathyroïdienne* (Imprimerie E. Warny, Louvain, 1966), 135 pp.; —, *J. Cell Biol.* **39**, 676 (1968).

35. Bowers, W. E., Finkenstædt, J. T., and de Duve, C., *J. Cell Biol.* **32**, 325 (1967); —, and de Duve, C., *ibid., p.* 339; — and de Duve, C., *ibid.,* p. 349; —, *J. Exp. Med.* **136**, 1394 (1972); —, *J. Cell Biol.* **59**, 177 (1973); —, *J. Immunol.* **113**, 1252 (1974).

36. Baggiolini, M., Hirsch, J. G., and de Duve, C., *J. Cell Biol.* **40**, 529 (1969); —, de Duve, C., Masson, P., and Heremans, J. F., *J. Exp. Med.* **131**, 559 (1970); —, Hirsch, J. G., and de Duve, C., *J. Cell Biol.* **45**, 586 (1970); Farquhar, M. G., Bainton, D. F., Baggiolini, M., and de Duve, C., *ibid.* **54**, 141 (1972).

37. Schultz, R. L., and Jacques, P. J., *Arch. Biochem. Biophys.* **144**, 292 (1971).

38. Peters, T. J., Müller, M., and de Duve, C., *J. Exp. Med.* **136**, 1117 (1972).

39. —, in *Peptide Transport in Bacteria and Mammalian Gut,* A Ciba Foundation Symposium (ASP, Amsterdam, 1971), pp. 107—122.

40. Tulkens, P., Beaufay, H., and Trouet, A., *J. Cell Biol.* **63**, 383 (1974).

41. Poole, B., and Wibo, M., in *Proceedings of Symposium on Intracellular Protein Catabolism* (Friedrichroda, GDR, May, 1973); in press; Wibo, M., and Poole, B., *J. Cell Biol.* **63**, 430 (1974).

42. Müller, M., Baudhuin, P., and de Duve, C., *J. Cell. Physiol.* **68**, 165 (1966); —, *Acta Biol. Acad. Sci. Hung.* **22**, 179 (1971); —, *J. Cell Biol.* **52**, 478 (1972).

43. Müller, M., Hogg, J. F., and de Duve, C., *J. Biol. Chem.* **243**, 5385 (1968).

44. —, *J. Cell Biol.* **57**, 453 (1973); Lindmark, D. G., and Müller, M., *J. Biol. Chem.* **248**, 7724 (1973); — and Müller, M., *J. Protozool.* **21**, 374 (1974); — and Müller, M., *J. Biol. Chem.* **249**, 4634 (1974).

45. Scheib-Pfleger, D., and Wattiaux, R., *Develop. Biol.* **5**, 205 (1962).

46. Eeckhout, Y., *Etude Biochimique de la Métamorphose Caudale des Amphibiens Anoures* (Académie Royale de Belgique, Mémoire, Classe des Sciences, 1969) **38**, No. 4, 113 pp.

47. de Duve, C., in *Ciba Foundation Symposium on Lysosomes* (Churchill, London, 1963), pp. 1—31; —, in *Injury, Inflammation and Immunity* (Williams & Wilkins Company, Baltimore, 1964), pp. 283—311; —, *Fed. Proc.* **23**, 1045 (1964); — and Wattiaux, R., *Ann. Rev. Physiol.* **28**, 435 (1966).

48. Dingle, J. T., and Fell, H. B., Eds., *Lysosomes in Biology and Pathology* (North-Holland, Amsterdam—London), Vol. 1 and 2 (1969), Vol. 3 (Dingle, J. T., ed., 1973).

49. de Duve, C., and Baudhuin, P., *Physiol. Rev.* **46**, 323 (1966); Hruban, Z., and Rechcigl, M., *Microbodies and Related Particles* (Academic Press, New York, 1968); de Duve, C., *Proc. Roy. Soc. Ser. B.* **173**, 71 (1969); Hogg, J. F., *Ann. N.Y. Acad. Sci.* **168**, 209 (1969); Tolbert, N. E., *Ann. Rev. Plant Physiol.* **22**, 45 (1971).

50. Deckers-Passau, L., Maisin, J., and de Duve, C., *Acta Unio Intern. Contra Cancrum* **13**, 822 (1957); de Duve, C., and Beaufay, H., *Biochem. J.* **73**, 610 (1959); Beaufay, H., Van Campenhout, E., and de Duve, C., *ibid,* p. 617.

51. Hers, H. G., *Biochem. J.* **86**, 11 (1963); Lejeune, N., Thinès-Sempoux, D., and Hers, H. G., *ibid.,* p. 16; Baudhuin, P., Hers, H. G., and Loeb, H., *Lab. Invest.* **13**, 1140 (1964).

52. Van Hoof, F., *Les Mucopolysaccharidoses en tant que thésaurismoses lysosomiales* (Vander, Louvain, 1972) 285 pp.

53. Hers, H. G., and Van Hoof, F., *Lysosomes and Storage Diseases* (Academic Press, New York, 1973).

54. Peters, T. J., and de Duve, C., *Exp. Mol. Pathol.* **20**, 228 (1974); Shio, H., Farquhar, M. G., and de Duve, C., *Am. J. Pathol.* **76**, 1 (1974); Takano, T., Black, W. J., Peters, T. J., and de Duve, C., *J. Biol. Chem.* **249**, 6732 (1974).

55. de Duve, C., Wattiaux, R., and Wibo, M., *Biochem. Pharmacol.* **9**, 97 (1962).

56. de Duve, C., de Barsy, T., Poole, B., Trouet, A., Tulkens, P., and Van Hoof, F., *Biochem. Pharmacol.* **23**, 2495 (1974).

57. Trouet, A., Deprez-De Campeneere, D., and de Duve, C., *Nature New Biology* **239**, 110 (1972); —, Deprez-De Campeneere, D., De Smedt-Malengreaux, M., and Atassi, G., *Europ. J. Cancer* **10**, 405 (1974).

58. Sokal, G., Trouet, A., Michaux, J. L. and Cornu, G., *Europ. J. Cancer,* **9**, 391 (1973); Cornu, G., Michaux, J. L., Sokal, G., and Trouet, A., *ibid.,* **10**, 695 (1974); Longueville, J., and Maisin, H., *in* "Adriamycin Review" (2d Intern. Symposium, Brussels), European Press, Ghent, p. 260 (1975).

GEORGE EMIL PALADE

I was born in November 1912 in Jassy (Iaşi), the old capital of Moldavia, the eastern province of Romania. My education was started in that city and was continued through a baccalaureate (continental style) at the "Al Hasdeu" Lyceum in Buzau. My father, Emil Palade, was professor of philosophy and my mother, Constanta Cantemir-Palade, was a teacher. The family environment explains why I acquired early in life great respect for books, scholars and education.

My father had hoped I was going to study philosophy at the University, like himself, but I preferred to deal with tangibles and specifics and—influenced by relatives much closer to my age than he was—I entered the School of Medicine of the University of Bucharest (Romania) in 1930.

Early in my student years, I developed a strong interest in basic biomedical sciences by listening to, and speaking with, Francisc Rainer and André Boivin, professors of Anatomy and Biochemistry, respectively. As a result, I started working in the Anatomy laboratory while still in medical school. I went, nonetheless, through six years of hospital training, mostly in internal medicine, but I did the work for my doctorate thesis in microscopic anatomy on a rather unusual topic (for an M.D.): the nephron of the cetacean *Delphinus delphi*. It was an attempt to understand its structure in terms of the functional adaptation of a mammal to marine life.

I graduated in 1940 and, after a short period as an assistant in internal medicine, I went back to Anatomy, since the discrepancy between knowledge possessed by, and expected from, the medical practitioners of that time made me rather uneasy.

During the second world war, I served in the medical corps of the Romanian Army and after the war—encouraged by Grigore Popa, Rainer's successor— I came to the United States in 1946 for further studies. I worked for a few months in the Biology Laboratory of Robert Chambers at New York University and, while there, I met Albert Claude who had come to give a seminar on his work in electron microscopy. I was fascinated by the perspectives opened by his findings and extremely happy when, after a short discussion following his seminar, he asked me to come to work with him at The Rockefeller Institute for Medical Research in the fall of the same year. This was truly a timely development, since Chambers was retiring that summer.

At The Rockefeller Institute, Claude was working in the department of Pathology of James Murphy with George Hogeboom and Walter Schneider as direct collaborators; Keith Porter was in the same department but had developed his own line of research on the electron microscopy of cultured animal cells. At the beginning, I worked primarily on cell fractionation procedures, and I developed with Hogeboom and Schneider the "sucrose method" for the homogenization and fractionation of liver tissue. This first "Rockefeller group" had a rather short existence: Schneider returned to the University of Wisconsin, Hogeboom moved to the National Cancer Institute, and Claude went back to Belgium in 1949 to assume the directorship of the Jules Bordet Institute. Only Porter and I remained at The Rockefeller Institute; two years later, upon Murphy's retirement, we became "orphans" and were adopted by Herbert Gasser then the director of the Institute, since none of us had the rank required to head a laboratory.

Aorund that time, I started working in electron microscopy with the general aim of developing preparation procedures applicable to organized tissue. This line of research had been tackled before by a few investigators, Claude included, but there was still ample room for improvement. Taking advantage of whatever techniques were already available, Porter and I worked out enough improvements in microtomy and tissue fixation to obtain preparations which, at least for a while, appeared satisfactory and gratifying. A period of intense activity and great excitement followed since the new layer of biological structure revealed by electron microscopy proved to be unexpectedly rich and surprisingly uniform for practically all eukaryotic cells. Singly, or in collaboration with others, I did my share in exploring the newly open territory and, in the process, I defined the fine structure of mitochondria, and described the small particulate component of the cytoplasm (later called ribosomes); with Porter, I investigated the local differentiations of the endoplasmic reticulum and with Sanford Palay I worked out the fine structure of chemical synapses. With all this activity, our laboratory became reasonably well known and started functioning as a training center for biological electron microscopy. The circumstances that permitted this development were unusually favorable: we didn't have to worry about research funds (since we were well supported by Herbert Gasser), we had practically complete freedom in selecting our targets, strong competitors who kept us alert, and excellent collaborators who helped us in maintaining our advance.

In the middle 1950's, I felt that the time was ripe for going back to cell fractionation as a means of defining the chemical composition and the functional role of the newly discovered subcellular components. The intent was to use electron microscopy for monitoring cell fractionation. I was starting from structural findings and morphological criteria seemed appropriate for assessing the degree of homogeneity (or heterogeneity) of the cell fractions. Philip Siekevitz joined our laboratory in 1955 and together we showed that Claude's microsomes were fragments of the endoplasmic reticulum (as postulated by Claude in 1948) and that the ribosomes were ribonucleoprotein praticles. To find out more about the function of the endoplasmic reticulum and of the attached ribosomes, we started an integrated morphological and biochemical analysis of the secretory process in the guinea pig pancreas.

In 1961, Keith Porter who had been the head of our group since 1953 joined the Biological Laboratories of Harvard University and, with his departure, the history of the second "Rockefeller group" came to an end. It was during this period that cell biology became a recognized field of research in biological sciences and that the Journal of Cell Biology and the American Society for Cell Biology were founded. Our group participated actively in each of these developments.

In the 1960's, I continued the work on the secretory process using in parallel or in succession two different approaches. The first relied exclusively on cell fractionation, and was developed in collaboration with Philip Siekevitz, Lewis Greene, Colvin Redman, David Sabatini and Yutaka Tashiro; it led to the characterization of the zymogen granules and to the discovery of the segregation of secretory products in the cisternal space of the endoplasmic reticulum. The second approach relied primarily on radioautography, and involved experiments on intact animals or pancreatic slices which were carried out in collaboration with Lucien Caro and especially James Jamieson. This series of investigations produced a good part of our current ideas on the synthesis and intracellular processing of proteins for export. A critical review of this line of research is presented in the Nobel Lecture (page 175).

In parallel with the work on the secretory process in the pancreatic exocrine cell, I maintained an interest in the structural aspects of capillary permeability, that goes back to the early 1950's when I found a large population of plasmalemmal vesicles in the endothelial cells of blood capillaries. Along this line of research, Marilyn Farquhar and I investigated the capillaries of the renal glomeruli and recognized that, in their case, the basement membrane is the filtration barrier for molecules of 100A diameter or larger; a byproduct of this work was the definition of junctional complexes in a variety of epithelia. Visceral (fenestrated) capillaries were investigated with Francesco Clementi, and muscular capillaries with Romaine Bruns and Nicolae and Maia Simionescu.

The capillary work has relied primarily on the use of "probe" molecules of known dimensions detected individually or in mass (after cytochemical reactions) by electron microscopy. It led to the identification of the passageways followed by large water-soluble molecules in both types of capillaries and by small molecules in visceral capillaries. The pathway followed by small, water-soluble molecules in muscular capillaries is still under investigation.

In the middle 1960's our laboratory began a series of investigations on membrane biogenesis in eukaryoic cells using as model objects either the endoplasmic reticulum of mammalian hepatocytes (with P. Siekevitz, Gustav Dallner and Andrea Leskes), or the thylakoid membranes of a green alga (*Chlamydomonas reinhardtii*) (With P. Siekevitz, Kenneth Hoober and Itzhak Ohad). These studies showed that "new" membrane is produced by expansion of "old" preexisting membrane (there is no *de novo* membrane assembly), and that new molecules are asynchronously inserted, and randomly distributed throughout the expanding membrane. Asynchrony also applies to the turnover of membrane proteins in the endoplasmic reticulum as shown by work done with P. Siekevitz, Tsuneo Omura and Walter Bock.

In 1973, I left the Rockefeller University to join the Yale University

Medical School. The main reason for the move was my belief that the time had come for fruitful interactions between the new discipline of Cell Biology and the traditional fields of interest of medical schools, namely Pathology and Clinical Medicine. Besides, my work at the Rockefeller University was done: when I left there were at least five other laboratories working in different sectors of cell biology.

At present I am investigating together with my collaborators the interactions which occur among the membranes of the various compartments of the secertory pathway, namely the endoplasmic reticulum, the Golgi complex, the secretion granules, and the plasmalemma.

I have been a member of the National Academy of Sciences (U.S.A.) since 1961, and I have received in the past a number of awards and prizes for my scientific work, among them: the Lasker Award (1966), the Gairdner Special Award (1967), and the Hurwitz Prize—shared with Albert Claude and Keith Porter (1970).

Since my high school years I have been interested in history, especially in Roman history, a topic on which I have read rather extensively. The Latin that goes with this kind of interest proved useful when I had to generate a few terms and names for cell biology.

I have a daughter, Georgia Palade Van Duzen, and a son Philip Palade from a first marriage with Irina Malaxa, now deceased. In 1970 I married Marilyn Gist Farquhar who is a cell biologist like myself.

INTRACELLULAR ASPECTS OF THE PROCESS OF PROTEIN SECRETION

Nobel Lecture, December 12, 1974

by

GEORGE E. PALADE

Yale University Medical School, New Haven, Connecticut, USA

A SHORT HISTORY OF THE WORK

In the early 1950's, during the near avalanche of discoveries, rediscoveries, and redefinitions of subcellular components made possible by electrons microscopy, those prospecting in this newly opened field were faced with the problem of what to do with their newly acquired wealth. It could be increased by extending the inquiry on the horizontal to many other cell types prepared by many other techniques; it could be extended in further depth, instrumental resolution permitting ("ultra" was the preferred prefix of the period); or it could be used as a guide to monitor cell fractionation procedures of the type previously developed by Claude (1). The last alternative seemed particularly attractive since the small dimensions of many of the newly discovered structures suggested that they were relatively simple macromolecular assemblies. At their level, structure—as traditionally envisaged by the microscopist—was bound to merge into biochemistry, and biochemistry of mass-isolated subcellular components appeared to be the best way to get at the function of some of the newly discovered structures. The example provided by the work on isolated mitochondria was recent and still shining (2, 3).

At the time the structures of interest were the "small particulate component of the cytoplasm" (4) soon to become in succession "ribonucleoprotein particles" (5) and "ribosomes" (6), and the endoplasmic reticulum originally discovered by Porter, Claude and Fullam (7) and then studied by Porter (8) and by Porter and myself (9—11). Philip Siekevitz joined me in 1955 and together we started a long series of integrated morphological and biochemical studies on the pancreas of the guinea pig using primarily a combination of electron microscopy and cell fractionation procedures.

The croice of the pancreatic exocrine cell, a very efficient protein producer, as the object for our studies reflected in part our training, and in part our environment. I was coming from a medical school where I had acquired an interest in "microscopical anatomy" and "physiological chemistry" and great respect for the work of Claude Bernard, Rudolf Heidenhain and Charles Garnier. Philip Siekevitz was coming from a graduate school with a Ph.D. in Biochemistry and had recently worked out one of the first *in vitro* systems for protein synthesis (12). Our environment was the Rockefeller Institute for Medical Research where a substantial amount of work had been carried on the isolation, crystallization and characterization of pancreatic secretory proteins (cf. 13). But perhaps the most important factor in this selection was the appeal of the amazing organization of the pancreatic acinar cell whose cytoplasm is packed with stacked endoplasmic reticulum cirsternae studded with ribosomes. Its pictures had for me the effect of the song of a mermaid: irresistable and half transparent. Its meaning seemed to be buried only under a few years of work, and reasonable working hypotheses were already suggested by the structural organization itself.

The general aim of the project was to define the role played by the ribosomes, endoplasmic reticulum and other subcellular components in the synthesis and subsequent processing of the proteins produced for export by the exocrine cells of the gland. The approach worked rather well for a while (14, 15), but after a few years we ran into the common limitations of the cell fractionation procedures then in use: imperfect separation, incomplete recovery, and incomplete representation of subcellular components in the fractionation scheme. To resume the advance of the inquiry, Lucien Caro and I shifted to radioautography adapted to electron microscopy and obtained, in experiments carried out *in vivo*, a reasonable approximation of the route and timetable followed by newly synthesized, radioactive proteins from their site of synthesis to their site of discharge from the cell (16). Radioautography has, however, its own limitations connected primarily with its low resolution, so that in subsequent experiments uncertain radioautographic findings had to be checked by going back to cell fractionation procedures—this time with an advised mind. The experimental protocols were also changed to obtain better time resolution of the events under study, the major changes being the use of an *in vitro* subcellular system (17) and the adaptation by James Jamieson of an *in vitro* slice system (18) which later on evolved into a lobule system (19, 20).

Analysis of the Secretory Process in the Pancreatic Exocrine Cell

Out of his combination of complementary techniques came a coherent representation of the secretory process, a "model" which has stood well the test of time. The current trend is to move from the subcellular to the molecular level in the analysis of the model, which means that its subcellular stage has been widely enough accepted.

The analysis of the secretory process of the pancreatic exocrine cell has not been the only research line pursued in our laboratory; membrane biogenesis, intercellular junctions and structural aspects of capillary permeability are other examples. But the corresponding bodies of information are either less fully developed or still under scrutiny by us and by others; besides none of them has affected the general thinking in our field to the same extent as the story of the secretory process. With these considerations in mind, I believe that this unique and solemn occasion would be put to good use if I were to depart from the apparent tradition, which favors a summary of past or current work, and assess instead the available evidence on the secretory process, pointing out its strengths as well as its weaknesses, and trying to figure out what can be done in the future to advance our knowledge still further.

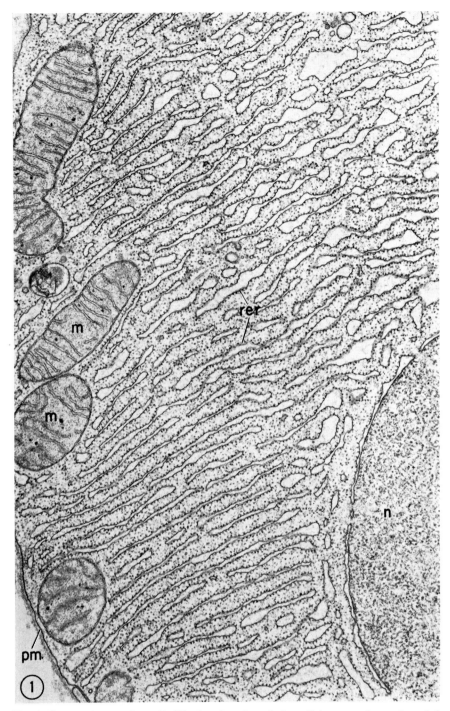

Fig. 1. Pancreatic exocrine cell. The basal region of the cell between the nucleus (n) and the plasmalemma (pm) is occuped by numerous cisternae of the rough endoplasmic reticulum (rer) and a few mitochondria (m).
× 12,000

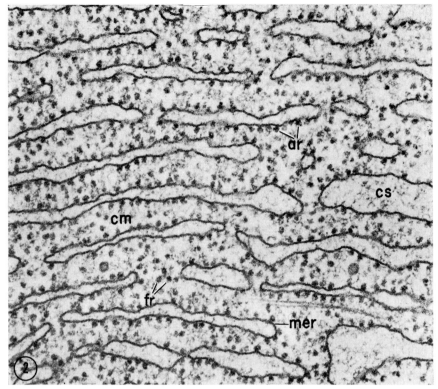

Fig. 2. Pancreatic exocrine cell. Array of cisternae of the rough surfaced endoplasmic reticulum.

cs, cisternal space; *cm,* cytoplasmic matrix (cell sol); *fr,* free ribosomes; *ar,* attached ribosomes; *mer,* membrane of the endoplasmic reticulum.
× 50,000

Our analysis recognizes in the secretory process[1] of the pancreatic exocrine cell 6 successive steps or operations of which the object is the secretory proteins. These steps are: *1) synthesis, 2) segregation, 3) intracellular transport, 4) concentration, 5) intracellular storage, and 6) discharge.* Each of them will be considered in some detail in what follows.

1. Synthesis

Proteins for export are synthesized on polysomes attached to the membrane of the rough endoplasmic reticulum (Fig. 1—2). The first clear indication that this is the case came from early work carried out with Philip Siekevitz. After a short *in vivo* exposure to [14C]leucine, radioactive chymotrypsinogen appeared preferentially associated with attached polysomes isolated from the guinea pig pancreas (21) (Table I). The products of free polysomes were not investigated, but by analogy with the situation studied by others in the liver (22, 23) these polysomes probably synthesize proteins for intracellular

---

[1] For convenience, the term "secretory process" will be used in the rest of the text as a shorthand for "the process of protein secretion".

170

Table I. Specific radioactivity of chymotrypsinogen isolated from attached and free poly-somes** after *in vivo* labeling with [^{14}C]leucine.

Fraction	Time after [^{14}C]leucine	
	1 min	3 min
Attached polysomes	22,100*	10,000*
Free polysomes	2,800	3,000

* cpm/mg chymotrypsinogen (estimated from enzyme activity).
** Guinea pig pancreas, from P. Siekevitz and G. E. Palade, J. Biophys. Biochem. Cytol. 7(1960)631.

use. Yet in all these cases, the results are—to some extent—ambiguous, since —as isolated—both polysome classes carry newly synthesized proteins irrespective of the latter's final destination. The differences are not qualitative as would be expected for strict specialization; they are definitely large, but only quantitative.

This finding could have a trivial explanation: e.g., leakage of newly synthesized proteins from cell compartments ruptured during tissue homogenization, followed by relocation by adsorption on the "wrong" class of polysomes. Available data indicate that artifactual relocation definitely occurs under these circumstances (24), but so far there is no reliable information concerning its extent. Alternatively the dual location may have functional significance since the position of the polysomes at the time of the initiation of translation is still unknown. Initiation in the free condition followed by enough elongation to expose either enzymic active sites or antigenic determinants before attachment seems unlikely but may occur, in principle. And the special sequence detected at the N-terminal of IgG light chains synthesized on detached polysomes (25) may function as a signal for attachment (cf. 26). To understand the situation, we need more information than we have at present on the relationship between free and attached ribosomes, on the position of polysomes at the time of initiation, and on the duration of polysomes attachment to the ER membrane.

Another aspect that should be considered at this point is the existence of two subclasses of attached polysomes: one synthesizing proteins for export and the other involved in the production of ER membrane proteins coupled with their insertion in this membrane (27). Much less is known about this second subclass, except that in its case the same uncertainties apply as to the location of the polysomes at the time of initiation. By analogy with a rather different system (chloroplast polysomes attached to thylakoid membranes during the synthesis of certain membrane proteins (28)), this type of attachment may be essentially transient, perhaps limited to a single round of translation for each site of attachment. It is generally assumed that all the soluble factors necessary for protein synthesis are present in molecular dispersion or in the form of soluble complexes in the cell sol or cytoplasmic matrix, but very few actual data are available in the case of the pancreatic exocrine cell—although this

171

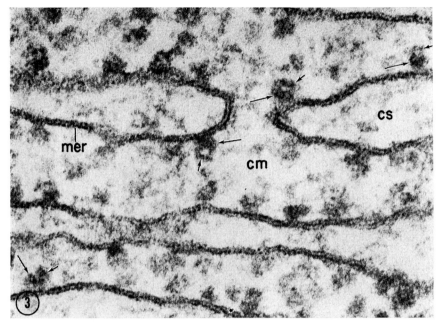

Fig. 3. Pancreatic exocrine cell. High magnification of a cytoplasmic region occupied by cisternal elements of the rough surfaced endoplasmic reticulum.
mer, membrane of the endoplasmic reticulum, *cs*, cisternal space, *cm*, cytoplasmic matrix (cell sol). The short arrows point to small subunits and the long arrows to large subunits of attached ribosomes.
× 275,000

cell is potentially a rich source of aminoacyl-t RNA synthetases, tRNAs and mRNAs. The presence of an active RNase among the secretory proteins produced by the cell has discouraged work along such lines, but this whole field may be open by using tissue taken from species known to have a very low pancreatic RNase content. Pancreatic proteolytic zymogens do not appear to constitute a problem, since their activation is either nil or controllable during cell fractionation.

2. SEGREGATION

The newly synthesized secretory proteins are segregated in the cisternal space of the rough endoplasmic reticulum. The first evidence that this is the case came from work carried out by Redman *et al* (17) on pigeon pancreatic microsomes synthesizing *in vitro* [^{14}C] amylase. This radioactive secretory protein, initially associated with attached polysomes, preferentially appeared after ∼ 3 min in the microsomal cavities. Experiments bearing on segregation were further refined in our laboratory by Redman and Sabatini (29) and Blobel and Sabatini (30). Their results indicate that the growing polypeptide chain is extruded through the microsomal membrane into the microsomal cavity which is the *in vitro* equivalent of the cisternal space of the rough endo-plasmic reticulum. Upon natural or experimentally induced termination, the

172

Segregation

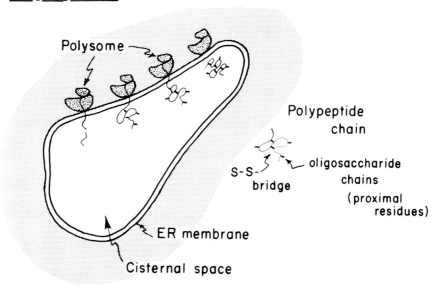

Fig. 4. Diagram of the segregation step.

newly synthesized chain separates with the microsomal vesicles and does not appear in the incubation medium, which topologically is the *in vitro* equivalent of the cell sol. Since it had already been established by Sabatini *et al* (31) that the ribosomes are attached to the ER membrane by their large subunits i.e., the bearers of nascent chains) (Fig. 3.), it was concluded that segregation is the result of a vectorial transport of the newly synthesized polypeptide from the large ribosomal subunit through the ER membrane to the cisternal space.

This conclusion provides a satisfactory explanation for the basic structural features of the endoplasmic reticulum: a cavitary cell organ of complicated geometry which endows it with a large surface. All these features make sense if we assume that one of the main functions of the system is the trapping of proteins produced for export. With the exception of Ca^{2+} accumulation in the sarcoplasmic reticulum, i.e., the equivalent cell organ of muscle fibers, no other recognized function of the endoplasmic reticulum (e.g., phosphatide— and triacylglycerol synthesis, mixed function oxygenation, fatty acid desaturation) requires compellingly and directly a cavitary organ, at least according to our current knowledge. In detail, however, the forces and reactions involved in the trapping operation remain unknown. The interaction of the large ribosomal subunit with the ER membrane is understood only in very general terms (30), and precise information bearing on specific molecules involved in attachment is still lacking. Segregation appears to be an irreversible step: the nascent polypeptide is extruded in the cisternal space and, once inside, it can no longer get out (Fig. 4).

The membrane of isolated microsomes was found to be highly permeable to

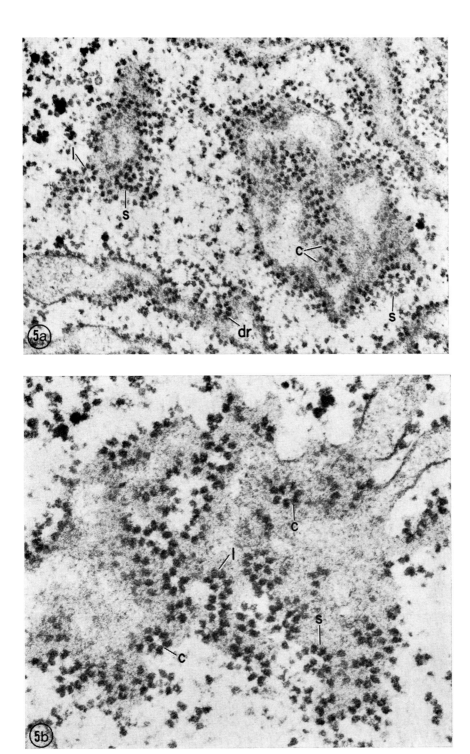

Fig. 5. Rat Hepatocyte. The attached ribosomes (polysomes) form spirals (*s*), loops (*l*), circles (*c*) and double rows (*dr*) on the surface of the endoplasmic reticulum membrane.
a: × 55,000
b: × 90,000

molecules of $\sim$ 10A diameter (32). Assuming that the same applies for the ER membrane *in situ*, it is reasonable to postulate that the imprisonment of the polypeptide is the consequence of its conversion into a globular protein too large ($>$ 20A diameter) to permeate the membrane. This postulate is in keeping with a series of findings which show that enzymes associated with the ER membrane, or present in the cisternal space, are responsible for disulfide bridge formation (33), hydroxylation of proline and lysine residues (34), proximal glycosylation of polypeptide chains (35), and perhaps partial proteolysis (cf. 25). All these modifying operations are expected to affect directly or indirectly the tertiary structure of the secretory proteins which, once assumed, could render the proteins impermeant and their segregation irreversible (Fig. 4). Letting disulfide bridge formation aside, it would be of interest to know to what extent modifications of the type mentioned affect proteins produced for intracellular use. If the extent were nil or negligible, the differential modification of secretory proteins would provide an additional explanation for their segregation.

Available evidence either indicates or suggests that vectorial transport of secretory proteins to the cisternal space occurs in many other cell types (e.g., plasma cells (36) fibroblasts (37), granulocytes (38) parotid acinar cells (39) etc.) in addition to hepatocytes and pancreatic exocrine cells. Vectorial transport and its corollary—segregation—are most probably obligate functional features for all protein secreting cells, but further work is needed to check on the actual extent of their occurrence, as well as on possible exceptions (40).

Although the ER membrane is characterized by high fluidity (41), the polysomes attached to its cytoplasmic aspect maintain regular, characteristic patterns (Fig. 5) of rather constant geometry (4). One may wonder what prevents them from assuming a random coil conformation; or, in other words, how does the cell succeed in securing fixed attachment sites on a highly fluid membrane. This riddle must have an interesting answer.

3. Intracellular Transport

From the cisternal space of the rough endoplasmic reticulum, the secretory proteins are transported to the Golgi complex. In the case we have studied, i.e., the pancreatic exocrine cell of the guinea pig, the terminus of the transport operations is a set of large vacuoles on the trans side of the complex (16, 18) which, on account of their function (to be discussed later on), are called condensing vacuoles.

Intracellular transport was first recognized in radioautographic experiments carried out with Lucien Caro (16), but the details and requirements of this operation became evident only after James Jamieson and I shifted from intact animals to *in vitro* systems based on tissue slices (18). In such systems, short tissue exposure to radioactive amino acids ("labeling pulse") followed by effective removal of unincorporated label ("chase") became possible and, as a result, time-resolution in our experiments was considerably improved.

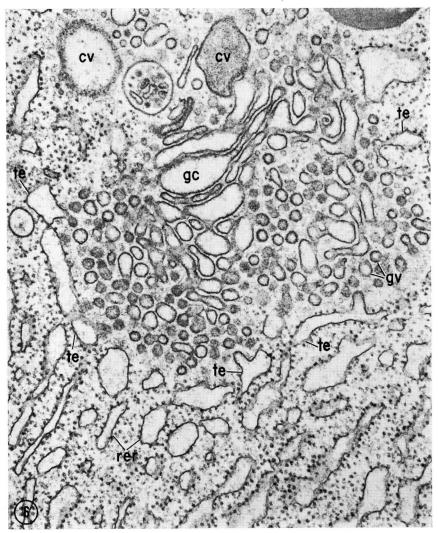

Fig. 6. Pancreatic exocrine cell. Golgi complex, partial view.
cv, condensing vacuoles; *gc*, Golgi cisternae; *gv*, Golgi vesicles; *te*, transitional elements; *rer*, rough endoplasmic reticulum.
× 26,000.

Results obtained in pulse-chase experiments showed that the pathway followed by the secretory proteins leads from the rough endoplasmic reticulum to the transitional elements of this system (Fig. 6), then to the small peripheral vesicles on the cis side of the Golgi complex (18) and finally, in about 30 min, to condensing vacuoles (42) (Table II, Fig. 7). An unexpected and intriguing finding was that intracellular transport requires energy (43) supplied (in the system investigated) by oxidative phosphorylation. In the absence of ATP synthesis, the secretory proteins remain in the rough endoplasmic reticulum, transport to condensing vacuoles being resumed upon resumption of ATP production. From these and other data, we concluded that the func-

Intracellular Transport

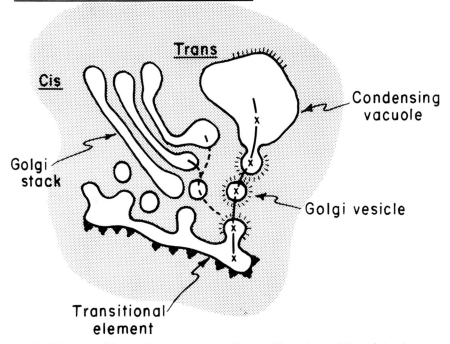

Fig. 7. Diagram of intracellular transport. X————X, pathway followed in the pancreatic exocrine cell of the guinea pig; - - - - -, pathway followed in other glandular cells.

Table II. Guinea pig pancreas. Slices incubated *in vitro**

Cell Compartments		% radioautographic grains			
		Pulse	chase minutes		
		3 min	+7	+37	+117
Rough endoplasmic reticulum		*86.3*	43.7	24.3	20.0
Golgi complex					
	peripheral vesicles	2.7	*43.0*	14.9	3.6
	condensing vacuoles	1.0	3.8	*48.5*	7.5
Zymogen granules		3.0	4.6	11.3	*58.6*
Acinar lumen		—	—	—	7.1
Other compartments**		7.0	4.6	1.1	3.2

* Simplified from J. D. Jamieson and G. E. Palade, J. Cell Biol. 34(1967)597.

pulse: 200 μCi/ml L-[^{3}H-4,5]leucine (40 μM).

chase: ^{1}H-leucine (2mM).

** Nuclei and mitochondria

For each compartment of the secretory pathway the maximal concentration figures are given in italics.

177

tional equivalent of a lock (or lock-gate) exists along the channels used for intracellular transport; that the lock is located at the level of the transitional elements of the endoplasmic reticulum, and that secretory proteins seem to flow vectorially to the Golgi complex, when the lock is opened.

The general pathway followed in intracellular transport appears to be the same in a variety of cell types (19, 44—48)), but direct evidence on the pre-Golgi lock has been obtained only in the case of the exocrine pancreatic cell. Extension to other systems of the inquiry dealing primarily with the lock-gate is clearly needed. In addition, many aspects of the transport operation remain either unknown or unsettled. The geometry of the connections between the endoplasmic reticulum and the Golgi complex is still a matter of debate: according to some investigators (49, 50), the two compartments are permanently connected by continuous tubules; according to us (18), the connection is intermittent and is probably established by shuttling vesicles. The energy-requiring reactions are unknown, and equally unknown are the forces involved in transport and the means by which macromolecules are moved from the endoplasmic reticulum to the condensing vacuoles against an apparent concentration gradient.

We have uncovered an interesting process, but we are only at the very beginning of its analysis. Every one of the points mentioned above remains to be elucidated by further work.

4. CONCENTRATION

The secretory proteins reach the condensing vacuoles in a dilute solution which is progressively concentrated at these sites to a level comparable to that eventually found in mature secretion granules. The exact concentration in each of the compartments involved in intracellular transport is unknown; but the increase in the density of the content in condensing vacuoles (as seen in electron micrographs), and the increase in number of radioautographic grains associated with the same vacuoles (42) (Fig. 8) suggest that the incoming solution is concentrated by a large factor. The final result of the concentration step is the conversion of the condensing vacuoles into mature secretion granules (16, 42), usually called zymogen granules in the case of the pancreatic exocrine cell.

Concentration is not dependent on a continuous supply of energy. *In situ,* neither condensing vacuoles nor zymogen granules swell when ATP production is blocked; and *in vitro,* isolated secretion granules are rather insensitive to the osmolality of the suspension medium at, or below, neutrality (51). They are instead highly sensitive to variations in pH and lyse promptly above pH 7.2 (52, 53). The findings rule out the hypothesis that concentration is achieved by ion pumps located in the membrane of the condensing vacuoles, and suggest that the cell uses for this step some other, energetically more economical mechanism. The synthesis of sulfate containing macrocolecules in Golgi elements and their presence in secretion granules in murine, pancreatic acinar cells (54) as well as in other murine glandular cells (55) have been

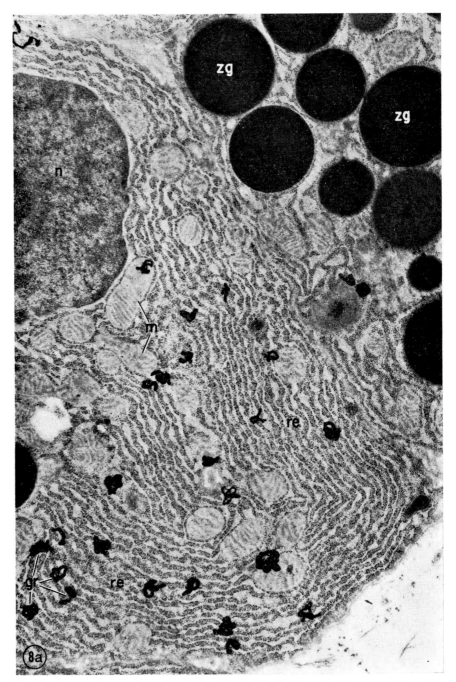

Fig. 8a. Pancreatic exocrine cell. (Guinea Pig). Distribution of radioautographic grains in specimen fixed at the end of a 3 min. pulse with L-[^{3}H-4,5]leucine.

gr, radioautographic grains; n, nucleus; m, mitochondria; zg, zymogen granules; re, region of the cytoplasm occupied by the rough surfaced endoplasmic reticulum. At this time, ∼ 85 % of the grains are found associated with such regions.

× 12,000

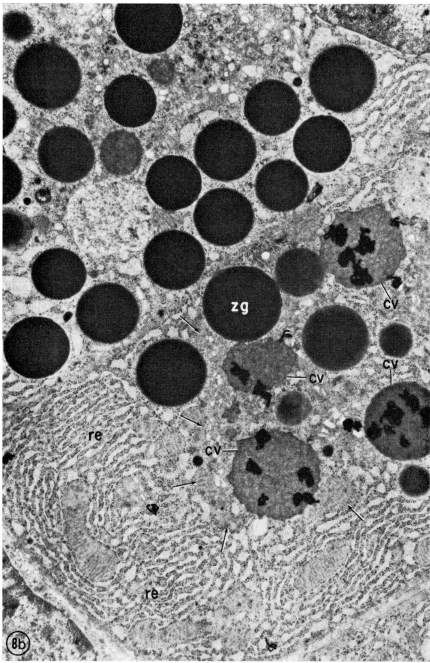

Fig. 8b. Pancreatic exocrine cell. (Guinea Pig). Distribution of radioautographic grains at the end of a 37 min chase (after a 3 min pulse as in Fig. 8a).

cv, condensing vacuoles; *zg*, zymogen granules; *re*, region of the cytoplasm occupied by the rough surfaced endoplasmic reticulum. The periphery of the Golgi complex is marked by arrows. At this time, $\sim 50\,\%$ of the radioautographic grains are associated with condensing vacuoles.

$\times$ 12,000

Figurs 8a and 8b are taken from J. D. Jamieson and G. E. Palade, J. Cell Biol. *34*, (1967) 597.

established by radioautography. Moreover, Tartakoff *et al* (56) have recently detected a sulfated polyanion (pI ≃ 3.4), presumably a sulfated peptidoglycan, in the content of zymogen granules and in discharged secretion in the guinea pig pancreas. The formation of large aggregates by ionic interactions between this polyanion and secretory proteins, which are known to be predominantly cationic (56), could cause a reduction in osmotic activity within condensing vacuoles with concomitant outflow of water. In this case, energy would no longer be required past the synthesis of the polyanion and concentration would depend primarily on the stability of the postulated aggregates.

This hypothesis remains to be validated by the isolation and characterization of the sulfated polyanion, and especially by the demonstration of relevant aggregate formation under conditions likely to prevail *in vivo* within condensing vacuoles. The hypothesis is particularly attractive because it could explain not only concentration *per se,* but also intracellular transport against an apparent chemical gradient. Such a gradient may not exist, or may be reversed, if the secretory proteins of every new batch were to be aggregated and thereby osmotically inactivated upon their entry into condensing vacuoles.

In the pancreatic exocrine cell of the guinea pig concentration is effected in trans Golgi condensing vacuoles, but in the same cell of other species (rat, for instance) the step under discussion takes places in the last cisterna on the trans side of each Golgi stack. Finally in many other glandular cells (cf. 57) the same operation is carried out in the dilated rims of the last 2—3 trans Golgi cisternae (Fig. 7). Moreover, in guinea pig pancreatic lobules hyperstimulated *in vitro*, the usual condensing vacuoles are no longer present, and concentration of secretory proteins begins already in the Golgi cisternae, preferentially in those located on the trans side of the stacks (58). There are, therefore, variations according to species, cell type, and physiological conditions in the location of concentration sites within the Golgi complex, and it would be of interest to find out whether these variations reflect changes in the distribution of the sulfated polyanion (or other functionally equivalent compounds) within the complex.

Radioautographic findings (45—47, 59) and cell fractionation data (60) obtained on a variety of tissues indicate that terminal glycosylation of secretory proteins occurs in the Golgi complex. This operation is expected to affect only a fraction, not the totality, of the proteins produced for export.

In addition, the Golgi complex appears to be the site of partial proteolysis of proinsulin (61) and perhaps other secretory proteins. It is also the site of synthesis of polysaccharides in plant cells (cf. 62). The Golgi apparatus has, therefore, a multiplicity of functions in the processing of secretory products, but—with the exception of concentration—the location of the other activities among its elements is either uncertain or still unknown.

On the one hand, there is a rather extensive literature dealing with differences in cytochemical reactions within the same cisterna (63, 64) or among the cisternae of the same stack (65, 66) without any obvious functional correlation. On the other hand, we begin to have biochemical data on Golgi subfractions, but so far they reveal no differences between Golgi cisternae and Golgi vacuoles (67).

Finally, at the level of the Golgi complex the secretory product is transferred from a high permeability membrane (i.e., the membrane of the endoplasmic reticulum), to a membrane whose lipid composition approaches that of the plasmalemma by its high content of cholesterol and sphingomyelin, and by the low degree of unsaturation of fatty acids in its phospholipids (68, 69)). Such a membrane is expected to have a low permeability, and therefore to be "exposable" without danger to the external medium at the time of discharge (see below).

In general, our knowledge of the functions of the complex is still rudimentary primarily because the isolation of Golgi fractions from tissue homogenates was achieved only recently (70—73) and is still limited to a few sources (liver, pancreas (68) and kidney (74)). The extent of compartmentation within the complex as well as the precise pathway followed by secretory products through it is still unknown. Finally, as a telling measure of our ignorance, it is worthwhile pointing out that we do not have any good idea about the functional meaning of the most prominent structural feature of the Golgi complex: the stacking of its cisternae.

5. INTRACELLULAR STORAGE

Secretory proteins are temporarily stored within the cell in secretion granules which, as already mentioned, are condensing vacuoles that have reached the end of the concentration step. Their membrane comes, therefore, from the Golgi complex and their content is the product of attached polysomes, modified at subsequent steps as already described in the previous sections.

In the cases so far investigated, i.e., the exocrine pancreas of the cow (53, 75), rat (76), and guinea pig (56), and the parotid of the rabbit (77), the content of the secretion granules (more precisely, the extract obtained from reasonably homogeneous secretion granule fractions) and the physiologically discharged secretion contain the same proteins in the same relative amounts (Fig. 9). Since no other intracellular sources has been revealed or suggested by our evidence, we have concluded that the content of these granules is the sole precursor of the proteins found in the juice secreted by the gland.

In the case of glands which, like the exocrine pancreas, consist of an apparently homogeneous population of secretory cells which produce a complex mixture of secretory proteins, the question of specialization at the cellular or subcellular level was asked repeatedly and answered only in part. So far all the proteins looked for in the bovine pancreas (trypsinogen (78), chymotrypsinogen, DNase (79) and RNase (80)) were detected by immunocytochemical procedures in all the secretion granules of all cells examined. Each granule probably contains a sample of the mixture discharged by the gland, but it is hard to believe that all these microsamples are quantitatively strictly identical. Specialization at the cellular level is well established in a

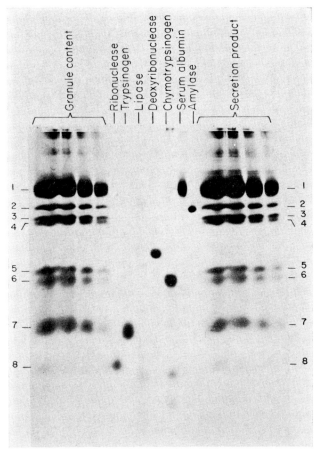

Fig. 9. Sodium dodecyl sulfate—polyacrilamide gel electropherograms of (left to right) zymogen granule content, standards, and secretion discharged by pancreatic lobules incubated and stimulated in vitro. Identification of bands: 1, unknown secretory protein and carrier bovine plasma albumin; 2, amylase; 3—4, procarboxypeptidases A and B and unknown secretory proteins; 5, unknown protein; 6, chymotrypsinogen; 7, trypsinogen; 8, ribonuclease.

From A. M. Tartakoff, L. J. Greene and G. E. Palade, J. Biol. Chem., *249*, (1974) 7420.

number of endocrine glands which are characterized by a morphologically heterogeneous cell population (cf. 57). Specialization at the subcellular level exists in polymorphonuclear neutrophil granulocytes (35). The formula used in the pancreas, i.e., intracellular storage of a complex mixture in apparently equivalent quanta, probably explains the lack of short term qualitative modulation of the secretory output (see (20, 81) for a more detailed discussion of this point). It can be assumed that this type of modulation is rendered unnecessary by the specialized nutritional habits of each species.

In the exocrine cells of the pancreas, secretion granules usually occupy the apical region between the Golgi complex and the acinar lumen. There are few microtubules in this region and few microfilaments, and there is no consistent pattern in their organization and distribution (except for the micro-

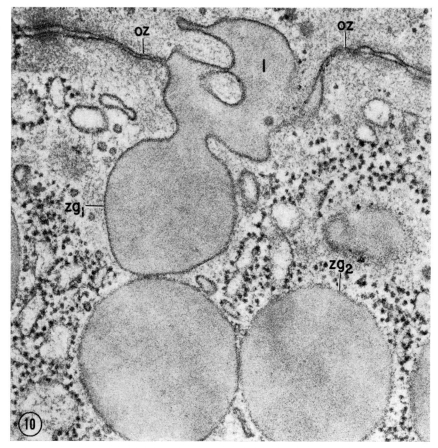

Fig. 10. Pancreatic exocrine cell. Apical region. *l*, lumen; *oz*, occluding zonules; *zg₁*, discharging zymogen granule; *zg₂*, zymogen granule still in storage.
× 110,000

filaments associated with junctional elements and microvilli). In other cell types, it has been postulated that microtubules and microfilaments play a role in effecting secretory discharge (se below), as well as in directing or moving secretory granules to their sites of discharge. In pancreatic acinar cells, radio-autographic findings show that newly formed, i.e., labeled, granules are distributed at random within the preexisting granule population (42), and biochemical data indicate that newly synthesized and preexisting proteins are discharged at random from the total zymogen granule population (20, 81). With the evidence at hand, these results can be ascribed to slow diffusion leading to thorough mixing of old and new granules within the apical region. In other cell types, the situation may be different on account of incomplete mixing within the granule population and uneven distribution of discharge sites (see below).

6. DISCHARGE

Relatively early in the investigation of the secretory process it was found that

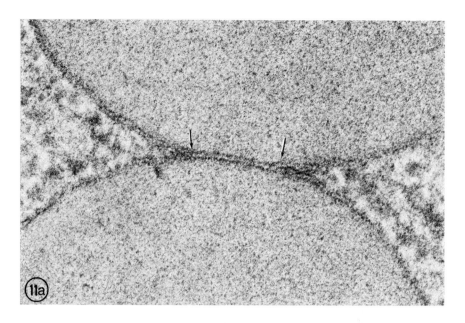

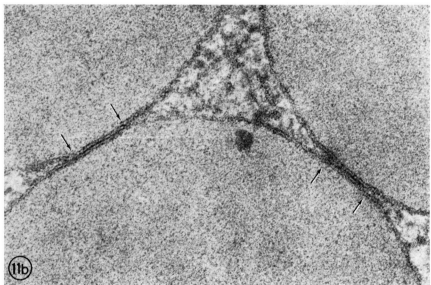

Fig. 11a, b. Pancreatic exocrine cells, Apical region. a. fusion of zymogen granule membranes followed by partial elimination of membrane layers (arrows), b. fusion of zymogen granule membranes (arrows);

a: × 220,000
b: × 160,000

secretion granules discharge their content into glandular lumina (Fig. 10) by a process originally called "membrane fusion" (82) and later on exocytosis (83). Morphological findings suggest that in preparation for discharge the membrane of the secretion granule fuses with the plasmalemma and that subsequent reorganization (i.e., progressive elimination of layers (Figs. 11, 12))

185

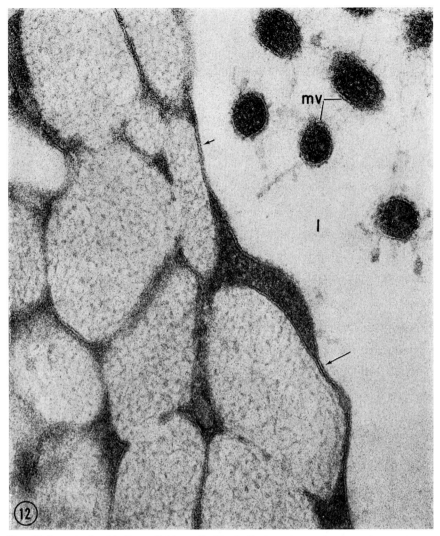

Fig. 12. Intestinal epithelium, Goblet cell. (Rat). Fusion of secretion granule membranes with the plasmalemma. Long arrows: simple fusion; short arrow: fusion with partial elimination of membrane layers.

l, lumen; *mv*, microvilli.

× 140,000

leads to fission of the fused membranes within the area of fusion. The final result is continuity established between the granule compartment and the extracellular medium (lumen), concomitantly with continuity of the granule membrane with the plasmalemma all around the orifice through which the granule content reaches the lumen (Fig. 13). This operation allows the discharge of the secretory product while insuring the maintenance of a continuous diffusion barrier between the cell sol and the extracellular medium. At the beginning, a few alternatives were considered, but by now exocytosis is recognized as a widely occurring, probably general mechanism for the dis-

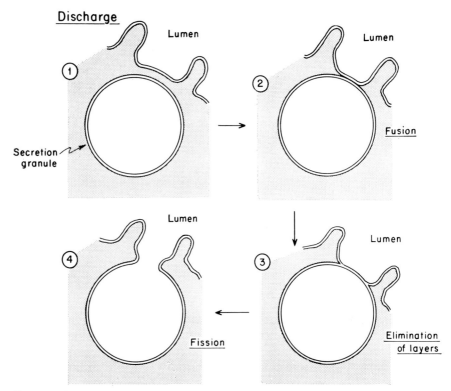

Fig. 13. Diagram of membrane interactions during secretory discharge.

charge of macromolecular secretory products.

The membrane fusion involved in secretory discharge has a high degree of specificity. The membrane of secretion granules fuses only with the plasma-lemma, although there are at the time of this event and at comparable distances around the interacting pair many other types of cellular membranes. In the exocrine cells the specificity is even more stringent since ability to fuse is limited to the apical or luminal domain of the plasmalemma. The only permanently operative alternative is preliminary fusion of granule membrane to granule membrane leading eventually to discharge of two or more secre-tion granules in tandem (84). This type of specificity suggests the existence of complementary recognition sites in each interacting membrane which may be involved in binding preliminary to fusion. In some respects the postulated situation is reminiscent of the interaction between a hormone and its mem-brane receptor (85), except that in this case the events are intracellular and receptors as well as agonists are assumed to be membrane-bound.

Exocytosis has been extensively studied in a variety of secretory cells and by now its basic requirements for Ca^{2+} and energy are well established (86—88). Our own data demonstrated a stringent energy requirement for secretory discharge in the exocrine pancreatic cell and, hence, the existence of a second energy-dependent lock that controls the flow of secretory products from secre-tion granules in to the acinar lumina (58). Our data also showed that dis-

187

charge can proceed in the absence of continuous protein synthesis (58).

In certain glandular cells, pancreatic exocrine cells included, discharge is intermittent and well integrated with other activities of the organism. In such cases, the cell which without stimulation discharges at a slow, liminal rate, responds to stimulation by either hormones or neurotransmitters by a dramatic step-up in the rate of exocytosis. The stimulus-secretion coupling (87) often involves of cyclic nucleotide generating system (adenylate cyclase in most cases) and one or more protein kinases (89). But this coupling also involves a depolarization of the plasmalemma. In the case of the pancreatic exocrine cell stimulation definitely leads to membrane depolarization (90), while the activation of a cyclic nucleotide system is still uncertain (91 vs. 89). The final target of the protein kinases is unknown in secretory cells. A hypothesis advanced a few years ago ascribes this role to tubulin (92), but the evidence in case is open to question. Results obtained on other systems (93, 94) suggest that the target might be a membrane protein.

In recent years, a number of agents activating or inhibiting exocytosis have been described and among the latter colchicine and the vinca alkaloids have received considerably attention (95, 96), the general assumption being that their inhibitory effect implies the involvement of microtubules in exocytosis. At present the situation is rather confused and a reasonable interpretation of the numerous and in part contradictory data is hardly possible. A distinction should be made between agents affecting directly membrane fusion-fission, and agents affecting the superimposed regulatory systems which activate and inactivate the coupling between stimulation and secretion. Colchicine appears to affect the basic mechanism, rather than its controls, since it inhibits discharge in hepatocytes, (97, 99), i.e., in cells that appear to lack a stimulus—secretion coupling. In these cells the effect has been localized at discharge, the last step in the secretory process, all previous steps being unaffected (99). But the involvement of microtubules remains open to question since, at least in hepatocytes, the inhibitory effect is prompt and reaches its maximum long before the depolymerization of the microtubules becomes morphologically detectable. Hence, alternative targets should be considered, especially because colchicine binds to membranes (100) and inhibits a number of transport mechanisms in the plasmalemma (101).

As already mentioned, there is no elaborate organization involving microtubules and microfilaments in the apical region of the pancreatic exocrine cells. A rather modest fibrillar feltwork (terminal web) is found under the luminal plasmalemma, but there is no fibrillar lining on the cytoplasmic aspect of the membrane of the zymogen granules while still in storage. However, a fibrillar shell[2] often appears around discharging zymogen granules when their membrane is already in continuity with the plasmalemma. It is continuous with the terminal web, it may consist of contractile proteins (actin?

---

[2] A fibrillar feltwork exists also at the periphery of the Golgi complex in association with the transitional elements of the ER. Its function, and the function of fibrillar coats or layers occasionally found around Golgi vesicles and vacuoles are unknown.

myosin?), and it may promote the expulsion of the secretion granule content.

EFFECTS OF EXOCYTOSIS AND INTRACELLULAR TRANSPORT ON
MEMBRANE DISTRIBUTION

The end result of exocytosis is—on the one hand—discharge of a secretory product, and—on the other hand—relocation of secretory granule membranes in the plasmalemma. Under normal steady state conditions, excess membrane must be removed from the receiving compartment (lumen) and membrane added to the donor compartment (secretion granules, or Golgi complex), since the distribution of membrane amounts among these compartments remains relatively constant with time.

The procedures used by the cell to recover and redistribute membrane after exocytosis are unknown. Morphological findings suggest coupled endocytosis and in a few cases, namely in nerve endings (102, 103) and in anterior pituitary cells (104, 105), recovery of organized membrane in the form of endocytic vesicles has convincingly been demonstrated with the help of cytochemical tracers. Moreover, in the case of pituitary cells the recovered membrane was eventually traced to trans Golgi vacuoles and cisternae (104, 105). But the exact nature of this membrane and its ultimate fate remain a matter of speculation.

In the case of discharge, the membranes of the secretory granules can be viewed as a set of individual vesicular containers which move forward from the Golgi complex to the surface during exocytosis and presumably back to the Golgi during coupled endocytosis. In the pancreas (106) as well as in the parotid (107), the rate of synthesis of the proteins of the granule membranes is generally slower than the rate of synthesis of the secretory proteins contained in the granules. Hence, reutilization or recycling of the membrane containers is possible, in principle, but so far it has not been proven.

Assuming that a similar shuttling system of membrane containers operates between the rough endoplasmic reticulum and the Golgi complex, recently obtained evidence indicates that there is no mixing among either the lipid (68, 69) or the protein (67, 108) components of the membranes of the two compartments in the pancreas (guinea pig) and in the liver (rat). These findings impose stringent limitations on membrane interactions since they suggest that lateral diffusion of components is prevented at the time the membranes of the two compartments establish continuity, and that incoming membrane is removed from the receiving compartment according to a non-random formula (67).

The situation may appear unexpectedly complicated, even confusing, but in fact it makes sense since the final result of the restrictions mentioned is the preservation of functional specificity for the membrane of each compartment. This specificity is implied in both the old concept of "marker enzyme," and the newer ideas on sequential modification of secretory proteins as they move along the secretory pathway. The most convincing example is that of the successive glycosylation of glycoproteins (45—47, 60). The main difficulty is that we do not have at present any clear idea about the means used by the cell to carry through the various steps of the secretory process while imposing and maintaining the restrictions mentioned.

These are intriguing and challenging problems which stress the need for extending the inquiry from the processed product to the processing apparatus, expecially to the membranes that outline the compartments which form the processing apparatus. Further understanding of the secretory process is now becoming dependent on adequate information on the chemistry of these membranes and on the reactions involved in their interactions.

VARIATIONS ON A COMMON THEME

The functional analysis of the pancreatic exocrine cell gave us a reasonably good representation of the steps generally involved in the secretory process. In addition, it helped us understand a series of special cases in other cell types which now appear to be recognizable variations on the theme already described. (Table III).

Table III. Secretory Process. Variations on a common theme.

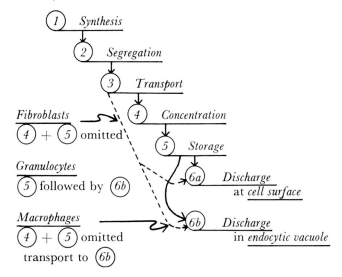

Endocrine cells producing peptide or protein hormones follow the same sequence of operations but apparently discharge their secretory product along the entire plasmalemma (57), instead of discharging within restricted plasma-lemmal domains as exocrine cells do. In many secretory cells (e.g., fibro-blasts, chondrocytes, plasma cells), the concentration step is omitted, secretion granules of usual appearance are absent, intracellular storage is reduced in duration or eliminated, and discharge seems to take place continuously. In such cells, the applicability of the last 3 steps of the general scheme was in doubt and the possibility of direct discharge from the cisternal space of the endoplasmic reticulum was considered (109). But recently, equivalents of secretion granules were recognized in special fibroblasts, i.e., odontoblasts (110), as well as in ordinary fibroblasts after treatment with colchicine (111). Their secretory process now appears as a variation on the common theme with the variant step resulting from lack of extensive concentration in the Golgi complex. In plasma cells the equivalent of secretion granules is still not yet identified (47).

In polymophonuclear neutrophil and eosinophil granulocytes, secretion granules are preferentially discharged into endocytic vacuoles (112, 113), discharge at the cell surface occurring only under special conditions (114). In eosinophils, the entire population of secretion granule consists of primary lysosomes, while in neutrophils the population includes "specific granules" in addition to primary lysosomes. In both cell types, all secretory proteins—irrespective of their nature—appear to be produced and processed according to the general scheme worked out for the pancreatic exocrine cell, except for the variant already mentioned at the discharge step.[3]

In macrophages, discharge of secretory proteins is also preferentially effected into endocytic vacuoles, but in addition the concentration step is apparently omitted. A dilute solution of acid hydrolases is carried probably by small vesicles (the local equivalent of primary lysosomes) from the Golgi complex to endocytic vacuoles. The latter are also able to fuse with secondary lysosomes which provide a second hand source of hydrolases (115). The variation on the common theme used by macrophages seems to be applied in all cells capable of autophagy and low efficiency heterophagy including cells specialized in protein production for export, like the hepatocytes, exocrine cells of the pancreas and cells of the anterior pituitary. A special problem arises in this case in connection with the separation of regular exportable proteins from lysosomal hydrolases. The separation seems to be reasonably efficient, though not perfect, since acid phosphatase activity has been repeatedly detected by histochemical procedures within regular secretion granules—mature and immature—and within trans Golgi cisternae (65, 116). In addition, it has been postulated that in a number of cell types lysosome formation takes place in a special compartment, called GERL (117), intercalated between the endoplasmic reticulum and trans Golgi elements. It is evident that all these cells are capable of handling concomitantly, and probably in the same production apparatus two "incompatible" lines of secretory proteins, but the means by which the products are separated or their inactivation prevented (in case of mixing) remain unknown. This riddle must also have an interesting answer.

Finally, another variation on the common theme has been found in glandular cells which produce protein or glycoprotein hormones, and are faced with an excess of stored product (116, 57). In this case the secretion granules are discharged directly into secondary lysosomes by simple membrane fusion. The process, called crinophagy was originally discovered in pituitary mammotrophs (116), but further work has shown that it probably occurs in all the cells of

[3] And except also for the fact that specific granules and primary lysosomes are formed on opposite sides of the Golgi complex of the neutrophil granulocytes (38).

the anterior pituitary (57) and probably in those of many other glands. The use of lysosomes for degrading excess secretory proteins stresses once more the need for understanding protective means against lysosomal hydrolases which must be at work along the entire secretory pathway beginning with the endoplasmic reticulum.

On the Generality of the Secretory Process

The evidence already discussed stresses the role played by the endoplasmic reticulum and the Golgi complex in the production and processing of secretory proteins. The stress put on secretion leads, however, to an apparent impasse. Since every eukaryotic cell possesses both an endoplasmic reticulum and a Golgi complex, it follows that all eukaryotic cells secrete proteins or that the organs of the secretory pathway have additional, perhaps more general and more important functions than secretion, which have been ignored or are still unknown.

This problem actually concerns fewer cell types than generally assumed since secretion of macromolecules has been recognized in recent years as an important activity in a wide variety of cells. Interestingly enough, all plant eukaryotes are secretory cells since they produce and discharge the polysaccharides and proteins of their cell walls (118). Among animal eukaryotes, male (119) and female (120, 121) gametes produce protein for extracellular use[4] and so do secretory nerve cells (122) including adrenergic (87) and presumably cholinergic (123) neurons. Smooth muscle cells have been recently recognized as producers of collagen, elastin and other proteins of the intracellular matrices (124), and the same probably applies for a variety of epithelia (including the vascular endothelium) in relation to the production of the corresponding basement membranes (125, 126).

For those animal cells for which a protein product for extracellular use has not been identified, an acceptable answer is provided by the production of lysosomal enzymes. As already mentioned, the production of these enzymes involves the same secretory apparatus (i.e., the endoplasmic reticulum and the Golgi complex) and the same sequence of steps (except for extracellular discharge) as in bona fide glandular or secretory cells. It appears, therefore, that—for the moment and with the evidence at hand—the problem can be solved in favor of the first alternative, i.e., all eukaryotic cells produce secretory proteins, the basic general secretory functions being the production of cell wall components in plant cells and the production of lysosomal enzymes in animal cells. To some extent, each type of basic production must be represented in the other kingdom. On top of these lowly but ubiquitous secretory activities, appears to be superimposed the production of highly specialized proteins exported by a variety of differentiated cell types. Our attention has been focused on the latter long enough to lose proper perspective and to

---

[4] In many species, female gametes produce vitellus proteins by using in part or in toto the secretory pathway (127).

assume (as we did until recently) that the secretion of proteins is a specialized function restricted to a few, highly differentiated, glandular cells.

Notwithstanding the conclusion reached in the preceding paragraph, the second alternative, i.e., the involvement of the secretory pathway in another general, but still unrecognized function, is not excluded. Among the non-secretory functions postulated for the endoplasmic reticulum and the Golgi complex is the production of cellular membranes, plasmalemma included (cf. 62). At present this postulate rests only on suggestive evidence, most of it morphological. This situation brings us back to the necessity of obtaining detailed and—if possible—comprehensive data on the chemistry and function of the different membranes of the secretory pathway and on their interactions. With this type of information, the second alternative could be put to test, and in the same time our understanding of the secretory process and of the basic organization of eukaryotic cells could be further advanced.

REFERENCES

1. Claude, A., J. Exper. Med., *84* (1946) 51, 61.
2. Hogeboom, G. H., Schneider, W. C., and Palade, G. E., J. Biol. Chem., *172* (1948) 619.
3. Kennedy, E. P., and Lehninger, A. L., J. Biol. Chem., *179* (1949) 957.
4. Palade, G. E., J. Biophys. Biochem. Cytol., *1* (1955) 59.
5. Palade, G. E., in Microsomal particles and protein synthesis, Roberts, R. B., editor, Pergamon Press, 1958.
6. Roberts, R. B. in Introduction to Microsomal particles and protein synthesis, Roberts, R. B., editor, Pergamon Press, 1958.
7. Porter, K. R., Claude, A. and Fullam, E., J. Exper. Med. 81 (1945) 233.
8. Porter, K. R., J. Exper. Med., *97* (1953) 727.
9. Palade, G. E., and Porter, K. R., J. Exper. Med., *100* (1954) 641.
10. Porter, K. R., and Palade, G. E., Biophys. Biochem. Cytol., *3* (1957) 269.
11. Palade, G. E., J. Biophys. Biochem. Cytol., *2* (suppl.) (1956) 85.
12. Siekevitz, P., J. Biol. Chem., *195* (1952) 549.
13. Northrop, J. H., Kunitz, M., and Herriott, R. M., Crystalline Enzymes, Columbia University Press (1948).
14. Palade, G. E., and Siekevitz, P., J. Biophys. Biochem. Cytol., *2* (1956) 171, 671.
15. Siekevitz, P., and Palade, G. E., J. Biophys. Biochem. Cytol., *4* (1958) 203, 309, 557; *5* (1959) 1.
16. Caro, L. G., and Palade, G. E., J. Cell Biol., *20* (1964) 473.
17. Redman, C. M., Siekevitz, P., and Palade, G. E., J. Biol. Chem., *241* (1966) 1150.
18. Jamieson, J. D., and Palade, G. E., J. Cell Biol., *34* (1967) 577.
19. Castle, J. D., Jamieson, J. D., and Palade, G. E., J. Cell Biol., *53* (1972) 290.
20. Scheele, G. A., and Palade, G. E., J. Biol Chem., *250* (1975) 2660.
21. Siekevitz, P., and Palade, G. E., J. Biophys. Biochem. Cytol., *7* (1960) 619, 631.
22. Redman, C. M., J. Biol. Chem., *244* (1969) 4308.
23. Hicks, S. J., Drisdale, J. W., and Munro, H. N., Science (Washington) *164* (1969) 584.
24. Tartakoff, A., and Palade, G., unpublished observations.
25. Milstein, C., Brownlee, G .G., Harrison, T. M., and Mathews, M. B., Nature, *239* (1972) 117.
26. Blobel, G., and Sabatini, D. D., in Biomembranes 2 (1971) 193; L. A. Menton

193

editor, Plenum Publish. Co., New York.

27. Dallner, G., Siekevitz, P., and Palade, G. E., J. Cell Biol., *30* (1966) 73, 97.
28. Chua, N. H., Blobel, G., Siekevitz, P., and Palade, G. E., Proc. Nat. Acad. Sci., U.S.A., *70* (1973) 1554.
29. Redman, C. M., and Sabatini, D. D., Proc. Nat. Acad. Sci., U.S.A. *56* (1966) 608.
30. Blobel, G., and Sabatini, D. D., J. Cell Biol., *45* (1970) 146.
31. Sabatini, D. D., Tashiro, Y., and Palade, G. E., J. Mol. Biol., *19* (1966) 503.
32. Tedeschi, H., James, J. M., and Anthony, W., J. Cell Biol., *18* (1963) 503.
33. Anfinson, C. B., Harvey Lectures *61* (1966) 95.
34. Olsen, B. R., Berg, R. A., Kishida, Y., and Prockop, D. J., Science (Washington) *182* (1973) 825.
35. Molnar, J., Robinson, G. B., and Winzler, R. J., J. Biol. Chem., *240* (1965) 1882.
36. Mach, B., Koblet, H., and Gros, D., Proc. Nat. Acad. Sci., U.S.A. *59* (1968) 445.
37. Grant, M. G., and Prockop, D. J., New England J. Med., *286* (1972) 194.
38. Bainton, D. F., and Farquhar, M. G., J. Cell Biol., *39* (1968) 299 and *45* (1970) 54.
39. Herzog, V., and Miller, F., Z. Zellforsch. Mikrosk. Anat., *107* (1970) 403.
40. Lisowska-Berstein, B., Lamm, M. E., and Vassali, P., Proc. Nat. Acad. Sci., U.S.A. *66* (1970) 425.
41. Rogers, M. J., and Strittmatter, P., J. Biol. Chem. *249* (1974) 895, 5565.
42. Jamieson, J. D., and Palade, G. E., J. Cell Biol., *34* (1967) 597.
43. Jamieson, J. D., and Palade, G. E., J. Cell Biol., *39* (1968) 589.
44. Swenson, R. M., and Kern, M., Proc. Nat. Acad. Sci., U.S.A. *57* (1967) 417.
45. Wuhr, P., Herscovics, A., and Leblond, C. P., J. Cell Biol., *43* (1969) 289.
46. Haddad, A., Smith, M. D., Herscovics, A., Nadler, N. J., and Leblond, C. P., J. Cell Biol., *49* (1971) 856.
47. Zagury, D. Uhr, J. W., Jamieson, J. D., and Palade, G. E., J. Cell Biol., *46* (1970) 52.
48. Hopkins, C. R., and Farquhar, M. G., J. Cell Biol., *59* (1973) 276.
49. Morré, D. J., Keenan, T. W., and Mollenhauer, H. H., in Advances in Cytopharmacology, Clementi, F., and Ceccarelli, B., editors, Raven Press, New York 1971.
50. Claude, A., J. Cell Biol., *47* (1970) 745.
51. Jamieson, J. D., and Palade, G. E., J. Cell Biol., *48* (1971) 503.
52. Hokin, L. E., Biochim. et Biophys. Acta *18* (1955) 379.
53. Greene, L. J., Hirs, C. H. W., and Palade, G. E., J. Biol. Chem. *238* (1963) 2054.
54. Berg, N. B., and Young, R. W., J. Cell Biol., *50* (1971) 469.
55. Young, R. W., J. Cell Biol., *57* (1973) 175.
56. Tartakoff, A. M., Greene, L. J., and Palade, G. E., J. Biol. Chem., *249* (1974) 7420.
57. Farquhar, M. G., Memoirs Soc. for Endocrinology, *19* (1971) 79.
58. Jamieson, J. D., and Palade, G. E., J. Cell Biol., *50* (1971) 135.
59. Neutra, M., and Leblond, C. P., J. Cell Biol., *30* (1966) 137.
60. Schachter, H., Jabbal, I., Hudgin, R. L., Pinteric, L., McGuire, J., and Roseman, S., J. Biol. Chem., *245* (1970) 1090.
61. Steiner, D. F., Clark, J. L., Nolan, C., Rubenstein, A. H., Margoliash, E., Melani, F., and Oyer, P. E., Proc. 13th Nobel Symposium, (1970) 123.
62. Dauwalder, M., Whaley, W. G., and Kephart, J. E., Subcell. Biochem., *1* (1972) 225.
63. Farquhar, M. G., Bergeron, J. J. M., and Palade, G. E., J. Cell Biol., *60* (1974) 8.
64. Ovtracht, L., and Thiéry, J. P., J. Microscopie, *15* (1972) 135.

65. Novikoff, A. B., Essner, E., and Goldfischer, S., in The Interpretation of Ultra-structure, Harris, R. J. C., editor, Acad. Press, New York. (1962).

66. Friend, D. S., J. Cell Biol., *41* (1969) 269.

67. Bergeron, J. J. M., Ehrenreich, J. H., Siekevitz P., and Palade, G. E., J. Cell Biol., *59* (1973) 73.

68. Meldolesi, J., Jamieson, J. D., and Palade, G. E., J. Cell Biol., *49* (1971) 109, 130.

69. Keenan, T. W., and Morré, D. J., Biochemistry, *9* (1970) 19.

70. Fleischer, B., Fleischer, S., and Ozawa, H., J. Cell Biol., *43* (1969) 59.

71. Fleischer, B., and Fleischer, S., Biochim. Biophys. Acta, *219* (1970) 301.

72. Morré, D. J., Hamilton, R. L., Mollenhauer, H. H., Mahley, R. W., Cunning-ham, W. P., Cheetham, R. D., and LeQuire, V. S., J. Cell Biol., *44* (1970) 484.

73. Ehrenreich, J. H., Bergeron, J. J. M., Siekevitz, P., and Palade, G. E., J. Cell Biol., *59* (1973) 45.

74. Fleischer, B., and Zambrano, F., J. Biol. Chem., *249* (1974) 5995.

75. Keller, P. J., and Cohen, E., J. Biol. Chem., *236* (1961) 1407.

76. Palla, J. C., Thèse de Doctorat-ès-Sciences, Marseilles, 1970.

77. Castle, J. D., Jamieson, J. D., and Palade, G. E., J. Cell Biol., *64* (1975) 182.

78. Kraehenbuhl, J. P., and Jamieson, J. D., Proc. Nat. Acad. Sci., U.S.A. *69* (1972) 1771.

79. Kraehenbuhl, J. P., and Jamieson, J. D., unpublished observations.

80. Painter, R. G., Tokuyashu, K. T., and Singer, S. J., Proc. Nat. Acad. Sci., U.S.A., *70* (1973) 1649.

81. Tartakoff, A. M., Jamieson, J. D., Scheele, G. A., and Palade, G. E., J. Biol. Chem., *250* (1974) 2671.

82. Palade, G. E., in Subcellular Particles, Hayashi, T., editor, Ronald Press, New York, 1959.

83. de Duve, C., in Lysosomes, Ciba Foundation Symposium, (1963) 126.

84. Ishikawa, A., J. Cell Biol., *24* (1965) 369.

85. Cuatrecasas, P., Proc. Nat. Acad. Sci., U.S.A. *68* (1971) 1264.

86. Douglas, W. W., and Rubin, R. P., J. Physiol., *159* (1961) 40 and *167* (1963) 288.

87. Douglas, W. W., Br. J. Pharmacol., *34* (1968) 451.

88. Schramm, M., Annu. Rev. Biochem., *36* (1967) 307.

89. Rasmussen, H., Science *170* (1970) 404.

90. Mathews, E. K., and Petersen, O. H., J. Physiol., *231* (1973) 283.

91. Kulka, R. G., and Sternlicht, E., Proc. Nat. Acad. Sci., U.S.A. *61* (1968) 1123

92. Goodman, D. P. B., Rasmussen, H., DiBella, F., and Guthrow, C. E., Jr., Proc. Nat. Acad. Sci., U.S.A., *67* (1970) 652.

93. Dilorenzo, R. J., Walton, K. G., Curran, P. F., and Greengard, P., Proc. Nat. Acad. Sic., U.S.A., *70* (1973) 880.

94. Johnson, E. M., Ueda, T., Moeno, H., and Greengard, P., J. Biol. Chem., *247* (1972) 5650.

95. Lacy, P. E., Howell, S. L., Young, D. A., and Fink, C. J., Nature, *219* (1968) 1177.

96. Williams, J. A., and Wolff, J., J. Cell Biol., *54* (1972) 158.

97. LeMarchand, Y., Single, A., Assimacopoulos-Jeannet, F., Orci, L., Rouillier, C., and Jeanrenard, B., J. Biol. Chem., *248* (1973) 6862.

98. Stein, O., and Stein, Y., Biochim. Biophys. Acta *306* (1973) 142.

99. Redman, C. M., Banerjee, D., Howell, K., and Palade, G. E., J. Cell Biol., *64* (1975) in press.

100. Stadler, J., and Franke, W. W., J. Cell Biol., *60* (1974) 297.

101. Wilson, L., Bamberg, J. R., Mizel, S. B., Grisham, L. M., and Creswell, K. M.,

Fed. Proc., *33* (1973) 158.

102. Heuser, J. E., and Reese, T. S., J. Cell Biol., *57* (1973) 315.
103. Ceccarelli, B., Hurlbut, W. P., and Mauro, A., J. Cell Biol., *57* (1973) 449.
104. Pelletier, G., J. Ultrastructure. Res. *43* (1973) 445.
105. Farquhar, M. G., Skutelsky, E., andHopkins, C. R., in The Anterior Pituitary, Tixier-Vidal, A., and Farquhar, M. G., eds. Academic Press, New York 1975, p. 83.
106. Meldolesi, J., J. Cell Biol., *61* (1974) *1*.
107. Castle, J. D., Thesis, Rockefeller University, 1974.
108. van Golde, L. M. G., Fleischer, B., and Fleischer, S., Biochim. Biophys. Acta *249* (1971) 318.
109. Ross, R., and Benditt, E., J. Cell Biol., *27* (1965) 83.
110. Weinstock, M., and Leblond, C. P., J. Cell Biol., *60*(1974) 92.
111. Olsen, B. R., and Prockop, D. J., Proc. Nat. Acad. Sci., U.S.A. *71* (1974) 2033.
112. Zucker-Franklin, D., and Hirsch, J. G., J. Exper. Med., *120* (1964) 569.
113. Bainton, D. F., in Phagocytic mechanisms in health and disease, Williams, R. C., and Fudenberg, H. H., eds. Intercontinental Medical Book Corp., New York, (1972).
114. Henson, P. M., J. Immunol. *107* (1971) 1547.
115. Cohn, Z. A., Fedorko, M. E., and Hirsch, J. G., J. Exp. Med., *123* (1966) 157.
116. Smith, R. E., and Farquhar, M. G., J. Cell Biol. *31* (1966) 319.
117. Novikoff, P. M., Novikoff, A. B., Quintana, N., and Hauw, J., J. Cell Biol., *50* (1971) 859.
118. Albersheim, P., Bauer, W. D., Keestra, K., and Talmadge, K. W., in Biogenesis of plant cell wall polysaccharides, Loewus, F., ed. Academic Press, New York (1973).
119. Fawcett, D. W., Biology of Reproduction, 2 (1970) 90.
120. Anderson, E., J. Cell Biol., *37* (1968) 514.
121. Szollosi, D., Anat. Record, *159* (1967) 431.
122. Douglas, W. W., and Poisner, A. M., J. Physiol. *172* (1964) 1.
123. Whittacker, V. P., in Advances in Cytopharmacology, 2 (1973) 311, Raven press, New York.
124. Ross, R., J. Cell Biol., *50* (1971) 172.
125. Hay, E. D., in The Epidermis, Montagna, W., and Lobitz, W. C., eds., Academic Press, New York, 1964, p. 97.
126. Hay, E. D., and Dodson, Y. W., J. Cell Biol., *57* (1973) 190.
127. Kessel, R. G., Zeitschr. Zellforschung, *89* (1968) 17.

DEDICATION

This lecture is dedicated with affection and gratitude to Keith Porter, Philip Siekevitz, James Jamieson, Lucien Caro, Lewis Greene, Lars Ernster, David Sabatini, Colvin Redman, Jacopo Meldolesi, Gustav Dallner, Yutaka Tashiro, Tsuneo Omura, Gunter Blobel, Alan Tartakoff, David Castle and George Scheele, my good colleagues and companions in the work carried out on the endoplasmic reticulum and secretory process.

EYVIND JOHNSON

Född 1900 i Svartbjörsbyn nära Boden, Överluleå socken, Norrbottens län.

Föräldrar: stenhuggaren Olof Petter J. från Värmland och Cevia Gustafs-dotter från Blekinge. Sex syskon av vilka E. J. var nästyngst. Fadern drabbades av silikos omkring 1904, och E. J. togs då om hand av sin barnlösa moster och hennes man, stenhuggaren Anders Johan Rost. I fjortonårsåldern lämnade han de avhållna fosterföräldrarna för att söka arbete nära föräldrahemmet.

Hans arbeten blev många: först vid timmergallringsbommen nära Sävast vid Luleälven, sedan vid Björns tegelbruk. Åren 1915—1919 var han sågverksar-betare, biljettförsäljare och biljettmottagare på en bio, och biomaskinist. Där-efter hantlangade han åt rörmokare och elmontörer. 1918 var han lokputsar-aspirant vid lokstallarna i Boden, och på vintern ett tag vedlämpare på gods-tåg mellan Boden och Haparanda. Åter en tid sågverksarbetare och sedan hö-pressare, därefter arbetslös, lånade ihop pengar och reste ner till Stockholm där han fick arbete på LM Ericsons stora verkstad vid Thulegatan. Så kom metallarbetarstrejken 1920, och han försökte leva på vad han skrev, och det var ett magert levebröd. Samtidigt hade han med några jämnåriga författare in spe grundat den litterära tidskriften Vår Nutid som kom ut i sex nummer. Han tillhörde då den blivande-diktarförening som kallade sig De gröna.

Hösten 1920—hösten 1921 arbetade han jämte ett par tre vänner, som slåt-terkarl och sedan timmerhuggare på ett småbruk i Uppland. Där fanns bl. a. läsfrid och skrivfrid.

Hösten 1921 for han till Tyskland — lastbåt till Kiel, tåg till Berlin, och om några månader fortsatte han via Rhenlandet till Paris där han försörjde sig bl. a. med att skriva i svenska blad, vara betongarbetare, och sedan diskare på ett stort hotell nära Gare du Nord. Sedan åter till Berlin där han stannade till hösten 1923 då han reste hem till Sverige.

Hans första bok, novellsamlingen De fyra främlingarna blev färdig våren 1924 och kom ut under hösten. Under ett vinterbesök i Norrbotten blev hans andra bok färdig, och gavs ut hösten 1925. Då var E. J. sedan åtskilliga må-nader åter i Frankrike, där han kom att bo i drygt fem år.

År 1927 vigdes han i Saint-Leu-La-Forêt vid Aase Christofersen. Deras son Tore föddes där 1928.

1930 flyttade familjen hem till Sverige.

Efter Aase Johnsons död gifte sig E. J. med Cilla Frankenhaeuser. De har två barn, Maria f. 1944, och Anders, f. 1946.

1947—1950 bodde E. J. med familj i Schweiz och England, och sedan 1950 i Saltsjöbaden.

Born in 1900 at Svartbjörsbyn near Boden in the north of Sweden.

Parents: Olof Petter J., stonecutter from Värmland, and Cevia Gustafsdotter from Blekinge. Six children, of whom E. J. was the youngest but one. His father fell ill with silicosis about 1904 and E. J. was taken care of by his childless aunt and her husband, stonecutter Anders Johan Rost. At the age of fourteen he left his foster-parents, of whom he was very fond, to look for work near the home where he was born.

He did many different kinds of work, first at the timber sorting boom near Sävast on the Lule River, then at the Björn brickworks. Between 1915 and 1919 he was a sawmill worker, a ticket seller and usher at a cinema, and a projectionist, then he was assistant to plumbers and electricians. In 1918 he was a locomotive cleaner at the engine sheds in Boden, and for a time during the winter a stoker on goods trains between Boden and Haparanda. Again sawmill worker for a while, then hay-presser, then out of work. Borrowing money, he travelled down to Stockholm, where he got work at LM Ericsson's big workshop in Thulegatan. The metalworkers' strike broke out in 1920 and he tried to live on what he wrote, with very meagre results. At the same time, together with some other young budding writers, he founded the literary magazine *Vår Nutid* (Our Present Day), which appeared for six numbers. He then belonged to the society of future writers which called itself *De gröna* (The Green Ones).

From the autumn of 1920 to the autumn of 1921, together with two or three friends, he worked at hay-making and timber-felling on a small farm in Uppland, where he had spare time and peace in which to read and write.

In the autumn of 1921 he went to Germany—cargo boat to Kiel, train to Berlin, and a few months later he continued via the Rheinland to Paris, where he earned his living writing for Swedish papers, as a cement worker and then as a dish-washer at a big hotel near the Gare du Nord. Then back to Berlin, where he remained until the autumn of 1923, when he returned home to Sweden.

His first book *De fyra främlingarna* (The Four Strangers), a collection of short stories, was finished in the spring of 1924 and published during the autumn. During a winter visit to the North, he finished his second book, which was published in the autumn of 1925. By then E. J. was back in France, where he was to live for over five years.

In 1927 he was married at Saint-Leu-La Forêt to Aase Christofersen. Their son Tore was born there in 1928.

In 1930 the family moved home to Sweden.

After Aase Johnson's death E. J. married Cilla Frankenhaeuser. They have two children, Maria, b. 1944, and Anders, b. 1946.

From 1947 to 1950 E. J. and his family lived in Switzerland and England, and since 1950 he has been living at Saltsjöbaden.

Bibliografi:

De fyra främlingarna (1924)

Timans och Rättfärdigheten, 1925

Stad i mörker (1927)

Lettre Recommandée (Stad i ljus på franska) (1927)

Stad i ljus (1928)

Minnas (1928)

Kommentar till ett stjärnfall (1929)

Avsked till Hamlet (1930)

Natten är här (1932)

Bobinack (1932)

Regn i gryningen (1933)

Romanen om Olof: 1. Nu var det 1914 (1934), 2. Här har du ditt liv! (1935), 3. Se dig inte om! (1936), 4. Slutspel i ungdomen (1937)

Nattövning (1938)

Den trygga världen (1940)

Soldatens återkomst (1940)

Krilonromanen: 1. Grupp Krilon (1941), 2. Krilons resa (1942), 3. Krilon själv (1943)

Strändernas svall (1946) (Romanen)

Strändernas svall (En teaterversion av romanen) (1948)

Dagbok från Schweiz (1949)

Drömmar om rosor och eld (1949)

Lägg undan solen (1951)

Romantisk berättelse (1953)

Tidens gång (forts. på Romantisk berättelse) (1955)

Vinterresa i Norrbotten (1955)

Molnen över Metapontion (1957)

Vägar över Metaponto — en resedagbok (1959)

Hans Nådes tid (1960)

Spår förbi Kolonos — en berättelse (1961)

Livsdagen lång (1964)

Stunder, vågor — anteckningar, berättelser (1965)

Favel ensam (1968)

Resa hösten 1921 (1973)

Några steg mot tystnaden (1973)

Harry Martinson

HARRY MARTINSON

Harry Martinson är född i Jämshög, 1904. Han blev tidigt föräldralös och efter en växlingsrik barndom där hemmen och upptagningsanstalterna var lika många som rymningarna kom han vid 16 års ålder till sjöss där han tillbringade sex år av sitt liv ombord i olika fartyg och inom olika yrken i främmande länder.

Det var från dessa resor och arbetsår i de mest olikartade miljöer som han senare kom att hämta stoff och inspiration till sina första litterära arbeten, ett par prosaböcker med glimtar, vyer och minnen från de koleldade fartygens värld under 1920-talet.

Dessa skildringar följdes några år senare av ett par böcker med självbiografiska inslag och diktade återinlevelser i ett bortackorderat barns tillvaro, särskilt barnets eget sätt att uppfatta och försöka förstå mänskorna och livet.

Jämsides med denna psykologiska avlyssning av minnets barndomsland, tillkom en rad diktböcker som så småningom fick sin fortsättning i en räcka naturstudier på prosa där ord och iakttagelse förenas i vad författaren kallat "tänkandet ute på ängen".

I ett senare arbete, romanen "Vägen till Klockrike" är beskrivningen av det mänskliga helt ägnat förhållandet mellan den bofaste och den resande mänskan inom oss själva.

En resevärld i ännu mer vidgad betydelse stiger fram i Aniara, ett epos om en diktad rymdfärd med djupperspektiv hän mot vår egen tid. Där sammanträngs till samma medvetanderum våra farhågor och våra frågor om vart det bär hän med oss själva och med den planet som vårt släkte behandlar så som nu sker.

Translation

Harry Martinson was born at Jämshög in 1904. He was left an orphan at an early age, and after a chequered childhood, in which the children's homes and institutions were as numerous as the escapes, he went to sea at the age of sixteen, spending six years of his life on board various ships and as a workman in foreign countries.

It was from these travels and years of work in environments of all kinds that he later drew material and inspiration for his first literary efforts—a couple of books of prose with glimpses, views and memories of the world of coal-heated ships during the 1920s.

These accounts were followed a few years later by one or two books with an autobiographical strain and fictional recollections of a boarded-out child's existence, especially the child's own way of perceiving and trying to understand life and the people in it.

Side by side with this psychological cognition of the childhood land of memory, there appeared some collections of poetry which were continued by degrees in a series of nature studies in prose, in which words and observation are combined in what the author has called "thinking out in the meadow".

In a later work, the novel *Vägen till Klockrike*, the description of the human side is devoted entirely to the relationship between the settled and the itinerant man within ourselves.

A world of journeying in a still wider sense emerges in *Aniara*, an epic work about an imagined space flight with a perspective in depth towards our own time. In it, jostling for room in our consciousness, are our fears and our questions as to where we are heading, together with the planet that our generation is treating as it does.

Seán Cearra MacBride

SEÁN MAC BRIDE

Mr. Seán Mac Bride was born on January 26th 1904 in Paris. Took an active part in the movement for Irish independence and suffered imprisonment on several occasions.

1947—1958 Member of Dail Eireann (Irish Parliament).

1948—1951 Minister for External Affairs for Ireland in Inter-Party Government. In 1954 was offered but declined, Ministerial Office in Irish Government.

1948—1951 Vice-President of the Organization for European Economic Co-operation (O.E.E.C.).

1949—1950 President, Committee of Ministers of Council of Europe.

1963—1971 Secretary General, International Commission of Jurists.

1966—19.. Consultant to the Pontifical Commission Justice and Peace.

1961—1974 Chairman Amnesty International Executive.

1968—19.. Chairman (1968—1974) and President since 1974 Executive International Peace Bureau.

1968—1974 Chairman Special Committee of International Non-Governmental Organizations (N.G.O.s) on Human Rights (Geneva).

1973—19.. Vice-Chairman Congress of World Peace Forces (Moscow, October 1973) and Continuing Committee.

1973—19.. Vice-President World Federation of United Nations Associations.

1973—19.. Elected by the General Assembly of the United Nations to the post of United Nations Commissioner for Namibia with rank of Assistant Secretary-General of the United Nations.

THE IMPERATIVES OF SURVIVAL

Nobel Lecture, December 12, 1974

by

Seán Mac Bride

Excellencies, Ladies and Gentlemen,

It is nearly with a feeling of despair that I come to your beautiful country and city to receive this hardly deserved honour. Despair partly because we are living in a world where war, violence, brutality and ever increasing armament dominate the thinking of humanity; but, more so, because humanity itself gives the appearance of having become numbed or terrified by its own impotence in the face of disaster.

Little thought seems to have been given to the effects of the fundamental changes that have taken place around us in the course of the last 30 years; and that are still taking place. Yet, the tremendous scientific and material developments that have taken place in this period have altered radically the whole structure of human society—and even threatened the survival of the human race. This stupendous scientific and material revolution has brought basic changes into every aspect of our lives and of the ecology in which we live. These scientific developments were accompanied by equally radical changes in our social and political structures. Of these, the demolition of colonialism begun the dismantling, not before its time, of the most unjust system of racial, social and economic discrimination that could exist. During this period an ill-defined effort was developed to replace colonialism and economic dominance based on wealth or military supremacy, by a just social order that would ensure freedom from hunger, justice and security based on equality. The strivings for these results, let us face it, have not been universally successful. Hunger and famine still stalk vast areas of the world causing death and spreading disease.

In the midst of this rapid revolution man discovered nuclear energy and harnessed it to weapons of destruction. Now, for the first time in the history of humanity, human beings have it within their power to destroy all living beings on this planet. Nearly as soon as it was discovered, the nuclear bomb was used and annihilated the populations of Hiroshima and Nagasaki. Since then additional countless and unknown thousands have been killed or damaged by nuclear "fall out" used experimentally.

This stupendous scientific and material revolution has changed practically every factor in our ecology and society. There has never been in the history of mankind a revolution so fundamental or far reaching. Never before has humanity been presented with so many or such grave problems. Perhaps as a result of this scientific revolution, or coincidentally with it, there has taken place a near total collapse of public and private morality in practically every sector of human relationship. The previously existing standards of public and private morality may have left a lot to be desired but at least they existed. They were regarded as standards and did command a certain degree of observance. Now they have ceased to be either accepted or observed.

It is a rule of international law that weapons and methods of warfare which do not discriminate between combatants and civilians should never be used. Aerial bombings from balloons were outlawed; the use of "dum-dum" bullets was outlawed and made a crime, on the grounds that they inflict unnecessary suffering. The bombing of hospitals and civilian targets was outlawed. All these principles and standards have suddenly vanished. They are not even mentioned by those whose responsibility it is to uphold them. The use of the most cruel, terrible and indiscriminate weapon of all time, the nuclear weapons, is not even outlawed. The manufacture and development of these doomsday weapons throughout the world is regarded as "normal" and "quite respectable". One of the frightening, if not shocking, aspect of this particular breakdown in our public standards of morality has been the comparative silence of many of the established guardians of humanitarian law.

Governments go to war directly or by proxy without declaring war. Force, or threat of force, are constantly used to dominate other countries. In these undeclared wars civilians, men, women and children are bombed and massacred indiscriminately; chemical agents are used to destroy humans, animals and crops. Prisoners are not only ill-treated but are tortured systematically in a worse manner than at any barbaric period of history. In many cases this is done with the direct or tacit approval of governments that claim to be civilised or even Christian. In some cases special courses in torture are conducted by army and police forces and new torture techniques are exported from country to country. Secret services are used to assassinate political opponents or to provoke internal dissension in another country or to procure the overthrow of a democratically elected government. In many cases leaders of governments have used their positions improperly to remain in power or to amass wealth. In other cases the overthrow of a government is followed by a massacre of its members and supporters. Again cases occur when one ethnic group seeks to supplant another in order to impose its domination and, for this purpose resorts to outright genocide.

From a survey of the contemporary scene it is only too obvious that it is often those in authority who set the bad example. If those vested with authority and power practice injustice, resort to torture and killing, is it not inevitable that those who are the victims will react with similar methods? This does not condone savagery or inhuman conduct but it does provide part of the explanation for the increasing violence and brutality of our world.

The rising generation are dismayed and deceived by the world we have created for them. I insist that it is "WE", the mankind of this century, that have created the doomsday world in which we live. A section of the youth of today have not unnaturally lost faith in the future and faith in God; some have become cynical; some seek escape "from it all" by creating escapist fantasies of their own or by resorting to drugs; some, on the other hand, seek

209

to pursue actively and idealistically the objective set out in the Universal Declaration of Human Rights and the achievement of General and Complete Disarmament. These, however, are often disheartened by the credibility gap between the ideas enunciated by governments, by religious leaders and by the United Nations itself. This credibility gap leads to a loss of confidence in all institutions.

It is clear from this recital, that Albert Schweitzer was absolutely correct when he pointed out that man had lost the capacity "to foresee and to forestall the consequences of his own acts". Not only has man lost this capacity but he does not realise that knowledge without wisdom and idealism is dangerous. What does wisdom involve in this context? A realisation that the world was not created by man and that in tampering with nature and creation man is endangering human survival. And what does idealism involve? An ethical belief in a duty to help human beings to survive and to benefit from the natural goodness and beauty with which Providence has surrounded humanity. It is clear that it is not man who has created the universe—whether you believe in God, or in gods or deny any divine presence—man cannot alter the laws that govern the universe without damaging it.

I have drawn attention to these philosophical and ethical issues to underline the responsibility that rests on the religious leaders of the world in this situation. The breakdown in public and private morality is in no small measure due to their failure to adjust to the tremendous scientific revolution through which we are passing. Churches, by the very reason of their structures are monolithic and do not adapt easily. But, in many cases they, too, have allowed themselves to become allied or even part of an unjust establishment or system. Often they have remained silent when they should have led the demand for justice; often they have resisted reform when they should have been leading the demand for it. It is the duty of the religious to give an unequivocal lead in the struggle for justice and peace. Those who believe in divine providence should insist that their religious structures provide such a lead.

It is important that rulers and religious and political leaders should realise that there can be no peace without justice. Likewise, that economic conditions which condemn human beings to starvation, disease or poverty constitute in themselves aggression against their victims. Structures which deprive human beings of their human rights or of their human dignity prevent justice from being realised. Racial and religious discrimination also constitute acts of aggression. Very often those who are defending the maintenance of the *status quo* are in fact defending the continuance of oppression or of an order which is unjust. This is so, particularly in the regions of southern Africa where the political and economic structures are built upon racial discrimination and colonial exploitation.

Presumably Alfred Nobel by his bequest intended that the individual selected to receive his Award would avail of the occasion which he thus created to propound his suggestions for world peace. If I have appeared to complain against the existing complacency of institutional establishments—governmental and religious—it is to permit me to make concrete suggestions. The first I would like to make, deals with what Alfred Nobel properly describes as "the horrors of horrors and the greatest of all crimes"—war. This is the threat that hangs over all humanity at the moment. War destroys all human values and is the greatest danger to everything which human beings desire and cherish. I think that it is only right that I should quote here in Oslo a former Swedish Ambassador to Norway, Governor Rolf Edberg, who is now Chairman of SIPRI and who describes the meaninglessness of war in the nuclear age:

"In earlier wars, aggressions could be unleashed against a visible enemy; not so in the clinically impersonal war envisaged for the future, in which a human automaton, perhaps directed by a computer, presses a button to annihilate people on the other side of an ocean. Earlier wars, including the corporal's were a more or less naked struggle for living spaces and territories; in a nuclear war there is no territory to conquer nor any to defend, since the attacked and the attackers are alike threatened with annihilation. In earlier wars the man at the front was presuming to be sacrificing himself out of loyalty to his group and in the belief that he had a reasonable chance to defend his family and his nation; in a war of hydrogen bombs everything he was supposed to defend will perish with him.

"Some meaning, whatever it was, could be imputed to earlier wars. The hydrogen bomb has made the waging of war an exercise in global futility.

"Truly, once we feel at liberty to monkey with the forces of nature, the possibilities for doing mischief are innumerable."

Peace then has to be the DESPERATE IMPERATIVE of humanity. Many imperatives flow from this only too obvious conclusion. These imperatives would be comparatively easier of achievement if those in authority throughout the world were imbued with an ethic that made world peace the primary objective and if they were inspired by a moral sense of social responsibility. It should be the primary role of the Churches to build this new morality.

The practical imperatives for peace are many and far reaching. But there is no short-cut and each must be tackled energetically. They are:
1. General and Complete Disarmament—including nuclear weapons
2. The glorification of peace and not of war
3. The effective protection of human rights and minorities at national and international levels
4. Automatic and depoliticised mechanism for the settlement of international and non-international disputes that may endanger peace or that are causing injustices
5. An international order that will ensure a fair distribution of all essential products
6. An International Court of Justice and legal system with full automatic jurisdiction to rectify injustice or abuse of power
7. An international peace-keeping force and police force with limited function
8. Ultimately, a world parliament and government.

I can already hear many say "Utopia". "Impossible of achievement". Of course, it will be difficult but what is the alternative? The nearly certain destruction of the human race.

I cannot deal comprehensively in this paper with each of the 8 imperatives I have outlined but I can emphasize some immediate steps that can be taken and point to some of indefensible contradictions that exist in our present endeavours.

GENERAL AND COMPLETE DISARMAMENT

This was the accepted aim of all governments and of the United Nations up to the end of 1961. Why has this objective been dropped? Why is it never even mentioned now? The extent to which agreement had been reached in 1961 may be gauged from the two opening paragraphs of the joint Soviet-United States statement of 20 September 1961:

"1. The goal of negotiations is to achieve agreement on a programme which will ensure

(a) that disarmament is general and complete and war is no longer an instrument for settling international problems, and

(b) that such disarmament is accompanied by the establishment of reliable procedures for the peaceful settlement of disputes and effective arrangements for the maintenance of peace in accordance with the principles of the Charter of the United Nations.

"2. The programme for general and complete disarmament shall ensure that States will have at their disposal *only such non-nuclear armaments,* forces, facilities and establishments as are agreed to be necessary to maintain internal order and protect the personal security of citizens; and that States shall support and provide agreed manpower for a United Nations peace force."

The Soviet and American draft treaties prepared at that period represented an extremely wide measure of agreement and few points of controversy remained. Yet, in a matter of a very few years these objectives were dropped and replaced by the "cold war". Is it not time that we got back to General and Complete Disarmament?

Far from considering General and Complete Disarmament the major powers are engaged in the greatest armaments race that has existed in the world. Negotiations are only aimed at limiting the *increase* of defensive weapons and the *increase* of ballistic nuclear weapons. And this, only because the armament race is so costly that it is bankrupting their economies; they can no longer afford further escalation. The present negotiations do not relate to disarmament—they relate to phased armament.

NUCLEAR ARMAMENT

While strictly speaking nuclear weapons come within the scope of General

212

and Complete Disarmament, they should also be dealt with in the context of Humanitarian Laws.

The arsenal of nuclear weapons is now such that there are now enough nuclear missiles to destroy the world twenty times over. Despite conferences and what are euphemistically called "Partial Disarmament Measures", no progress has been made to outlaw nuclear weapons. The nuclear arsenal is growing day by day. Nuclear warheads are spread all over the world in bases, aircraft, ship and submarines to a greater extent than ever before. The Nuclear Test Ban Treaty and the Non-Proliferation Treaty have been of little value but have been used to defuse public anxiety.

There is probably no field in which the credibility gap between profession and performance is greater than in the field of nuclear armament. As pointed out weapons which are unnecessarily cruel, or weapons which are indiscriminate in their effect on combatants and civilian targets are outlawed by The Hague and Geneva Conventions. These are the basic cardinal principles of Humanitarian Law enshrined in International Conventions and in many United Nations resolutions. What weapon could be more cruel or more indiscriminate than a nuclear bomb or warhead? Why outlaw a "dum-dum" bullet and not an atomic bomb? Yet, for some unexplained reason, there has been a refusal to include nuclear weapons among the weapons to be specifically outlawed in the revised texts of the Geneva Conventions. If any meaningful credibility is to be given to humanitarian law or to the ban on nuclear weapons, the first concrete measure which should be taken is to OUTLAW THE *USE* OF NUCLEAR WEAPONS. A simple Convention, or article in a Convention outlawing the *USE* of nuclear weapons would be a first simple step. Yet, this has not been done. Of course, this step should be accompanied by provisions to outlaw the manufacture, sale, transfer or stockpiling of nuclear weapons and the destruction of all existing stock. All kind of problems, of course, arise as to control verification and inspection; but it is difficult often to escape the impression that many of these issues are raised only to find difficulties and to block or delay agreements. Why not begin simply by outlawing the USE, MANUFACTURE, SALE, TRANSFER and STOCK-PILING of nuclear weapons or components thereof? Why not *now* stop completely the production of all nuclear weapons?

Is not the real truth that all or some of the nuclear powers want to be free to manufacture, sell, transfer, stockpile and use nuclear weapons? If this is the case, the truth should be exposed starkly to world public opinion. The distribution of drugs and narcotics is outlawed. Yet, self-righteous and civilised governments claim the right to make and distribute these engines of nuclear mass destruction.

For many years some governments sought to create the impression that they, and only they, had the secret to make nuclear weapons and that so long as it was only they which possessed this secret the world was safe. It was, of course, an idiotic fantasy to suggest that the technique of nuclear destruction could remain the secret of a few selected "trustworthy" powers. Or that the particular powers in question were worthy of such a trust. The conduct of governments in this era does not encourage one's trust in their judgement or in their integrity.

THE PROPOSED UNITED NATIONS WORLD DISARMAMENT CONFERENCE

It must be admitted that the efforts made through the United Nations for disarmament have been fairly negative; not for fault of trying but, of course, the United Nations can only go as far, or as fast, as its members will let it go. The major nuclear powers have the right to veto all decisions of the Security Council; in addition, out of the 138 Member States only a few have been very active on disarmament. The impression has been created that it is so complex that it must be left to the big powers; that there is an aura of magic relating to nuclear weapons that only the major powers really understand. In any event, many of the smaller States are too preoccupied with their own immediate problems and that of economic survival to get involved in disarmament; also many of them, for one reason or another, are themselves busy trying to build up armies. Let me immediately make an honourable exception of the Nordic countries whose steadfast and constructive initiatives on disarmament have been of considerable value. I should also mention the valuable contributions of Ghana (under the late President Nkrumah, which I hope will be revived by contemporary Ghana), Poland, Romania, Canada and India—and even if India has now become a nuclear power. It is sincerely hoped that the Non-Aligned States will again now turn their attention actively and persistently to the achievement of General and Complete Disarmament. It is they and the countries that I have mentioned that have the greatest interest in peace.

It is now generally recognised that the CCD (the Conference of the Committee on Disarmament) which has been virtually in existence, in one form or another, since 1961 has achieved little or nothing; it seems in recent years to have successfully buried both the Soviet "Draft Treaty on General and Complete Disarmament Under Strict International Control" and the United States "Outline of Basic Provisions for a Treaty on General and Complete Disarmament in a Peaceful World". Perhaps the failure of the CCD was due to its structure; or perhaps the failure of the CCD was due to the lack of a real desire by some, or all, of the major powers to disarm.

Because of the failure or lack of progress of the CCD, 36 Non-Aligned States in 1965 recommended the convening by the United Nations of a World Disarmament Conference. Somehow or another this proposal vanished into thin air and was forgotten until 1971 when the Soviet Union revived the idea. The Soviet proposal was received frigidly, and even with animosity, by some countries. However, finally a resolution was adopted by the General Assembly expressing the conviction that:

"... it is more desirable to take *immediate* steps in order that careful consideration be given to the convening, following adequate preparation, of a world disarmament conference open to all States".

Someone, sometime should make a compendium of the gobbledegook ver-

214

biage used in United Nations resolutions. It is this meaningless language and everlasting procrastination at the U.N. that disenchant people, who have faith and who realise the dangers which our world faces. It is not the fault of the Secretariat but rather of those who torture words in order to say nothing. To talk of "taking immediate steps" after ten years of feet-dragging was encouraging; but we are now at the end of 1974 and there is not yet a United Nations Disarmament Conference in sight—despite the call for *immediate* steps. Conferences are being held all over the world about every imaginable topic; why this slowness and hesitancy on the United Nations World Conference on Disarmament?

These are the reasons which prompted the International Peace Bureau at its International Conference on Disarmament at Bradford to call on the General Assembly to announce on or before the 17th June 1975 the date on which it is proposed to convene the United Nations World Disarmament Conference.

Many will ask "what is the use of calling another conference, after all the conferences there have been?" It is a valid question. The answer is that it would be nearly useless if it were to be left to governments only. This brings me to what I regard as a most single important factor in the struggle for peace and disarmament. Unfortunately, it is the rule rather than the exception that in all matters relating to war, peace and disarmament it is not the people who decide the issues but the governments. In fact, while it is nominally the governments, which take decisions, the decisions are definitely influenced by a number of powerful vested interests.

VESTED INTERESTS AND EXPERTS

I use the words "vested interests" here in a broad sense to include, not only financial vested interests but also professional vested interests, sectarian and political vested interests. The issues of peace or war, or the armament race versus disarmament, are never put to the people. The people are never given the opportunity of either knowing the facts or of deciding the issues. Even parliaments are often by-passed on such issues or only partially consulted. The real decisions relating to armament are taken behind closed doors by the Joint Chiefs of Staffs or by the General Staffs of the Defence Forces. It is they who are the "experts" to whom all questions relating to armament, disarmament, nuclear weapons, war and peace are referred. It is even to them that questions on Humanitarian Laws are referred. They are the experts to whom governments turn for advice on all these vital questions on which depend the future of humanity. It is natural that members of governments should do so; the members of a government are not military experts. Therein lies the nerve centre of our problems in regard to Complete and General Disarmament.

Who are these "experts"? Military officers, often drawn from a particular caste or class of society, whose profession it is to prepare for war; defensive or offensive war, it matters not; it depends on circumstances. But to prepare for war they require arms. Their professional objectives must be to have the best army and armament possible. What is the best armament possible? The armament that will wreak the greatest destruction on any potential enemy. Therefore, the experts the governments rely on for advice are generals whose profession is war and whose objective is the building of a military machine equipped with the biggest and best engines of destruction it is possible to obtain. Their ambition is to have the greatest land, sea and air fire power possible. Of course, an atom bomb is more effective than a conventional one and therefore the experts do not want the use of atomic bombs outlawed. Of course, a fragmentation bomb will kill more people than an ordinary one, therefore it is desirable. Nerve gases and napalm are very effective killers, therefore we must be free to use them. "Dum-dum" bullets are of little value therefore they can be outlawed without any real inconvenience. An army looks more respectable and is less unpopular if it makes minor concession to a few humanitarian concepts such as the outlawing of "dum-dum" bullets.

So, the experts upon whom the governments rely for ultimate advice on disarmament are those whose profession it is to make war and who want bigger and more destructive arms. By training, by philosophy, by formation and by profession they are against "General and Complete Disarmament" and in most cases against any form of disarmament or weapon prohibition. They are probably very decent, sincere and God-fearing men; but their profession is war and armament. They cannot help a bias or vested interest by reason of their profession and training. No conscientious objector or peace leader is ever likely to be consulted by a government! Why not?

In addition to the military experts who advise governments on armament, there are the financial interests which make money out of armament and also the industrial-military complex that live by increased armament. To the industrial-military complex and to the banks and financial interests that finance the industrial-military complex, the arms race is a boon. A war far-away, such as in South-East Asia or in the Middle East means increased arms sales and more profits to the industrial-military complex; it is not un-welcome. Peaceful conditions in the world are not welcome to the arms in-dustry. General and Complete Disarmament would spell disaster to the industrial-military complexes in the United States, France, Britain and Ger-many, to mention but a few of the countries that thrive on increased armament.

The socialist countries do not have a profit-motivated industrial-military complex. They can therefore adjust more readily to disarmament. The military-industrial complex is State owned and controlled. To them disarmament means an automatic switch from increased arms production to increase in production for industrial development and for the consumer and export markets. They cannot lose by disarmament, they can only gain. This, no doubt, accounts for the much more sincere and far reaching approach of the Soviet Union to General and Complete Disarmament than that of the western powers.

While vested interests arising from the military-industrial complexes in the communist countries favour disarmament, the industrial-military complexes in the West are very powerful factors in favour of every increase in armament. It would be foolish to underrate the massive influence of the organised lobbies of military-industrial complexes in the United States and western Europe. They constitute an unseen and unmentioned powerful force operating silently in the corridors of NATO and of most western governments. Their resources are unlimited and their influence is great. This constitutes a huge vested interest which works silently against General and Complete Disarmament.

In addition to the military and industrial vested interest there are also the vested interests arising from political or ideological considerations and that favour armament as part of the processus for the imposition of policies or ideologies on other areas. These obstacles to disarmament unfortunately exist all over the world. They are not the monopoly of one side.

If I have drawn attention to the importance of the military, financial and ideological vested interest that oppose General and Complete Disarmament, it was to enable me to emphasise the importance of the role of Non-Governmental Organisations and of public opinion in the field of disarmament.

PUBLIC OPINION — "WE THE PEOPLE . . ."

Many of the results of the tremendous scientific revolution which has taken place in the last 30 years have been conterproductive and dangerous, e.g. the atomic bomb. However, this revolution has also brought with it some means which may enable us to protect ourselves from the atomic bomb and other engines of destruction. The advent of the mass media of communication (radio and T.V.) coupled with higher standards of literacy and education are giving a much greater degree of influence to public opinion in the world than it has ever had in the past. The public can now be informed as to current events and policies. Governments can no longer keep their actions and policies secret from their public. There can no longer be an impenetrable curtain which can prevent the spread of news and views. The press, radio, T.V. and political commentators probe deep into the secret activities of governments and inform public opinion. Once informed and alerted to the issues involved, in turn, public opinion can be formed and can make itself heard.

This is a new development which is leading to a change in the centre of gravity of power from governments to the public through the press and the mass media. This is a new development; it began to make itself noticed during the Viet-Nam War. It was American and world public opinion that forced the United States to withdraw from Viet-Nam. It was the first time that a country at war was stopped in its tracks by its own and by world public opinion. Before that, a government at war, rightly or wrongly, received the support of its people. Now, because the public can learn and see what its government is doing, it is able to curb its government. The same thing has happened and is happening in the Soviet Union in regard to human rights and the right to intellectual freedom. This is a new and welcome development which neither governments nor the non-governmental sector have as yet understood fully. It will give tremendous new powers to the press and the mass media. Greater vigilance than ever will have to be exercised to ensure that the press and the mass media do not become controlled by governments or financial interests. The non-governmental sector will have to use this new power constructively.

In no field is it more necessary, and at no time was it more urgent than now, to alert public opinion to the danger of war that exists and to the imperatives of peace.

Why do I think it necessary to inject this note of urgency? The answer is simple. The armament build up has soared so high and is so costly that, at any time, the General Staff of one side or the other may warn its government "We have armament superiority *now* but we will not have it in six months time; therefore now is the time to strike." It does not matter how wrong the generals who give this advice may be; it is the kind of advice which influences governments and which may cause a crisis to explode into a full blown war.

These are the reasons why the time has come for "WE THE PEOPLE . . ." referred to in the Charter of the United Nations to assert ourselves and to demand the outlawing of all nuclear weapons and the achievement of General and Complete Disarmament. It is essential that the ordinary people of the world should have a say as to their own survival. The non-governmental sector is just as qualified as the "experts" of those who have a vested interest in armament and war.

The International Conference of the International Peace Bureau at Bradford has formulated a demand for the representation of "We the people . . ." at the proposed United Nations World Disarmament Conference by not less than 30 representatives from the non-governmental sector. Quite rightly the International Peace Bureu Conference pointed out:

"It is essential if the Conference is to succeed that effect be given to the spirit of the Charter so that "WE THE PEOPLE" can be heard. In the absence of direct democratic representation at the United Nations this must be done through non-governmental organizations which are concerned with general and complete disarmament. Otherwise the World Disarmament Conference will represent in the main the official, military and industrial establishments that have vested interest in maintaining and increasing armaments. It is the governments and the industrial-military complexes that have failed so far to achieve disarmament. It is they who have been responsible for the increased military establishments and the arms race."

Unless this is done and governments can be persuaded to take a much more enlightened view as to the urgency of General and Complete Disarmament, the proposed Conference will be of little value.

The Special Role of Women

Just as the questions relating to disarmament are usually left to military ex-

218

perts and to those with a vested interest in armament, these questions are also usually regarded as the exclusive prerogative of men. Women (with the honourable exception of Mrs. Alva Myrdal) are excluded from disarmament negotiations, indeed, as they generally are from important government posts. Yet, it is their children and their homes that will be ravaged by war. In my life I have found that women have a much better understanding of the imperatives of peace and are much less easily "taken in" by the specious arguments of experts or diplomats. They should be given a real decisive role in all disarmament negotiations and conferences. War and peace is surely the concern of women as much as it is that of men—and perhaps much more so.

Peace and Human Rights are Interrelated

The fundamental relationship between peace and human rights is now recognised. Structures which deprive persons of their human rights and dignity prevent justice from being realised; and systems which condemn people to starvation or to substandard conditions are a denial both of human rights and human dignity. It is these conditions which compel people to resort to violence. Hence the Universal Declaration of Human Rights proclaimed:

"It is essential, if man is not to have recourse, as a last resort, to rebellion against tyranny and oppression, that human rights should be protected by the rule of law."

Recognition that violations of human rights were among the causes of war, led to the adoption by the nations of the world of the Universal Declaration of Human Rights on the 10th December 1948. This historical instrument was, and remains, the most important declaration ever adopted by mankind. It should be taught as a text in all the schools; it should be displayed in all parliaments; it should be used as a text by the churches.

Magna Carta (England, 1215), the American Declaration of Independence (1776), La Déclaration des Droits de l'Homme (France, 1789), Karl Marx's "Das Kapital" (1867) were all important historical documents but they were all limited in scope or territory. The Universal Declaration of 1948 is both universal and comprehensive. I cannot over-emphasise the importance of the Universal Declaration. It provides a basis for the relationship between human beings and States inter se. The political and religious leaders of the world should utilise it as part of an effort to rebuild standards of morality that have crumbled in the decadence of this age.

However, it is deplorable that so little progress has as yet been made towards its implementation. The two Covenants to implement it, which took over fifteen years to draw up are still not yet in operation. They were adopted unanimously but can only come into operation when signed and ratified by 35 States. The position in regard to these two Covenants is as follows:
International Covenant on Economic, Social and Cultural Rights, 1966
(adopted unanimously on 16 December 1966).
As of December 1974 this Covenant was:

— Signed by 51 States
— States that have Ratified or Acceeded: 29 States
— Number of Ratifications or Accessions required to enable entry into operation: 35 States

International Covenant on Civil and Political Rights, 1966
(adopted unanimously on 16 December 1966).
As of December 1974 this Covenant was:
— Signed by 50 States
— States that have Ratified or Acceeded: 28 States
— Number of Ratifications or Accessions required to enable entry into operation: 35 States.

In addition to the two Covenants there are also many other Human Rights Conventions that require ratification and implementation. But above all, there is a need for effective implementation mechanism at domestic and at international levels. May I suggest that the universities and youth organisations should concentrate actively on these questions and make their voices heard. The rising generation are entitled to demand of their governments that they ratify and implement the principles which they proclaim as being theirs and which are enshrined in the Universal Declaration. An active public opinion campaign should be mounted in every country on these issues.

There is nothing more damaging to the concept of world order and peace than the massive violations of human rights that continue to occur in various parts of the world. The torture and massacres of political prisoners have spread like a malignant contagious disease from country to country. The detailed Reports of Amnesty International, which are not seriously challenged, provide an index to the extent and ramification of this malignant disease. In Southern Africa the imposition of racial discrimination and of slave like conditions on the African populations are an affront to the principles of the United Nations. Likewise South Africa's refusal to relinquish its illegal occupation of Namibia and its flogging of Namibian political prisoners are acts that call for determined action by the governments.

To the rights enshrined in the Universal Declaration of Human Rights one more might, with relevance be added. It is "The Right to Refuse to Kill". Both at the World Conference on Religion and Peace at Kyoto (1970) and at the Baden Consultation of Churches (1970) very clear cut Conclusions were adopted:

"We consider that the exercise of conscientious judgment is inherent in the dignity of human beings and that, accordingly, each person should be assured the right, on grounds of conscience or profound conviction, to refuse military service, or any other direct or indirect participation in wars or armed conflicts. The right of conscientious objection also extends to those who are unwilling to serve in a particular war because they consider it unjust or because they refuse to participate in a war or conflict in which weapons of massdestruction are likely to be used. This Conference also considers that members of armed forces have the right, and even the duty, to refuse to obey military orders which may involve the commission of criminal offenses, or of war crimes, or of crimes against humanity."

I have drawn attention to the issues raised in these Conclusions because they appear to be of particular relevance to the present day world. The right of an individual to refuse to kill, to torture or to participate in the preparation for the nuclear destruction of humanity seem to me to be fundamental.

THE ROLE OF THE UNITED NATIONS

It is easy to criticise the United Nations but it must be borne in mind that it is dependant upon the goodwill of its Member States and that its Secretariat can only go as far as the States will allow it to go. Again I would like to emphasise the importance of the role of public opinion in regard to the United Nations. The more public opinion can be interested in the work of the United Nations the further will governments be prepared to go. Unfortunately, however, much of what transpires at the United Nations does not reach public opinion and has little effect on it. Also, it would be useful if governments and parliaments themselves could participate in and follow more closely the work of the United Nations. The World Federation of United Nations Associations plays a useful role in this field but should receive greater direct assistance from the United Nations and governments to enable it to step up its work considerably.

There are certain things that could usefully be done to make the United Nations more effective:

(a) The provision of conciliation machinery that would automatically initiate discussions and mediation wherever the likelyhood of a conflict can be foreseen.

(b) Conciliation mechanism that would continue to operate during the existence of any conflict that is taking place.

(c) A United Nations mechanism to enable the receipt of complaints, and their investigation in all cases of allegations of violations of Humanitarian Laws in the course of armed conflicts.

(d) Full authority to the Secretary-General to send fact finding missions in any cases involving gross violations of human rights and in particular in cases involving the torture of prisoners.

(e) An extended compulsory jurisdiction for the International Court of Justice and a wider jurisdiction to pronounced advisory opinions.

These are not very far reaching reforms but I think that they would prove of value. Much more fundamental changes involving a surrender of partial sovereignty should also be envisaged at a later stage, particularly when General and Complete Disarmament is in sight.

IMPORTANCE OF VOLUNTARY ORGANISATIONS

By reason of higher educational standards and of the mass media, public opinion is now capable of influencing events more than ever before. In recent years the non-governmental organisations have been playing an increasingly important role. They are virtually the only independent voices that are heard and that can alert public opinion through the press and the media. The International Commission of Jurists and the International Association of Democratic Lawyers have rendered valuable services in the process of integrating human rights into the practical application of the Rule of Law. Amnesty International has succeeded in focusing attention very successfully on the torture of prisoners. These three organisations have also rendered invaluable humanitarian service by sending missions to areas wherein human rights were being violated and by sending observers to trials. In the field of *apartheid* the work of the Anti-Apartheid Associations coupled with that of the World Council of Churches has been of considerable value. In regard to Disarmament, the Society of Friends, the Women's International League for Peace and Freedom, the International Peace Bureau, the International Confederation for Disarmament and Peace and the World Peace Council have made all valuable contributions. In particular, special credit should be given to the Soviet Peace Council for its initiative in organising and hosting the World Congress of Peace Forces.

In my view the role of voluntary organisations is becoming more and more essential. They are the only bodies that will have the necessary independence and initiative to restore some faith and idealism in our world. They deserve a great deal more support and encouragement.

If disarmament can be achieved it will be due to the untiring selfless work of the non-governmental sector. This is what Alfred Nobel appreciated in his days. It is more urgent than ever now. The big powers are travelling on the dangerous road of armament. The signpost just ahead of us is "Oblivion". Can the march on this road be stopped? Yes, if public opinion uses the power it now has.

Eisaku Sato

EISAKU SATO*

1. Eisaku Sato was born on March 27, 1901 in Tabuse, Yamaguchi Prefecture, Japan.

In 1921, completing the course of senior high school, he entered Tokyo Imperial University (now Tokyo University) and majored in German jurisprudence.

In 1923, he passed the senior civil service examinations, and in the following year, upon graduating from the University, he joined the Ministry of Railways. In the Ministry, he held various important posts, such as Director of the Osaka Railways Bureau from 1944 to 1946 and Vice-Minister for Transportation from 1947 to 1948.

He married Hiroko Sato on February 23, 1926 and has two sons. The elder son, Ryutaro, is Managing Director of the Asian Drilling Co. Ltd. and the younger son, Shinji, is a member of the House of Councillors.

His hobbies include golf, fishing, and performing the traditional Japanese tea ceremony (chanoyu) with his wife.

2. His first contact with the political world was on his appointment to the post of Chief Cabinet Secretary of the second Yoshida Cabinet in 1948.

In 1949, he was elected to the House of Representatives and since then he has held the following Government and Party posts:

February 1949 to April 1950
  Chairman of the Policy Affairs Research
  Council of the Liberal Party
April 1950 to May 1951 and
January 1953 to July 1954
  Secretary General of the Liberal Party
July 1951 to July 1952
  Minister of Postal Services and Telecommunications
October 1952 to February 1953
  Minister of Construction and concurrently Minister of State in charge of
  Hokkaido Development
December 1957 to June 1958
  Chairman of the Executive Council of the Liberal Democratic Party
June 1958 to July 1960
  Minister of Finance
July 1961 to July 1962
  Minister of International Trade and Industry
July 1963 to June 1964
  Minister of State in charge of Hokkaido Development and concurrently

* Eisaku Sato died on June 3rd, 1975.

15—753278. *Les Prix Nobel en 1974*

Minister of State in charge of Science and Technology, Minister of State
in charge of the 18th Olympic Games
December 1964 to June 1972
President of the Liberal Democratic Party and Prime Minister.

THE PURSUIT OF PEACE AND JAPAN IN THE NUCLEAR AGE

Nobel Lecture, December 11, 1974

by

Eisaku Sato

Excellencies, Ladies and Gentlemen,

Having the exceptional honour to receive the Nobel Peace Prize, rich in tradition and honoured throughout the world, before such a distinguished assembly, was, indeed, the most memorable occasion of my life.

I believe that it is not upon me alone that this rare honour has been bestowed; the Japanese people share it with me. All through the years since World War II, the Japanese people have, I am convinced, made strenuous efforts to preserve and promote world peace, contributing to the progress and prosperity of mankind.

It is, therefore, on behalf of the Japanese people as well that I respectfully express my profound gratitude to the Nobel Committee of the Norwegian Parliament for their decision to award this prize to us. It is with great pride as a Japanese and with deep humility as an individual that I accepted this prize.

I have held the post of Prime Minister of Japan for one-third of the 22-year period since the San Francisco Peace Treaty entered into force. It seems to me that this is an appropriate opportunity to look back upon the Japanese people's opting for peace, and the efforts they have made to give substance to that decision.

If the attainment of peace is the ultimate objective of all statesmen, it is, at the same time, something very ordinary, closely tied to the daily life of each individual. In familiar terms, it is the condition that allows each individual and his family to pursue, without fear, the purpose of their lives. It is only in such circumstances that each individual will be able to devote himself, without the loss of hope for the future of mankind, to the education of his children, to an attempt to leave upon the history of mankind the imprint of his own creative and constructive achievements in the arts, culture, religion and other activities fulfilling social aspirations. This is the peace which is essential for all individuals, peoples, nations, and thus for the whole of humanity.

Though frequent turmoils vitiated life in other parts of the world during the two and half centuries from the beginning of the 17th century, Japan managed to live in tranquility in a state of isolation, neither threatening other nations nor threatened by them. It was only in the mid-nineteenth century that Japan, faced with the growing presence of European powers in Asia, abandoned its policy of isolation, and opened its doors to the outside world, and, with the Meiji Restoration, began to move towards the creation of a modern nation state.

Subsequently, the Japanese people experienced a variety of vicissitudes and were involved in international disputes, eventually, for the first time in their history, experiencing the horrors of modern warfare on their own soil during World War II. Japan is the only country in the world to have suffered the ravages of atomic bombing. That experience left an indelible mark on the hearts of our people, making them passionately determined to renounce all wars.

Fully conscious of the bitter lessons of defeat in 1945, and unswervingly determined to seek an enduring peace, our people revised the old Constitution. The new Constitution is founded on the principles of the protection of human rights on the one hand, and the renunciation of war on the other.

Article 9 of the Japanese Constitution stipulates as follows:

"Aspiring sincerely to an international peace based on justice and order, the Japanese people forever renounce war as a sovereign right of the nation and the threat or the use of force as means of settling international disputes."

Such a declaration renouncing the use of force in the settlement of international disputes, incorporating the philosophy of the Kellogg-Briand pact, has been made by peoples other than the Japanese. It is noteworthy, however, that a major power like Japan should have persevered in this direction by national consensus and be determined to retain this attitude in the future.

Japan has changed greatly during the thirty years since the period of confusion following defeat—rebuilding the nation's life and regaining its sovereign independence, with vigorous economic and social development complemented by scientific and technological progress in the sixties. In the meantime, our people made certain important choices.

The first among them was the spontaneous formation of a national consensus not to be armed with nuclear weapons. It has often been pointed out that, with the rise in the level of economic activity and the great strides made in science and technology, Japan has the capacity to produce nuclear arms. However, it is, in spite of Japan's potential, or precisely for that reason, that our people have, on their own initiative, made the firm choice not to be armed with nuclear weapons. This is also the firm policy of the Japanese Government. I wish to take this opportunity to declare this again unequivocally, and beg that my distinguished audience will bear this fact in mind.

It is only natural that for any statesman at the helm of any government the question of his country's security should be a concern of the utmost importance.

Upon assuming the reins of government, I adopted, always conscious of the importance of the role of the United Nations, a policy of following a formula of collective security based on the Charter of the United Nations for the maintenance of my country's security in the prevailing international situation. In the light of the circumstances in which my country was placed, this meant the maintenance of the Japan—U.S. Mutual Security and Cooperation Treaty which took effect in 1960. This treaty is not directed against any country but rather seeks to establish the basic conditions prerequisite for the maintenance of peace. This is the meaning of the treaty.

228

We, in the latter part of the 20th century, are, however, living in the nuclear age. I pointed out in a basic policy speech delivered in the National Diet early 1968, that the common task confronting all countries today is the question of how we are to survive this nuclear age.

I established three non-nuclear principles as a policy of the Japanese Government after deep reflection on the course Japan should take as a country which will not possess nuclear arms. This policy states that we shall not manufacture nuclear weapons, that we shall not possess them and that we shall not bring them into our country. This was later reaffirmed by a resolution of our Diet. I have no doubt that this policy will be pursued by all future governments.

It was also during my tenure of office that the Japanese Government agreed to the conclusion of a Nuclear Non-Proliferation Treaty and signed it, pursuing a policy in harmony with the avowed desire of the people. Under the terms of our Constitution, the assent of the Diet is required before ratification procedures can be completed; it is my desire to see these procedures completed with the least possible delay.

Thermo-nuclear energy, used as a means of warfare, has terrifying potential for destruction. In fact, the proliferation of nuclear weapons may well jeopardize the very survival of mankind. Nuclear disarmament has now become a matter of the utmost urgency. Consequently, it is gratifying that the Strategic Arms Limitation Talks between the United States and the Union of Soviet Socialist Republics have made a certain amount of progress.

Nevertheless, this progress represents only a freezing at present level. It is the earnest hope of our people that the world may see the day when all nuclear weapons are abolished. If I may, however, be allowed to put this in more realistic, if more modest, terms, the nuclear Powers, with the United States and the U.S.S.R. taking the lead, should, at least, cease their quantitative and qualitative nuclear arms race, and sincerely explore effective and practical means for the gradual reduction and international control of nuclear arms.

In this context, I wish to point out to the five nations which at present possess nuclear weapons that they have especially heavy responsibilities for assuring the peace and security of the world. The Japanese people hope most earnestly that constructive efforts will be made by these nuclear powers with a view to bringing about some epoch-making progress in nuclear arms control and disarmament.

II

The second achievement during my tenure of office that I should like to refer to was Japan's attainment of the reversion to Japan of the Ogasawara and Okinawa Islands.

The international order established at the end of World War II could certainly have been worse. However, this order did contain certain factors which bore within them the seeds of instability. The divided countries provide the most vivid example of this situation. Moreover, the fact that the majority of the divided countries in the world are in Asia indicates how global tensions might concentrate in that continent.

Under the Japanese Peace Treaty, signed in San Francisco in 1951, Okinawa and Ogasawara, integral parts of our national territory, were placed under the administration of the United States, with Japan retaining residual sovereignty. The fact of defeat obliged our country to acquiesce in this arrangement.

However, with the passing of time, the world gradually moved towards stability and prosperity, while our country regained sufficient economic and diplomatic potential to contribute to the progress and development of the community of nations. As these developments took place, the desire that the arrangements I have mentioned should be revised gradually gained ground in our national consciousness.

It was a clearly anomalous situation for one million Japanese people to be still under foreign domination more than twenty years after the termination of hostilities. The desire to see Okinawa returned to Japan developed into a broad national consensus among our people.

By that time, Okinawa had come to occupy a key strategic position in Asia in the framework of the Cold War. Nevertheless I declared soon after my assumption of office as Prime Minister my conviction that: "Until Okinawa is returned, Japan will not have completely emerged from her postwar period." For I had come to the conviction that to leave Okinawa in such an anomalous state would create greater tension in Asia because of the very important position of this group of islands and that to realize the reversion of Okinawa would contribute to a stable peace in the Western Pacific.

I came to be convinced that between countries like Japan and the United States, each with a democratic system and a high standard of living, it would, by means of peaceful negotiations, not be at all impossible to avoid a confrontation, even given considerable differences of interest. The negotiations on the reversion of Okinawa did indeed present a challenge. Fortunately, owing to the wisdom and foresight of its drafters, Article 3 of the San Francisco Peace Treaty left us with ways to obtain a readjustment.

In the light of the mutually shared basis of friendship and trust in the soundness of Japan—U.S. relations, and with the purpose of relaxing tensions in Asia, with the ultimate aim of achieving a stable world peace, I sought from the United States the return of Okinawa in the form of a peaceful alteration of the then-prevailing situation.

It cannot be said that these negotiations were easy. However, the United States, as a friendly country, lent a willing ear to the Japanese request. Finally, the great achievement of realizing the return of territory through diplomatic negotiations, an event rarely witnessed in world history, was achieved.

As a result of this political solution, peace and stability in the East Asian region surrounding Japan have been strengthened. Furthermore, the friendly relations existing between America and Japan, which are the key to this peace and stability, have been placed on an even firmer foundation. A situation had been created, moreover, which would serve as the basis for a gradual relaxation of tension with China.

It is my belief that the return of Okinawa is a shining example of a peaceful modification of the status quo and that it also contributed to the relaxation of tension in Asia, and to stability in the Western Pacific region. As for Japan, the return of Okinawa has served as a major factor in fostering political stability.

III

In the area of foreign relations, I have always sought to maintain friendly relations with all countries, indeed to improve them further. Prince Shotoku who lived from the end of the 6th century to the 7th century was a distinguished political leader of ancient Japan, as well as a great religious leader of the period when Buddhism was introduced into Japan. Japan's first constitution established by Prince Shotoku begins with the declaration "Harmony is the basic principle to be respected." This spirit is a national and popular ideal which has run throughout Japanese history.

As for myself, I have expressed this spirit of harmony in the words "magnanimity and harmony", making it one of the guiding principles of my political life. There is a favourite saying of mine: "Here I stand and there stand you; but we remain friends." It is only natural that people should differ. Nevertheless, all should accept these differences with tolerance and seek a way in which they can live together in peace through mutual understanding. This, indeed, is the moral principle which has guided me in the reality of politics. I am happy to say that it has the support of many people of good will in Japan and elsewhere.

This spirit, when applied in the fields of external relations, can develop into policies for the maintenance of peaceful and fraternal relations, whatever differences may exist among countries whose ideologies, social systems and policies differ.

Prompted by this spirit, I emphasized first and foremost the development of good-neighbour diplomacy in Asia. Depending on the countries and the problems involved, there were occasions when it was not easy to put this policy into practice. However, I never adopted a policy which meant that we looked upon a foreign country with hostility, and I always conducted myself with the utmost sincerity, always being ready for dialogue.

It was with this viewpoint in mind that I undertook in earnest, negotiations to normalize relations with the Republic of Korea soon after my assumption of office as Prime Minister. These negotiations encountered numerous difficulties, due largely to national feeling on the part of both the Japanese and Korean peoples, attributable to the historical fact of the past domination of Korea by Japan and to the reality of the Korean Peninsula being divided into two camps.

Nevertheless, the guiding spirit of equality and mutual advantage and the realistic approach of seeking to establish friendship with close neighbours first proved effective. In January, 1966, the Treaty on Basic Relations between Japan and the Republic of Korea and the related agreements became effective, thus solving a major pending issue in post-war Japanese diplomacy.

Now to look at Southeast Asia in the 1960s. The economy developed over the entire area at a comparatively steady pace, despite the grave problem of the Vietnam War which fortunately did not spread beyond the Indo-China Peninsula.

This progress was the fruit of the unceasing initiatives and efforts made by various countries under the wise leadership of their leaders. I believe that Japan was also able to make some contribution to this progress. Japan was in the forefront of the nations participating in the establishment of the Asian Development Bank in 1966, took an active part in the convening of the first Ministerial Conference for the Economic Development of Southeast Asia, and also participated in the Asian and Pacific Council. She, thus, made every effort to further the development of regional cooperation and mutual solidarity. The leaders of Southeast Asia rate highly the role our country has played in the non-military areas of the economy and technology. I believe we must continue this cooperation ever more actively in order to achieve tangible results. In addition, the activities of the Youth Overseas Cooperation Corps, whose members devote themselves to working hand-in-hand with and sweat alongside the local people for the improvement of the standard of living in developing countries, not only in Southeast Asia but throughout the developing world, greatly increased during my premiership.

I like to believe that, thanks to numerous opportunities for heart-to-heart talks with Asian leaders in order to deepen mutual understanding, I was able to contribute to the cultivation of friendly and good-neighbourly relations in our part of the world.

IV

By an interesting coincidence, my life began in 1901, the year in which the first Nobel Peace Prize was awarded. For 74 years the Nobel Prize has witnessed the bright and dark phases in the quest for world peace. During my lifetime, I have also shared the same experiences. Therefore, I feel that I might be allowed to venture some observations on one of the subjects confronting our contemporary civilization.

That subject is none other than the problem of the utilization of thermo-nuclear energy.

One of the aspects of thermo-nuclear energy is its massive, and potentially destructive, power. For this reason, this energy source could clearly pose a dire threat to humanity, depending on the manner in which it is used. Another aspect which cannot be denied is that it is a source of potentially limitless energy which could well open up new vistas for the civilization of tomorrow.

Today, humanity faces difficult challenges in such problems as population, food, natural resources, energy and the environment.

These are grave problems which could destroy peace in this world should we make mistaken choices in our efforts to find solutions. The discord among the advanced industrialized countries, the countries possessing natural resources and the developing countries is growing greater. Unless this difficulty is overcome by the promotion of new sources of energy, especially the peaceful use of nuclear energy, which could assure a stable supply of energy throughout the world, we shall come to an impasse.

However, this peaceful utilization of atomic energy confronts us with problems such as the disposal of waste materials and safety, and one has the impression that its development has come to a standstill. Such a standstill, however, is an unavoidable stage we must accept until technological innovation achieves a major breakthrough. I am convinced that so long as we maintain an unshakable confidence in the progress of science and technology, and provided the world's most brilliant minds are united in their efforts, humanity is capable of building a new civilization of untold possibilities for the future. However, research and development in nuclear fusion—which is considered to be the cleanest source of nuclear energy—face grave problems when reaching the stage of practical use, unless an international system and organization for research and cooperation is established.

Several years ago, I set down the three non-nuclear principles which gave concrete expression to the determination of the Japanese people to achieve peace. As I said before, this was because the entire nation is against the use of thermo-nuclear energy as a means of killing their fellow men.

However, I am entirely in favour of the peaceful utilization of nuclear energy. That is why I wish to express here today three views on the peaceful uses of this energy.

First of all, we need the creation of international safety standards. I believe that research and development in the peaceful use of nuclear energy should be carried on under common worldwide regulations that take environmental problems into account. One of the basic requirements for this is the establishment of internationally unified safety standards. I hope to see early progress in the establishment of such standards by the International Atomic Energy Agency, which is contributing effectively towards the promotion of the peaceful uses of atomic energy.

Next, an international agreement on the exchange and allocation of nuclear fuel will have to be concluded. In view of the trend towards a worldwide shortage of energy resources, there is the risk that at some time in the future an unbridled race for the acquisition of nuclear fuel may develop. Needless to say, such a development would be a threat to peace and detrimental to the well-being of mankind. Therefore, I believe that effective steps should be taken now, based upon a sound vision for the future.

In the light of the above, it would be most desirable to see the establishment of a system where, under the terms of an agreement to be concluded for the exchange and allocation of nuclear fuel, such fuels would be placed under the control of an international agency, which would see to it that countries needing fuel would be assured of a stable supply. However, an immediate issue upon which the development of the peaceful use of atomic energy hinges is an international agreement providing for, at the very least, mutual accomodation with regard to nuclear fuel needs.

Lastly, there is the problem of international cooperation in research and development work on nuclear fusion. The rapid development of a system for the effective use of thermo-nuclear energy seems to be beyond the capacity of a single nation, no matter how great its resources may be. I suppose that if we could bring together the greatest minds of the world, the time required to bring nuclear fusion into practical use might be considerably shortened, as against present predictions that such a breakthrough may require another twenty to thirty years.

Japan has reached an advanced stage in science and technology. I have no doubt that, should an international research facility be created, young and able brains from among us will gladly volunteer to participate in its work.

I would like to state the three points I have referred to as the "Three Principles for the Peaceful Uses of Nuclear Energy". For a considerable time now, warnings have been given of an approaching fossil fuel energy resources crisis. In spite of these warnings, only inadequate progress has been made in the peaceful uses of atomic energy. One of the reasons for this has been attributed to narrow-minded nationalism. It is true that nationalism has played a role as a symbol of the freedom and equality of each of the countries which make up the community of nations. Politically speaking, the historical role of nationalism has not as yet been played out in the world.

However, it is clear that, when looked at from the point of view of enlarging the future of mankind, narrow-minded and near-sighted nationalism does indeed hamper progress in the peaceful utilization of atomic energy. It certainly does not promote its progress. All peoples should be united in positive efforts to make peace a reality and to strengthen the foundations on which that peace rests so as to secure for all humanity progress and a better life.

V

I feel extremely fortunate to have been awarded the Nobel Peace Prize at this point in time, as a result of the decision of the distinguished members of the Peace Committee. I am deeply moved, because this means that my sustained efforts for peace over the years have received international recognition. However, when I look back on Japan's history, I am inclined to think that there were people in my country before me who worked for peace, whose achievements far exceeded my own, and who might have been worthier than I to receive the Peace Prize.

I am thinking not only of contributions to peace in the narrow sense of the term. I am convinced that our people, by dint of their ability and efforts, are intrinsically capable of making a great contribution to world civilization.

Had the Nobel Prize been established a thousand years ago, the first recipient of the Prize for Literature might well have been a Japanese woman. Also, had Japan taken part in the life of the international community several centuries earlier, Japanese recipients of the physics, chemistry, biology and economic science prizes might well have been numerous. At present, the Japanese recipients of Nobel Prizes, including myself, number only five. To me, it seems, this offers food for thought.

I say this because Japanese history and culture have followed very unique paths. It is a fact that, because of our long isolation from other nations, we suffer from social awkwardness and we as a people have been unable to contribute actively to world civilization in a measure commensurate with our potential. We should, I think, reflect deeply on the unfortunate inadequacy of our efforts to influence, or, rather, to communicate with, the peoples of the world. Especially in recent times, in our haste to absorb Western civilization and culture, we have been somewhat deficient, I fear, in our efforts to let foreign nations know about our own civilization and culture.

Japan is basically a difficult nation to understand because the foundation of our culture differs so much from those of the West and of other Asian countries. Because this was so, we should have tried to make ourselves better understood. I cannot but admit that at a time when international understanding was required, our efforts to promote such understanding were inadequate.

When I think of the geniuses and great men of our country who failed to obtain international recognition, I feel all the more fortunate to have been accorded this precious Prize. At the same time, I feel deeply the need to increase our own efforts to promote better international understanding.

I intend to make this award culturally meaningful. I, therefore, plan to use the prize I received to further the links between our country and the rest of the world.

The intention of Alfred Nobel in instituting the Nobel Prizes in his will was undoubtedly to promote peaceful relations among nations. I should like to stress that for my part, following in Alfred Nobel's steps, I shall devote myself to increasing still more my people's capacity to contribute to the well-being of the international community, and to obtaining the world's understanding for such efforts.

Thank you.

LE PRIX
EN MÉMOIRE
D'ALFRED NOBEL

EN 1974

INSTITUTION

Lors de son tricentenaire en 1968, LA BANQUE DE SUÈDE fit une donation à la FONDATION NOBEL pour décerner, par l'intermédiaire de l'ACADÉMIE ROYALE DES SCIENCES, un *Prix de sciences économiques en mémoire d'Alfred Nobel*.

Les status de la distribution du prix sont, mutatis mutandis, les mêmes que pour les Prix Nobel. La remise du prix doit avoir lieu à la cérémonie Nobel le 10 décembre en même temps que celle des Prix Nobel.

Le montant du prix correspond à celui du Prix Nobel de l'année. Un diplôme particulier ainsi qu'une médaille d'or sont remis à cette occasion.

En 1974, le Comité chargé de préparer les affaires était composé des membres suivants :

MM. B. OHLIN, anc. professeur de sciences économiques, *président du Comité;* E. LUNDBERG, professeur de sciences économiques; H. WOLD, professeur de statistique; A. LINDBECK, professeur de sciences économiques et bancaires; S. CARLSON, professeur de gestion des entreprises; *secrétaire du Comité :* M. R. BENTZEL, professeur de sciences économiques.

ATTRIBUTION DU PRIX

L'ACADÉMIE ROYALE DES SCIENCES

a décidé, le 9 octobre 1974, d'attribuer la moitié du Prix de Sciences Économiques institué en mémoire d'Alfred Nobel à

GUNNAR MYRDAL
de Suède,
et l'autre moitié à

FRIEDRICH VON HAYEK
d'Angleterre,

pour leurs travaux novateurs de théorie monétaire et de théorie des conjonctures ainsi que pour leurs analyses pénétrantes de l'interdépendance des facteurs économiques, sociaux et institutionnels.

Le nombre de propositions statutaires de candidatures s'est monté à 52.

LES INSIGNES ET LE MONTANT DU PRIX

Les lauréats ont reçu un *diplôme,* une *médaille* et un *document* indiquant le montant du prix.

Le montant du prix en mémoire d'Alfred Nobel comme celui des Prix Nobel s'élève à 550 000 couronnes suédoises.

Les diplômes aux lauréats de sciences économiques en mémoire d'Alfred Nobel G. Myrdal et F. A. von Hayek sont exécutés par l'artiste peintre suédois Karl-Axel Pehrson.

Commentaires aux images des diplômes :

Gunnar Myrdal
Une végétation luxuriante sur le fond d'un lac paisible qui reflète un paysage tropical, symbolisant l'engagement du lauréat dans les régions en voie de développement.

Friedrich von Hayek
Une termitière sur le fond d'un paysage lacustre verdoyant et entourée d'une végétation florale abondante, symbolisant la structure, l'économie et le travail de la société humaine. La termitière porte au sommet un œuf décoré de monnaies d'or.

F. A. von Hayek

Gunnar Myrdal

THE PRIZE FOR ECONOMIC SCIENCE, IN MEMORY OF ALFRED NOBEL

Speech by Professor ERIK LUNDBERG of the Royal Academy of Sciences
Translation from the Swedish text

Your Majesty, Your Royal Highnesses, Ladies and Gentlemen,

Hitherto the prize in Economic Science dedicated to the memory of Alfred Nobel has been awarded to researchers who have made pioneering contributions in what may be called "pure" economics. It has been awarded for work on economic theory at a high, abstract level with the theory of general equilibrium as the starting point, for work on analytical techniques on the basis of theoretical models with the aim of achieving quantitative precision of various relations and, finally, for work on historical-statistical analysis of economic development during long and short periods. However, there are prominent researchers in the field of the social sciences whose range of interests covers other and wider areas than those embraced by the term "pure economics". Among these prominent researchers are this year's prize winners, Professors Myrdal and Hayek.

Professors Myrdal and Hayek both began their careers with important contributions in pure economic theory. To a great extent their early work (during the 1920s and 30s) lay within the same field: business-cycle theory and monetary theory. But thereafter both Myrdal and Hayek greatly extended their range in order to deal with problems which cannot be studied only within a narrow economic framework. The need felt by both Myrdal and Hayek to expand the range of problems studied and the methodology applied is tellingly expressed in the following quotation from Hayek: "But nobody can be a great economist who is only an economist—and I am even tempted to add that the economist who is only an economist is likely to become a nuisance if not a positive danger".

Although these two economists have thus broadened their scope to cover more than purely economic problems, this does not mean that they have pursued the same line of development. Myrdal has, above all by directing his attention mainly to social problems (in the widest sense), especially as regards the negro question in the U.S.A. and the poverty of the underdeveloped countries, attempted to integrate economic analysis with a high measure of attention to social, demographic and institutional conditions. Hayek has extended his field of interest so as to take in the legal framework of the economic system and psychological-philosophical questions concerning the way in which individuals, organizations and different social systems work. Both scholars have shown a dominating interest in problems of economic policy, including possible changes in the organizational, institutional and legal structure of society. Here Myrdal has usually advocated reforms of a radical and unconventional kind, whereas Hayek has looked for ways of enhancing the viability of a liberal, individualistically orientated social system. These politically-coloured differences, however, are altogether subordinated to a common attitude towards social science research: the conviction that the major socio-economic questions of our time cannot be fully understood without an interdisciplinary broadening of the range of problems studied as well as of the methodology applied.

It is above all in the great work *An American Dilemma. The Negro Problem and Modern Democracy* that Myrdal has proved his eminent ability to combine economic analysis with a wide social science approach in studying the series of factors and relations which may determine the situation of the negro population and its possibilities of development. In order to support his analysis of the social situation of the negro population Myrdal makes use in a fruitful way of economic equilibrium models and of dynamic analysis of cumulative processes that follow from disturbances. He draws attention to the interdependence between a large number of economic and social factors and shows how cumulative processes of deterioration can arise ("vicious circles"), making it impossible to point to particular factors as "final causes". In fact Myrdal has in this work accomplished a many-faceted analysis of strategic factors which influence all underdevelopment (education, health, living conditions, job satisfaction, discriminatory attitudes on the part of employers and trade unions), factors which were not taken into account in the analytical models of the economists until the 1960s. The book has become a classic, and in addition has had an exceptional impact in the course of the years on American opinion and policies as far as the negro question is concerned.

It can be maintained that Myrdal's extensive contributions to the study of the problems of underdeveloped countries have to a considerable extent been of the same character as in *An American Dilemma*. Again it is a question of social science research in the widest sense, research where great importance is attached to political, institutional, demographic, educational and health factors. On a number of points Myrdal's ideas and research results have been of importance for the public debate on underdeveloped countries; this applies, for example, to the conceptions regarding the character and causes of unemployment, the nature of the inefficiency of farming, in particular in India, the way in which the diffusion effects from industrial development in a given country are functions of that country's cultural, social and economic levels, and, finally, the importance of social discipline.

Hayek's contributions in the fields of economic theory are both deep-probing and original. His scholarly books and articles during the 1920s and 30s sparked off an extremely lively debate. It was in particular his *theory of business cycles* and his conception of the effects of monetary and credit policy which aroused attention. He attempted to penetrate more deeply into cyclical interrelations than was usual during that period by bringing considerations of capital and structural theory into the analysis. Perhaps in part because of this deepening of business-cycle analysis, Hayek was one of the few economists who were able to foresee the risk of a major economic crisis in the 1920s, his warnings in fact being uttered well before the great collapse occurred in the autumn of 1929.

It is above all the analysis of the viability of different economic systems which is among Professor Hayek's most important contributions to social science research. From the middle of the 1930s onwards, he devoted increasing attention to the problems of socialist central planning. In this area, as in all others to which Hayek has devoted research, he presented a detailed exposition of ideas and conceptions in this field. He evolved new approaches in his examination of fundamental difficulties in "socialist calculation" and investigated the possibilities of achieving effective results through decentralized "market socialism". His guiding criterion in assessing the viability of different systems refers to the efficiency with which these systems utilize the knowledge and information spread among the great mass of individuals and enterprises. His conclusion is that it is only through a far-reaching decentralization in a market system with competition and free price formation that it is possible to achieve an efficient use of all this knowledge and information. Hayek shows how *prices* as such are the carriers of essential information on cost and demand conditions, how the price system is a mechanism for communication of knowledge and information, and how this system can mean an efficient use of highly decentralized resources of knowledge.

Hayek's ideas and analyses of the viability of economic systems, presented in a number of writings, have provided important and stimulating impulses to the great and growing area of research which is named comparative economic systems.

Thus, after their work in central economic theory, Professors Myrdal and Hayek have carried out important interdisciplinary research. The Royal Swedish Academy of Sciences has therefore decided to award the Prize in Economic Science in Memory of Alfred Nobel for 1974 in equal shares to Professor Gunnar Myrdal and Professor Friedrich August von Hayek *for their pioneering work in the theory of money and economic fluctuations and for their penetrating analysis of the interdependence of economic, social and institutional phenomena.*

It is a great honour for me to convey to both of you the congratulations of the Royal Swedish Academy of Sciences and to ask you, Professor Myrdal and Professor von Hayek, to accept from the hand of His Majesty the King the 1974 Prize in Economic Science dedicated to the memory of Alfred Nobel.

FRIEDRICH AUGUST VON HAYEK

Born Vienna 8 May 1899 as son of Dr. August von Hayek, Professor of Botany at the University of Vienna and Felicitas née Juraschek.

Gymnasium at Vienna.

War service in Austro Hungarian Army (Italian Front) 1917—1918.

Study at University of Vienna 1918—1921, Dr. jur. 1921, Dr. rer. pol 1923. In Austrian government service as legal consultant in temporary office for carrying out provisions of Peace Treaty, 1921—1926, interrupted by post-graduate work at New York University, March 1923—June 1924.

1927—1931 Director, Österreichisches Institut für Konjunkturforschung (Austrian Institute for Trade Cycle Research) 1927—1931, from 1929 to 1931 also Lecturer (Privatdozent) in Economics and Statistics, University of Vienna.

1931—1950 Tooke Professor of Economic Science and Statistics, University of London (London School of Economics and Political Science).

1950—1962 Professor of Social and Moral Science, University of Chicago (Committee on Social Thought).

1962—1968 Professor der Volkswirtschaftslehre at the Albert Ludwig Universität at Freiburg im Breisgau.

At various dates visiting Professor at the Universities of Stanford, Arkansas, Virginia, California (Los Angeles), Cape Town and Salzburg.

Fellow British Academy 1944.

Korrespondierendes Mitglied der Österreichischen Akademie der Wissenschaften, 1970.

Dr. jur.h.c. Rikkyo University, Tokyo, 1964, Universität Salzburg 1974.

Ehrensenator der Universität Wien, 1971.

Honorary Fellow, London School of Economics, 1972.

Books Published

Geldtheorie und Konjunkturtheorie, Wien 1929, also in English as *Monetary Theory and the Trade Cycle,* London 1933 as well as in Spanish and Japanese translations.

Prices and Production, London 1931, also in German, Chinese, French and Japanese translations.

Monetary Nationalism and International Stability, London 1937.

Profits, Interest, and Investment, London 1939.

The Pure Theory of Capital, London 1940, also in Japanese and Spanish translations.

The Road to Serfdom, London and Chicago 1944, also in Chinese, Danish, Dutch, French, German, Italian, Japanese, Norwegian, Portuguese, Spanish and Swedish translations.

Individualism and Economic Order, London and Chicago 1949, also in German and an abridged Norwegian translation.

John Stuart Mill and Harriet Taylor, London and Chicago 1951.

The Counter-Revolution of Science, Chicago 1952, also in German, Italian and an abridged French translation.

The Sensory Order, London and Chicago 1952.

The Constitution of Liberty, London and Chicago 1960, also in Spanish, German and Italian translations.

Studies in Philosophy, Politics, and Economics, London and Chicago 1967.

Freiburger Studien, Tübingen 1969.

Law, Legislation and Liberty, vol. I, Rules and Order, London and Chicago 1973.

Edited by F. A. Hayek:

Beiträge zur Geldtheorie, Wien 1931.

Collectivist Economic Planning, London 1935, also in French and Italian translations.

Capitalism and the Historians, London and Chicago 1954, also in Italian translation.

THE PRETENCE OF KNOWLEDGE

Nobel Memorial Lecture, December 11, 1974

by

Friedrich August von Hayek

Salzburg, Austria

The particular occasion of this lecture, combined with the chief practical problem which economists have to face today, have made the choice of its topic almost inevitable. On the one hand the still recent establishment of the Nobel Memorial Prize in Economic Science marks a significant step in the process by which, in the opinion of the general public, economics has been conceded some of the dignity and prestige of the physical sciences. On the other hand, the economists are at this moment called upon to say how to extricate the free world from the serious threat of accelerating inflation which, it must be admitted, has been brought about by policies which the majority of economists recommended and even urged governments to pursue. We have indeed at the moment little cause for pride: as a profession we have made a mess of things.

It seems to me that this failure of the economists to guide policy more successfully is closely connected with their propensity to imitate as closely as possible the procedures of the brilliantly successful physical sciences—an attempt which in our field may lead to outright error. It is an approach which has come to be described as the "scientistic" attitude—an attitude which, as I defined it some thirty years ago, "is decidedly unscientific in the true sense of the word, since it involves a mechanical and uncritical application of habits of thought to fields different from those in which they have been formed."[1] I want today to begin by explaining how some of the gravest errors of recent economic policy are a direct consequence of this scientistic error.

The theory which has been guiding monetary and financial policy during the last thirty years, and which I contend is largely the product of such a mistaken conception of the proper scientific procedure, consists in the assertion that there exists a simple positive correlation between total employment and the size of the aggregate demand for goods and services; it leads to the belief that we can permanently assure full employment by maintaining total money expenditure at an appropriate level. Among the various theories advanced to account for extensive unemployment, this is probably the only one in support of which strong quantitative evidence can be adduced. I nevertheless regard it

---

[1] "Scientism and the Study of Society", *Economica*, vol. IX, no. 35, August 1942, reprinted in *The Counter-Revolution of Science*, Glencoe, Ill., 1952, p. 15 of this reprint.

as fundamentally false, and to act upon it, as we now experience, as very harmful.

This brings me to the crucial issue. Unlike the position that exists in the physical sciences, in economics and other disciplines that deal with essentially complex phenomena, the aspects of the events to be accounted for about which we can get quantitative data are necessarily limited and may not include the important ones. While in the physical sciences it is generally assumed, probably with good reason, that any important factor which determines the observed events will itself be directly observable and measurable, in the study of such complex phenomena as the market, which depend on the actions of many individuals, all the circumstances which will determine the outcome of a process, for reasons which I shall explain later, will hardly ever be fully known or measurable. And while in the physical sciences the investigator will be able to measure what, on the basis of a *prima facie* theory, he thinks important, in the social sciences often that is treated as important which happens to be accessible to measurement. This is sometimes carried to the point where it is demanded that our theories must be formulated in such terms that they refer only to measurable magnitudes.

It can hardly be denied that such a demand quite arbitrarily limits the facts which are to be admitted as possible causes of the events which occur in the real world. This view, which is often quite naively accepted as required by scientific procedure, has some rather paradoxical consequences. We know, of course, with regard to the market and similar social structures, a great many facts which we cannot measure and on which indeed we have only some very imprecise and general information. And because the effects of these facts in any particular instance cannot be confirmed by quantitative evidence, they are simply disregarded by those sworn to admit only what they regard as scientific evidence: they thereupon happily proceed on the fiction that the factors which they can measure are the only ones that are relevant.

The correlation between aggregate demand and total employment, for instance, may only be approximate, but as it is the *only* one on which we have quantitative data, it is accepted as the only causal connection that counts. On this standard there may thus well exist better "scientific" evidence for a false theory, which will be accepted because it is more "scientific", than for a valid explanation, which is rejected because there is no sufficient quantitative evidence for it.

Let me illustrate this by a brief sketch of what I regard as the chief actual cause of extensive unemployment—an account which will also explain why such unemployment cannot be lastingly cured by the inflationary policies recommended by the now fashionable theory. This correct explanation appears to me to be the existence of discrepancies between the distribution of demand among the different goods and services and the allocation of labour and other resources among the production of those outputs. We possess a fairly good "qualitative" knowledge of the forces by which a correspondence between demand and supply in the different sectors of the economic system is brought about, of the conditions under which it will be achieved, and of the factors likely to prevent such an adjustment. The separate steps in the account of this process rely on facts of everyday experience, and few who take the trouble to follow the argument will question the validity of the factual assumptions, or the logical correctness of the conclusions drawn from them. We have indeed good reason to believe that unemployment indicates that the structure of relative prices and wages has been distorted (usually by monopolistic or governmental price fixing), and that to restore equality between the demand and the supply of labour in all sectors changes of relative prices and some transfers of labour will be necessary.

But when we are asked for quantitative evidence for the particular structure of prices and wages that would be required in order to assure a smooth continuous sale of the products and services offered, we must admit that we have no such information. We know, in other words, the general conditions in which what we call, somewhat misleadingly, an equilibrium will establish itself: but we never know what the particular prices or wages are which would exist if the market were to bring about such an equilibrium. We can merely say what the conditions are in which we can expect the market to establish prices and wages at which demand will equal supply. But we can never produce statistical information which would show how much the prevailing prices and wages *deviate* from those which would secure a continuous sale of the current supply of labour. Though this account of the causes of unemployment is an empirical theory, in the sense that it might be proved false, e.g. if, with a constant money supply, a general increase of wages did not lead to unemployment, it is certainly not the kind of theory which we could use to obtain specific numerical predictions concerning the rates of wages, or the distribution of labour, to be expected.

Why should we, however, in economics, have to plead ignorance of the sort of facts on which, in the case of a physical theory, a scientist would certainly be expected to give precise information? It is probably not surprising that those impressed by the example of the physical sciences should find this position very unsatisfactory and should insist on the standards of proof which they find there. The reason for this state of affairs is the fact, to which I have already briefly referred, that the social sciences, like much of biology but unlike most fields of the physical sciences, have to deal with structures of *essential* complexity, i.e. with structures whose characteristic properties can be exhibited only by models made up of relatively large numbers of variables. Competition, for instance, is a process which will produce certain results only if it proceeds among a fairly large number of acting persons.

In some fields, particularly where problems of a similar kind arise in the physical sciences, the difficulties can be overcome by using, instead of specific information about the individual elements, data about the relative frequency, or the probability, of the occurrence of the various distinctive properties of the elements. But this is true only where we have to deal with what has been called by Dr. Warren Weaver (formerly of the Rockefeller Foundation), with a distinction which ought to be much more widely understood, "phenomena of unorganized complexity," in contrast to those "phenomena of organized complexity" with which we have to deal in the social sciences.[2] Organized complexity here means that the character of the structures showing it depends not only on the properties of the individual elements of which they are composed, and the relative frequency with which they occur, but also on the manner in which the individual elements are connected with each other. In the explanation of the working of such structures we can for this reason not replace the information about the individual elements by statistical information, but require full information about each element if from our theory we are to derive specific predictions about individual events. Without such specific information about the individual elements we shall be confined to what on another occasion I have called mere pattern predictions—predictions of some of the general attributes of the structures that will form themselves, but not containing specific statements about the individual elements of which the structures will be made up.[3]

This is particularly true of our theories accounting for the determination of the systems of relative prices and wages that will form themselves on a well-functioning market. Into the determination of these prices and wages there will enter the effects of particular information possessed by every one of the participants in the market process—a sum of facts which in their totality cannot be known to the scientific observer, or to any other single brain. It is indeed the source of the superiority of the market order, and the reason why, when it is not suppressed by the powers of government, it regularly displaces other types of order, that in the resulting allocation of resources more of the knowledge of particular facts will be utilized which exists only dispersed among uncounted persons, than any one person can possess. But because we, the observing scientists, can thus never know all the determinants of such an order, and in consequence also cannot know at which particular structure of prices and wages demand would everywhere equal supply, we also cannot measure the deviations from that order; nor can we statistically test our theory that it is the deviations from that "equilibrium" system of prices and wages which make it impossible to sell some of the products and services at the prices at which they are offered.

Before I continue with my immediate concern, the effects of all this on the employment policies currently pursued, allow me to define more specifically the inherent limitations of our numerical knowledge which are so often overlooked. I want to do this to avoid giving the impression that I generally reject the mathematical method in economics. I regard it in fact as the great advantage of the mathematical technique that it allows us to describe, by means of algebraic equations, the general character of a pattern even where we are ignorant of the numerical values which will determine its particular mani-

---

[2] Warren Weaver, "A Quarter Century in the Natural Sciences", *The Rockefeller Foundation Annual Report 1958,* chapter I, "Science and Complexity".

[3] See my essay "The Theory of Complex Phenomena" in *The Critical Approach to Science and Philosophy. Essays in Honor of K. R. Popper,* ed. M. Bunge, New York 1964, and reprinted (with additions) in my *Studies in Philosophy, Politics and Economics,* London and Chicago 1967.

festation. We could scarcely have achieved that comprehensive picture of the mutual interdependencies of the different events in a market without this algebraic technique. It has led to the illusion, however, that we can use this technique for the determination and prediction of the numerical values of those magnitudes; and this has led to a vain search for quantitative or numerical constants. This happened in spite of the fact that the modern founders of mathematical economics had no such illusions. It is true that their systems of equations describing the pattern of a market equilibrium are so framed that *if* we were able to fill in all the blanks of the abstract formulae, i.e. *if* we knew all the parameters of these equations, we could calculate the prices and quantities of all commodities and services sold. But, as Vilfredo Pareto, one of the founders of this theory, clearly stated, its purpose cannot be "to arrive at a numerical calculation of prices", because, as he said, it would be "absurd" to assume that we could ascertain all the data.[4] Indeed, the chief point was already seen by those remarkable anticipators of modern economics, the Spanish schoolmen of the sixteenth century, who emphasized that what they called *pretium mathematicum*, the mathematical price, depended on so many particular circumstances that it could never be known to man but was known only to God.[5] I sometimes wish that our mathematical economists would take this to heart. I must confess that I still doubt whether their search for measurable magnitudes has made significant contributions to our *theoretical* understanding of economic phenomena—as distinct from their value as a description of particular situations. Nor am I prepared to accept the excuse that this branch of research is still very young: Sir William Petty, the founder of econometrics, was after all a somewhat senior colleague of Sir Isaac Newton in the Royal Society!

There may be few instances in which the superstition that only measurable magnitudes can be important has done positive harm in the economic field: but the present inflation and employment problems are a very serious one. Its effect has been that what is probably the true cause of extensive unemployment has been disregarded by the scientistically minded majority of economists, because its operation could not be confirmed by directly observable relations between measurable magnitudes, and that an almost exclusive concentration on quantitatively measurable surface phenomena has produced a policy which has made matters worse.

It has, of course, to be readily admitted that the kind of theory which I regard as the true explanation of unemployment is a theory of somewhat limited content because it allows us to make only very general predictions of the *kind* of events which we must expect in a given situation. But the effects on policy of the more ambitious constructions have not been very fortunate and I confess that I prefer true but imperfect knowledge, even if it leaves much indetermined and unpredictable, to a pretence of exact knowledge that is

[4] V. Pareto, *Manuel d'économie politique,* 2nd. ed., Paris 1927, pp. 223—4.
[5] See, e.g., Luis Molina, *De iustitia et iure,* Cologne 1596—1600, tom. II, disp. 347, no. 3, and particularly Johannes de Lugo, *Disputationum de iustitia et iure tomus secundus,* Lyon 1642, disp. 26, sect. 4, no. 40.

likely to be false. The credit which the apparent conformity with recognized scientific standards can gain for seemingly simple but false theories may, as the present instance shows, have grave consequences.

In fact, in the case discussed, the very measures which the dominant "macro-economic" theory has recommended as a remedy for unemployment, namely the increase of aggregate demand, have become a cause of a very extensive misallocation of resources which is likely to make later large-scale unemployment inevitable. The continuous injection of additional amounts of money at points of the economic system where it creates a temporary demand which must cease when the increase of the quantity of money stops or slows down, together with the expectation of a continuing rise of prices, draws labour and other resources into employments which can last only so long as the increase of the quantity of money continues at the same rate—or perhaps even only so long as it continues to accelerate at a given rate. What this policy has produced is not so much a level of employment that could not have been brought about in other ways, as a distribution of employment which cannot be indefinitely maintained and which after some time can be maintained only by a rate of inflation which would rapidly lead to a disorganisation of all economic activity. The fact is that by a mistaken theoretical view we have been led into a precarious position in which we cannot prevent substantial unemployment from re-appearing; not because, as this view is sometimes mis-represented, this unemployment is deliberately brought about as a means to combat inflation, but because it is now bound to occur as a deeply regrettable but inescapable consequence of the mistaken policies of the past as soon as inflation ceases to accelerate.

I must, however, now leave these problems of immediate practical importance which I have introduced chiefly as an illustration of the momentous conse-quences that may follow from errors concerning abstract problems of the philosophy of science. There is as much reason to be apprehensive about the long run dangers created in a much wider field by the uncritical acceptance of assertions which have the *appearance* of being scientific as there is with regard to the problems I have just discussed. What I mainly wanted to bring out by the topical illustration is that certainly in my field, but I believe also generally in the sciences of man, what looks superficially like the most scientific procedure is often the most unscientific, and, beyond this, that in these fields there are definite limits to what we can expect science to achieve. This means that to entrust to science—or to deliberate control according to scientific principles—more than scientific method can achieve may have deplorable effects. The progress of the natural sciences in modern times has of course so much exceeded all expectations that any suggestion that there may be some limits to it is bound to arouse suspicion. Especially all those will resist such an insight who have hoped that our increasing power of prediction and control, generally regarded as the characteristic result of scientific advance, applied to the processes of society, would soon enable us to mould society entirely to our liking. It is indeed true that, in contrast to the exhilaration which the discoveries of the physical sciences tend to produce, the insights

254

which we gain from the study of society more often have a dampening effect on our aspirations; and it is perhaps not surprising that the more impetuous younger members of our profession are not always prepared to accept this. Yet the confidence in the unlimited power of science is only too often based on a false belief that the scientific method consists in the application of a ready-made technique, or in imitating the form rather than the substance of scientific procedure, as if one needed only to follow some cooking recipes to solve all social problems. It sometimes almost seems as if the techniques of science were more easily learnt than the thinking that shows us what the problems are and how to approach them.

The conflict between what in its present mood the public expects science to achieve in satisfaction of popular hopes and what is really in its power is a serious matter because, even if the true scientists should all recognize the limitations of what they can do in the field of human affairs, so long as the public expects more there will always be some who will pretend, and perhaps honestly believe, that they can do more to meet popular demands than is really in their power. It is often difficult enough for the expert, and certainly in many instances impossible for the layman, to distinguish between legitimate and illegitimate claims advanced in the name of science. The enormous publicity recently given by the media to a report pronouncing in the name of science on *The Limits to Growth,* and the silence of the same media about the devastating criticism this report has received from the competent experts[6], must make one feel somewhat apprehensive about the use to which the prestige of science can be put. But it is by no means only in the field of economics that far-reaching claims are made on behalf of a more scientific direction of all human activities and the desirability of replacing spontaneous processes by "conscious human control". If I am not mistaken, psychology, psychiatry and some branches of sociology, not to speak about the so-called philosophy of history, are even more affected by what I have called the scientistic prejudice, and by specious claims of what science can achieve.[7]

If we are to safeguard the reputation of science, and to prevent the arrogation of knowledge based on a superficial similarity of procedure with that of the physical sciences, much effort will have to be directed toward debunking such arrogations, some of which have by now become the vested interests of established university departments. We cannot be grateful enough to such modern philosophers of science as Sir Karl Popper for giving us a

---

[6] See *The Limits to Growth: A Report of the Club of Rome's Project on the Predicament of Mankind,* New York 1972; for a systematic examination of this by a competent economist cf. Wilfred Beckerman, *In Defence of Economic Growth,* London 1974, and, for a list of earlier criticisms by experts, Gottfried Haberler, *Economic Growth and Stability,* Los Angeles 1974, who rightly calls their effect "devastating".

[7] I have given some illustrations of these tendencies in other fields in my inaugural lecture as Visiting Professor at the University of Salzburg, *Die Irrtümer des Konstruktivismus und die Grundlagen legitimer Kritik gesellschaftlicher Gebilde,* Munich 1970, now re-issued for the Walter Eucken Institute, at Freiburg i.Brg. by J. C. B. Mohr, Tübingen 1975.

test by which we can distinguish between what we may accept as scientific and what not—a test which I am sure some doctrines now widely accepted as scientific would not pass. There are some special problems, however, in connection with those essentially complex phenomena of which social structures are so important an instance, which make me wish to restate in conclusion in more general terms the reasons why in these fields not only are there only absolute obstacles to the prediction of specific events, but why to act as if we possessed scientific knowledge enabling us to transcend them may itself become a serious obstacle to the advance of the human intellect.

The chief point we must remember is that the great and rapid advance of the physical sciences took place in fields where it proved that explanation and prediction could be based on laws which accounted for the observed phenomena as functions of comparatively few variables—either particular facts or relative frequencies of events. This may even be the ultimate reason why we single out these realms as "physical" in contrast to those more highly organized structures which I have here called essentially complex phenomena. There is no reason why the position must be the same in the latter as in the former fields. The difficulties which we encounter in the latter are not, as one might at first suspect, difficulties about formulating theories for the explanation of the observed events—although they cause also special difficulties about testing proposed explanations and therefore about eliminating bad theories. They are due to the chief problem which arises when we apply our theories to any particular situation in the real world. A theory of essentially complex phenomena must refer to a large number of particular facts; and to derive a prediction from it, or to test it, we have to ascertain all these particular facts. Once we succeeded in this there should be no particular difficulty about deriving testable predictions—with the help of modern computers it should be easy enough to insert these data into the appropriate blanks of the theoretical formulae and to derive a prediction. The real difficulty, to the solution of which science has little to contribute, and which is sometimes indeed insoluble, consists in the ascertainment of the particular facts.

A simple example will show the nature of this difficulty. Consider some ball game played by a few people of approximately equal skill. If we knew a few particular facts in addition to our general knowledge of the ability of the individual players, such as their state of attention, their perceptions and the state of their hearts, lungs, muscles etc. at each moment of the game, we could probably predict the outcome. Indeed, if we were familiar both with the game and the teams we should probably have a fairly shrewd idea on what the outcome will depend. But we shall of course not be able to ascertain those facts and in consequence the result of the game will be outside the range of the scientifically predictable, however well we may know what effects particular events would have on the result of the game. This does not mean that we can make no predictions at all about the course of such a game. If we know the rules of the different games we shall, in watching one, very soon know which game is being played and what kinds of actions we can expect and what kind not. But our capacity to predict will be confined to such general characteristics of the events to be expected and not include the capacity of predicting particular individual events.

This corresponds to what I have called earlier the mere pattern predictions to which we are increasingly confined as we penetrate from the realm in which relatively simple laws prevail into the range of phenomena where organized complexity rules. As we advance we find more and more frequently that we can in fact ascertain only some but not all the particular circumstances which determine the outcome of a given process; and in consequence we are able to predict only some but not all the properties of the result we have to expect. Often all that we shall be able to predict will be some abstract characteristic of the pattern that will appear—relations between kinds of elements about which individually we know very little. Yet, as I am anxious to repeat, we will still achieve predictions which can be falsified and which therefore are of empirical significance.

Of course, compared with the precise predictions we have learnt to expect in the physical sciences, this sort of mere pattern predictions is a second best with which one does not like to have to be content. Yet the danger of which I want to warn is precisely the belief that in order to have a claim to be accepted as scientific it is necessary to achieve more. This way lies charlatanism and worse. To act on the belief that we possess the knowledge and the power which enable us to shape the processes of society entirely to our liking, knowledge which in fact we do *not* possess, is likely to make us do much harm. In the physical sciences there may be little objection to trying to do the impossible; one might even feel that one ought not to discourage the over-confident because their experiments may after all produce some new insights. But in the social field the erroneous belief that the exercise of some power would have beneficial consequences is likely to lead to a new power to coerce other men being confered on some authority. Even if such power is not in itself bad, its exercise is likely to impede the functioning of those spontaneous ordering forces by which, without understanding them, man is in fact so largely assisted in the pursuit of his aims. We are only beginning to understand on how subtle a communication system the functioning of an advanced industrial society is based—a communications system which we call the market and which turns out to be a more efficient mechanism for digesting dispersed information than any that man has deliberately designed.

If man is not to do more harm than good in his efforts to improve the social order, he will have to learn that in this, as in all other fields where essential complexity of an organized kind prevails, he cannot acquire the full knowledge which would make mastery of the events possible. He will therefore have to use what knowledge he can achieve, not to shape the results as the craftsman shapes his handiwork, but rather to cultivate a growth by providing the appropriate environment, in the manner in which the gardener does this for his plants. There is danger in the exuberant feeling of ever growing power which the advance of the physical sciences has engendered and which tempts man to try, "dizzy with success", to use a characteristic phrase of early communism, to subject not only our natural but also our human en-

257

vironment to the control of a human will. The recognition of the insuperable limits to his knowledge ought indeed to teach the student of society a lesson of humility which should guard him against becoming an accomplice in men's fatal striving to control society—a striving which makes him not only a tyrant over his fellows, but which may well make him the destroyer of a civilization which no brain has designed but which has grown from the free efforts of millions of individuals.

GUNNAR MYRDAL

Gunnar Myrdal was born in Gustafs parish, Sweden, on December 6, 1898. He graduated from the Law School of Stockholm University in 1923 and began practicing law while continuing his studies at the University. He received his juris doctor degree in economics in 1927 and was appointed docent in political economy. From 1925 to 1929 he studied for periods in Germany and Britain, followed by his first trip to the United States in 1929—1930, as a Rockefeller Fellow. During this period he also published his first books, including *The Political Element in the Development of Economic Theory*. Returning to Europe he first served for one year as Associate Professor in the Post-Graduate Institute of International Studies, Geneva, Switzerland. In 1933 he was appointed to the Lars Hierta Chair of Political Economy and Public Finance at the University of Stockholm as the successor of Gustav Cassel. In addition to his teaching activities Professor Myrdal was active in Swedish politics and was elected to the Senate in 1934 as member of the Social Democratic Party. In 1938 the Carnegie Corporation of New York commissioned him to direct a study of the American Negro problem. The material which he collected and interpreted was published in 1944 as *An American Dilemma. The Negro Problem and Modern Democracy*. Having come home to Sweden in 1942, he was reelected to the Swedish Senate, served as member of the Board of the Bank of Sweden, and was Chairman of the Post-War Planning Commission. From 1945—1947 he was Sweden's Minister of Commerce, a position which he left to accept an appointment as Executive Secretary of the United Nations Economic Commission for Europe. In 1957 he left this post to direct a comprehensive study of economic trends and policies in South Asian countries for the Twentieth Century Fund, which resulted in *Asian Drama. An inquiry into the Poverty of Nations* and *The Challenge of World Poverty. A World Anti-Poverty Program in Outline*. From 1961 he was back in Sweden and was appointed Professor of International Economics at the Stockholm University. He founded this same year the Institute for International Economic Studies at the University and is still a member of its Directorate. He was Chairman of the Board of the Stockholm International Peace Research Institute (SIPRI) and remains a board member. He was also Chairman of the Board of the Latin American Institute in Stockholm. During the academic year 1973—1974 he was visiting Research Fellow at the Center for the Study of Democratic Institutions at Santa Barbara, California, and during 1974—1975 Distinguished Visiting Professor at New York City University. Professor Myrdal is recipient of more than thirty honorary degrees beginning with Harvard University in 1938, where he gave the Godkin Lectures that year. He has received many prices, the last one the Malinowski Award by the Society of Applied Anthropology. He is member of the British Academy, American Academy of Arts and Sciences, Vetenskaps-akademien [the Royal Swedish Academy of Sciences], Fellow of the Econometric Society, honorary member of American Economic Association.

Gunnar Myrdal is married to the former Alva Reimer who held high posts in the United Nations and UNESCO, was the Swedish Ambassador to India and became Sweden's Minister of Disarmament and of Church. They have three grown children, two daughters, Sissela and Kaj, and one son, Jan.

A complete bibliography of his scentific publications is presently under preparation by the Royal Library of Stockholm.

THE EQUALITY ISSUE IN WORLD DEVELOPMENT

Nobel Memorial Lecture, March 17, 1975

by

GUNNAR MYRDAL

Stockholm

My first impulse, when brooding over what topic I should choose for this lecture, was that I should turn toward some specific problem, selected from the field where I am at present working. But then I felt that more appropriate for this very special occasion would be that I should talk in more sweeping terms about a broader problem, and I chose the equality issue in world development. I shall dwell upon the economic, financial, social, psychological and political conditioning of our thinking about that issue, which is at bottom, a moral issue.

Our knowledge, as well as our ignorance, at any time and on every issue, tends to be opportunistically conditioned, and thus brought to deviate from full truth. In every epoch and every problem, this opportunistic tendency operates also in our scientific work, if not critically scrutinized. This view dawned upon me more than forty years ago, when I analyzed the political element in the development of economic theory. I have then over the years found this hypothesis confirmed by my studies in many different fields and, of course, during my ten years as Executive Secretary of the United Nations Economic Commission for Europe, responsible for operational work in relations with governments, as well as for research.

I

When I am now working on a study of the broad social and economic dynamics of race relations in the United States since the time, more than thirty years ago, when I wrote *An American Dilemma*, it has struck me how different the whole outlook on the world could be during the late Roosevelt era, compared with now. In most respects the world issues seemed to be, and in a sense were then, simpler, much less complex.

Leaving all other differences aside, what then was referred to by the static term the "backward regions" were held at rest, within the colonial power structure. Their continued economic stagnation in great poverty was taken for granted, without exerting much interest on the part of the public in the rich countries, nor among their economic scientists.

Perhaps the most important effect of World War II was the rapid dissolution of that power structure—although not having been part of the war aims of any belligerent country and not expected anywhere. Beginning with the quasivoluntary decolonization of the British dependencies on the Indian subcontinent and the rest of South Asia, it swept over the globe like a hurricane, reaching also regions where there had been virtually no indigenous liberation movement foreboding and, in some measure, preparing for the change. The result was the coming into existence in a rapid sequence of a great number of new, politically independent countries, which all were very poor and mostly stagnant, economically and socially, but where the educated elite, who thought and acted on their behalf, now raised the demand for development.

In turn, as a subsequent effect of that political change the general public in the Western countries were suddenly forced to become aware of the huge income gap as between the poor majority of mankind and the rich minority, as well as the further fact that this income gap is continually widening, as indeed it had been doing for more than a century. An isolating wall of in-attention, and an ignorance made possible by that opportunistic bent of mind, had been broken through.

The poverty of what now came to be known as "underdeveloped countries", a dynamic term, became recognized to be a problem. This represented a momentous redirection of public interest. Within this movement there went also an equally radical redirection of economic research, for the first time giving importance to these countries' abject poverty and also to the policy methods, which could initiate progress there by planning for development.

This new awareness of the poverty in underdeveloped countries was bound to be morally disturbing in the Western world, where, particularly since Enlightenment, the ideal of greater equality has had an honored place in social philosophy. In economic science it had even been "proven" and placed at the basis of economic theory. The influence on practical policy of that recognized ideal had been minor, however, until towards the end of the last century economic conditions and power relations in one Western country after another began to make possible gradually to turn them into "welfare states." This process also implied greater awareness of existing inequalities.

From the beginning we find also that among the new policy proposals of economists aimed at instigating development in the underdeveloped countries, besides the prescriptions for economic planning, there was included a demand for economic assistance from the developed countries. In fact, much of the writings of economists in that early stage of the postwar era, as in many cases even later, became focused upon urging the politicians and the general public in the developed countries to be prepared to come forward with technical assistance, capital aid, and commercial concessions.

This was a new element in Western thinking. Until then, the colonial power system had served as a protective shield for consciences in Western developed countries. There anyhow existed no political basis for sensing any degree of collective international responsibility for what happened in the colonial de-pendiencies of some West European countries, for instance no surge for a discussion in the League of Nations about how to help them to develop.

And the otherwise highly idealistic charter of the United Nations, drawn up before the end of World War II, had little to say about the right to political independence for the peoples in the "backward regions." The Charter was still less outspoken about how to spur and aid development in the under-developed countries that would come to emerge.

But almost from the beginning, the United Nations and its specialized agencies became now the sounding boards for demands, raised by the representatives of the underdeveloped countries, for aid from, and commercial considerations of the developed countries. During the three decades of its existence, the effectiveness of the United Nations has, on the whole, tended to decrease, particularly in the field of peace and security and, more generally, all issues in which the developed countries feel they have important stakes. But this whole system of intergovernmental organizations has more and more become agencies for discussing, analyzing, and promoting development in underdeveloped countries. Their secretariats produce statistics and studies aimed at ascertaining, analyzing, demonstrating, and publicizing the pertinent elements of their poverty and the possible means of lifting them out of it. This is part of the process through which a compelling awareness of their plight has been engendered in the postwar period and forced itself upon every alert person.

Under the pressure of the underdeveloped countries, who have grown in number of votes and gradually learned to cooperate and work out a common stand, the developed countries have gradually been brought to make some, although minor concessions in their commercial policies and even to subscribe the funds for permitting old and newly created agencies in the United Nations family of intergovernmental organizations to provide technical assistance and capital aid. Still multilateral aid has remained only very small in relation to needs, and even compared with unilateral aid however it is calculated.

The aid urged in the economic literature and discussed in the several developed and underdeveloped countries at home and in the United Nations was at that time never thought of by anybody as needing to be more than marginal. Part of the explanation of this was undoubtedly the optimistic slant of early economic theorizing about the development problems in underdeveloped countries, originating from the common disregard for the "non-economic" factors, broadly attitudes and institutions and, in particular, the social and economic stratification, that raise so much greater inhibitions and obstacles to development in these countries which for ages have been stagnant. This optimism was, of course, also in the selfish interest of the developed countries as it implied that underdeveloped countries could develop with less aid.

But I must confess that when, twenty years ago in the middle of the Fifties, I delivered a series of lectures in Cairo focused on the same topic as my present lecture (later published in a volume, *Economic Theory and Underdeveloped Regions*), and in spite of my already then having attempted to redirect my thinking in an institutional direction, I could assert:

"What is needed is not primarily a redistribution of wealth and incomes. Indeed, aid can only be a very small part of a rational international equalization program ... None of the schemes which have been propounded for capital aid for development of underdeveloped countries has ever amounted to taking away more than a tiny fraction of the yearly increase of national income per head in the richer countries, which implied that no real sacrifice has ever been envisaged ... A wholesale income equalization by redistribution between nations is both impossible and, I am inclined to believe, an unimportant objective."

Among things which, at that time, besides defects in our theoretical approaches, contributed to our common overoptismism in regard to planning for development in underdeveloped countries, was that only gradually, toward the censuses around 1960, did we have reasons to worry much about a population explosion, as population increases as known up till then had not been proceeding at too alarming a rate. Also, the anxiety emerging in more recent years about depletion of not renewable resources had not then drawn our attention to the tremendous inequality in the use of resources. The challenge was not apparent of the virtual necessity of bringing down the consumption of these and other resources in the developed countries, if development should be possible in the underdeveloped ones.

To this new configuration of the problems in these underdeveloped countries and of our relations with them I will lead up to in the second part of my lecture.

In the developed world, the political climate at that early time did certainly not encourage economic scientists to raise more than very modest proposals for aid to the newly discovered world of age-old poverty.

In the beginning and continually for a long time, what of aid was given came almost only from the United States. Most European countries faced themselves a serious reconstruction problem. For a second time the United States had emerged from a world war richer than ever and with its productive assets undamaged. The Marshall aid program for Western Europe—on a much grander scale than any aid later afforded underdeveloped countries, given on much more generous terms, and lasting until the middle of the Fifties—undoubtedly tended to crowd out considerations to give much aid to the development of underdeveloped countries.

During the rapid decolonization, American aid to the newly independent countries had a very slow start and remained, for years, on a diminutive scale—with the partial exception of the aid given to the United States' former colony, the Philippines, which had also, like her European allies, suffered wartime destruction. When then in the Fifties American aid began to take somewhat larger proportions, it became, however, geared to the intensifying cold war and aimed at supporting politically allied governments or, sometimes, to reward a not unfriendly neutrality. This is clearly visible in the distribution of aid among countries.

Aid was from the beginning motivated as being "in the best interests of the United States", and these interests were primarily defined in the crude terms of political, strategic and military advantages for the United States. Most of the aid to underdeveloped countries became, directly and indirectly, military aid. It was nevertheless, at the same time, in some vague way also conceived to be an aid to development given for humanitarian reasons. This latter motivation was, however, increasingly pushed in the shadow.

Toward the middle and end of the Fifties West European countries became somewhat more important as providers of aid to underdeveloped countries. It was partly due to the prodding of the United States, that these countries as they regained economic viability should shoulder their share of the aid burden.

They, too, commonly tended to view aid from the point of view of their national interests, though those interests were conceived more in terms of export and the retention of cultural and, in particular, commercial links with former colonial dependencies, and less as offering political, strategic and military advantages.

Finally it should be recalled, that the aid coming from the Communist bloc was on an even smaller scale and more definitely geared to political interests in the raging cold war.

Aid did gradually rise towards the beginning of the Sixties, although the motivations on the part of the aid-giving governments had as a result a skewed distribution among countries. Then the solemn designation 1960 by the United Nations General Assembly of the next ten years as the Development Decade, at the proposal of the newly elected President of the United States, John F. Kennedy, did contain implicit and explicit but vague promises on behalf of the developed countries of more substantial aid for development.

But what actually happened was that from about that time on, the rising trend instead stagnated and began to steer downwards. In the United States this movement has continued until now. Because of its weight among developed countries, aid in real terms has even globally continually been decreasing and, what is even more important, the "quality" of aid has in several respects been deteriorating.

Even though in this brief lecture I cannot be more specific, I must refer to the fact that the statistics and budget figures for aid have been opportunistically juggled by the United States government and, to a lesser extent, by most other Western governments as, more lately, they became more important as providers of aid. Building upon these figures, the falsification has then been continued and given authority by the Development Assistance Committee (DAC) of OECD, the organization of all the non-Communist developed countries.

The misrepresentation of the facts has been most glaring in regard to what the DAC secretariat calls the "net flows" of private capital to the underdeveloped countries, where not only profits on foreign investments but also capital movements, often capital flight, are not accounted for. This was bluntly pointed out in DAC already in 1969 by the Swedish Minister of Industry, Krister Wickman.

But even the "public flows" of aid proper have been systematically beguiled to conceal the downward trend. Often the figures have been used without discounting for the rising trend of prices. Loans, which during the Sixties were continually substituted for grants, were without proper qualifications reckoned as aid. Tying aid to exports from the "donor country", which had gradually become the general rule in almost all Western countries, implies mostly higher import costs for the underdeveloped countries. Particularly in regard to the United States, items of military aid are often smuggled into the computations as aid to development.

As the Sixties progressed towards its close and continuing till now, the political character of aid has become ever more pronounced in the United

States. A prime operative factor was, of course, the increasing military involvement in the Vietnam war, which has implied "aid" on a large scale to the Saigon government and later to the Cambodian insurgent government, and some other satellite governments in South East Asia.

In spite of the fact that these easily detected opportunistic manipulations of the aid statistics have been demonstrated in some detail, the officially presented, misleading figures are, mostly without any qualifications, quoted and utilized by officials, politicians and journalists all over the world. In the same way they are used by the delegates and secretariats of intergovernmental organizations. They are usually accepted even by representatives of underdeveloped countries and by those in developed countries who argue for increasing the amount of aid.

The lack of zeal on the part of most professional economists to scrutinize the statistical figures on aid is to me embarrasing, like their often uncritical use of many other statistics from underdeveloped countries, their acceptance of a diplomatically twisted terminology and, more fundamentally, their use of systems of analytical concepts that are inadequate to the situation in underdeveloped countries.

The naked truth is, that when the present emergency came, aid in any real sense was low and tended to go even lower.

My next point is that the motivation given for a policy does matter, not only in a deeper moral sense, but also for its affectiveness.

In the United States, where aid to underdeveloped countries has been continuously argued as being in "our country's best interest", with these interests more and more specified as located in the military sphere, foreign aid has increasingly lost its popular appeal. The fact that the foreign policies supposedly served by this direction of aid has met defeat in Southeast Asia and also been less than successful in Latin America and other parts of the world, can only have made people in America ever more sceptical and adverse to foreign aid supposed to serve these purposes. Since long the American government has had to fight in every Congress to save the foreign aid appropriations from being cut down more than they have actually been.

Even liberal Congressmen have shown increasing resistance to stand for foreign aid. They fear even that aid, given that direction, may lead the United States into military involvements like the one in Vietnam. Conservative Congressmen have meant that any aid goes down in a rat hole, to use an American expression.

The United States' major West European allies and, in particular, Britain, France, and West Germany, have argued for foreign aid in a considerably less nationalistic spirit, and in any case not attached primary importance to their strategic and military interests in the cold war. They have, at the same time, been able to hold up their aid appropriations better than the United States.

In a few, mostly smaller developed countries, where aid has been allowed to increase and is mostly still increasing—and where aid is also accounted for in a generally more correct way—the arguments for aid in terms of national self-interest have been given less weight or been entirely absent.

Sweden, where the government has been committed to increase its aid by twenty-five per cent each year, is, of course, a case in point. None of the nationalistic motivs for aid in the United States and, to a lesser extent, present also in its major West European allied countries, could with any credibility be presented to the Swedish people. Aid has had to be argued in terms of human solidarity and compassion with the needy. Also in the other Scandinavian countries and, for instance, in the Netherlands or Canada, the situation is not too different.

My theory is that the selfish national interests, particularly as they so often turn out to have been spurious and misconceived, do not appeal to ordinary people, who in our type of countries determine the course of public policy over the years, while a motivation in moral terms carries weight. When in the United States the general public appears massively indifferent to foreign aid, this may be, as an American author has stated it, because the appeal has not been made to the humanitarianism and fundamental decency of the ordinary American. I cannot believe that Americans are basically less charitable than Swedes.

I find support for my theory in the consistent correlation between behavior in regard to aid and the reasons given for aid in the United States, its major West European allies, and the third group of smaller nations, respectively. If I had the time, I could furnish more specific reasons for my theory than this broad correlation. I insist that I am offering this theory not merely as the opinion of a moralist but as the conclusion of an economic scientist who has devoted study to the problem. When politicians and experts become timid about givig due importance to moral commitments, realism is absent.

I have stressed this theory, as I will have to come back to the fundamental moral problem, when I now come to deal with the present calamitous situation in the world. Meanwhile, I should note that even in those countries, that were more generous with aid, it was still on a marginal level, not implying much real sacrifice for their peoples.

II

In recent years there have been sudden, major changes in the world economy. They have radically affected the economic situation of all underdeveloped countries, though in different directions and degrees, and thereby the entire setting of the equality problem I am discussing in this lecture. For by far the larger part of the peoples in underdeveloped countries, these changes have been worsening their development prospects and in many countries are now threatening the survival of large numbers of their poor masses. The type of marginal foreign aid we have provided, is clearly not enough to meet their barest needs.

The underdeveloped countries are therefore now proclaiming the necessity of not only increased aid but fundamental changes of international economic relations. By their majority votes they can in the United Nations carry resolutions like the "Declaration on the Establishment of a New International Economic Order", passed at the conclusion of the Special Session of the United

269

Nations General Assembly held in April 1974 to consider the emergency situation.

At the World Food Conference in November of the same year a declaration was passed on the eradication of hunger and malnutrition, establishing the right of "every man, woman and child . . . to be free from hunger and malnutrition", and stressing the "fundamental responsibility of the governments to work together" for reaching that goal. The new commitments made by the developed countries and the new institutions created fell, however, far short of assuring even a modest beginning of implementing these ideals or even to prevent a further serious deterioration of the food situation in underdeveloped countries.

Particularly delegates from the group of smaller countries that had already in the earlier epoch consistently shown more sympathy for the cravings of underdeveloped countries and who have also maintained or even increased their modest aid, have often voted for the most general though noncommital declarations. And they have sometimes positively expressed agreement with the radical demands for a new world order, which logically must imply an infringement of their countries share of the world's resources. They must then have spoken and voted without much sincerety, as they cannot have been ignorant about the fact, that the nations they represent are not really prepared to give up privileges, least of all on a scale commensurate with their general promises. To this I shall come back.

In my further, utterly compressed and summary remarks on the profound changes that have brought about a critically new setting of the world equality problem, I will view these changes from the restricted viewpoint of their impact on underdeveloped countries and of the preparedness in developed countries to come to their aid.

A few of the underdeveloped countries, those having oil for export, have succeeded to form an effective cartel, the Organization of the Petroleum Exporting Countries, raising the price of oil four and a half to six and a half times the earlier price, depending upon what base year is chosen for comparison. They have suddenly become immensely rich. Except a few of them, like Nigeria and Indonesia, they were among the richer of the underdeveloped countries already before, or at least not so poor.

In an estimate, which is naturally very uncertain, the World Bank has reckoned that the accumulated surplus revenues could reach $450 and $550 billion by the end of 1980. The revenues for last year have been estimated to exceed those for 1973—when for some few months the oil prices had already been pressed up to a much higher level—by some $60 to $65 billion, of which about $10 billion have to be paid by underdeveloped countries. This more than swallows up all aid they had been getting, however inflated as in the faulty DAC statistics. And then is not counted the rise in prices of the fertilizers and other oilbased products they need to produce or import.

On the whole, other underdeveloped countries have avoided criticizing the OPEC countries. They apparently sensed a new power and admired as a novel phenomenon the authority and unity with which the OPEC countries conducted their negotiations with the foreign oil companies and the developed countries. Those few underdeveloped countries which export copper, bauxite and tin and even those exporting rubber, sugar, cocoa and coffee saw new opportunities, and they had for a time their hopes supported in the general commodity boom which lasted until almost a year ago.

Studies made generally tend to support the view, that the countries in OPEC will have good opportunity to hold up the oil prices—if there is not a new outbreak of war in the Middle East, or if the developed Western countries do not fall into a very serious slump, when in both cases the future of oil prices as well as many other things become entirely unpredictable. But the other commodity exporting underdeveloped countries will probably not succeed to follow the same pattern to any considerable extent. And they represent anyhow, like the oil exporting countries, only a small part of the peoples living in underdeveloped countries. On the whole, with clear exceptions, the under-developed world is rather less endowed with marketable resources of this type than the developed countries were when they developed, and are even now.

All underdeveloped countries which depend on oil imports will suffer a setback to their development programs. It can be shown to be broadly true, however, that the poorest among the underdeveloped countries, which also generally have had least of development, or no development, are particularly hard hit by the oil crisis. To those hardest hit belong the countries on the Indian subcontinent and also Ceylon with soon together a total population of one billion, the largest conglomeration in the world of desperately poor people.

By historical accident, with the oil crisis was compounded the food crisis. The latter actually preceded it by about a year. It was caused by bad crops in many parts of the world and by earlier attempt to decrease the bulging food stocks in the surplus countries, particularly in the United States but also Canada and Australia. These stock were expensive to store, and had up till that time almost made food aid to underdeveloped countries a not too burden-some policy of agricultural protection, holding up food prices at home and abroad.

Food prices now advanced suddenly and rapidly to the great disadvantage of the grain importing underdeveloped countries and contributed to the in-flationary trend even in the rich countries. We are now anxiously expecting news about what this year's crops will amount to. Any surplus will partly have to be used for building up stocks again, which are at a dangerous bottom level.

The oil crisis has had, and has, serious implications for agricultural pro-duction in underdeveloped countries, particularly but not only by raising the prices for fertilizers. The technocratic euphoria some ten years ago about a "green revolution" had already earlier been shown up as having nurtured undue optimism. There are many more reasons, but among them was also that the new high-yield grains could only be grown on land with plenty of water and by using much of fertilizers, which already at the lower prices restricted the favorable impact of the availability of the new seeds on agricultural pro-duction.

If the present acute food crisis was thus caused by short-term misfortunes, like droughts or floods and the increased prices of fertilizers, the reason for long-term anxieties for the future is primarily the ongoing population explosion. India, which pioneered attempts to check fertility earlier than any other country, has as present a population increase of more than 12 million per year, that is a rate of around 20 promille. I guess that at present the rate of population growth is still slightly rising in most underdeveloped countries.

The unfortunately much confused World Population Conference in Bucharest last year demonstrated that in many parts of the underdeveloped world, particularly in Latin America, Africa and the Middle East, though not in Asia proper, there is little understanding of what a high population increase means for keeping down levels of living and for holding back development in every underdeveloped country. Those effects are largely independent of how much of underutilized resources a country disposes of, though, of course, they are more serious in the already crowded countries. That population increase raises the demands for a substantial increase in agricultural production, is obvious.

I cannot in this lecture go deeper into the population problem but I want to stress, that the difficulties in bringing down the number of births are tremendous, even for a country that seriously tries a family planning policy, which India's example demonstrates. A condition for success is that individual couples among the masses can experience that they are living in a dynamic society which offers them opportunity to advance socially and economically. It is not so much the level of living as such that matters, but whether it is rising. A comparison between the relative success or failure of family planning in different underdeveloped countries broadly confirms this theory.

There is, therefore, a vicious circle inherent in the present trends. As development is frustrated and living levels brought downwards among the masses because of the oil crisis and the food crisis, any population policy, which might be inaugurated, becomes less effective. And so the food crisis becomes goaded in the way of circular causation with cumulative effects.

At a certain stage, which might stretch over a period of years with its ups and downs, the "Malthusian checks" on the population thrust come into operation. There are already now regions and groups in underdeveloped countries where the mortality trend has turned upwards.

But ahead of that point, and thereafter simultaneously, the morbidity will rise. A growing part of the poorest strata in a population may be more diseased, or at least be lacking in vigor, and may even become ever more inflicted, while the mortality rate is still decreasing, due to the cheap and powerful medical technology made available after the war. People will continue to live and breed, only to suffer debilitating conditions of ill health to an ever larger extent. Thus, they will be ever less efficient with serious effects also on the productivity of the labor force.

In this situation there are certainly moral and rational reasons for a new world order and, to begin with, for aid on a strikingly much higher level. In particular, people in the rich countries should be challenged to bring down their lavish food consumption. It is estimated that if the average American were to reduce his consumption of beef, pork and poultry by 10 per cent, 12 million tons or more of grain would be saved. This would mean making so much more food aid possible, saving perhaps five times as many million people as tons released, or even more, from starvation in the poorest countries. This reduction of meat consumption would be in the rational interest of the American people itself and much less than is recommended for health reasons by the American Heart Association: one third. To overeating comes the colossal waste by overserving and spoilage. To a varying and usually lesser extent the same holds true in all developed countries.

As has also been amply demonstrated, the cutting down of consumption, and of production for home consumption, of many other items besides food, and in all the developed countries, is rational and in our own interest. This is what the discussion of the "quality of life" is all about. Our economic growth in a true sense could certainly be continued, but it should be directed differently, and in a planned way, to serve our real interest in a better life. At the same time, it would release resources for aiding the underdeveloped countries on a much larger scale and to begin with for solving the acute food crisis.

I am in deep sympathy with the urgings of medical men, environmentalists and other colleagues in the natural sciences, when they speak for the rationality in our own interest, individually and still more collectively, of a much more frugal life style so far as growth in consumption, and production for home consumption, of many material products is concerned. This is whats sincerely mean is in line with our own welfare as well as our proclaimed ideals.

Real economic planning should be done in these rational terms. Such planning could help us to be more successful in solving the internal equality problems and would at the same time provide for a much larger aid to development in underdeveloped countries. In the first place, it could prevent the serious risk of human disasters for the majority of the poorest peoples in these countries. *The blunt truth is that without rather radical changes in the consumption patterns in the rich countries, any pious talk about a new world economic order is humbug.*

It is legitimate for an economist to analyze what the rational inferences in regard to economic policy would be from the value premises of what is in people's true interests and their acclaimed ideals. But if, instead, we raise the other problem of what is actually going to happen, it is difficult to believe that these rational policy conclusions are going to be followed out in the practical policies of developed countries. In the tradition of Western civilization we are quite well trained to combine base behavior with high ideals.

The so far very weak reaction on the part of developed countries to the urgent demand for very much higher appropriations for aid, directed not upon serving national interests but upon the needs for aid in the poorest underdeveloped countries, may be partly explained by these needs having burst forward and risen at the very time when the developed countries find themselves in difficulties. They are commonly experiencing an intensification of the stagflation trend toward which they were already steering, with unemployment rising intermittently with continued price inflation. This intensification of stagflation has been caused by the same oil crisis and, to an extent, the food crisis, which have been rendering the situation so utterly precarious for most underdeveloped countries. One effect is serious balance of payment difficulties in all developed countries.

This situation is apt to turn policy interests in developed countries inwards, to the national problems of how to stop stagflation at home and stabilize the balance of payments. Those international issues, which are felt to be important, concern the relations with other developed countries and with the OPEC countries, while from the point of view of narrowly conceived national interests what happens in the underdeveloped countries fades out from serious attention.

And the wider issue referred to above—about rational national planning for curtailment of consumption, and production for home consumption, of such commodities that are less necessary and often even harmful for health and happiness, which would also help to stabilize the economy and at the same time release so much resources for egalitarian reforms within the countries and between countries—has less appeal in a situation of high and, as a trend, rising unemployment. Even normally there are strong pressure groups defending all sorts of economic activity that results in incomes in the market. And indiscriminately supporting all consumption has became a standard policy means of counteracting unemployment.

Much more generally people keep conservatively to their consumption habits. They don't want to be reformed, even in their own interest. In our competitive society all groups are instead always brought to press for more of the same type of consumption. Commercial marketing does certainly not work for a more rational discussion of our consumption demands.

Our politicians, of all political parties, stick to the inapt concept of "growth" which is embodied in the gross national product or one of its derivatives. We economists, by not having scrutinized more intensively that even statistically rather spurious concept, and by ourselves commonly utilizing "growth" in that sense uncritically as a main value premise in our discussions of practical economic policy, have unfortunately contributed to restricting the mental horizon of politicians and of the common people.

It is in this general setting we have to understand the dawdling and in the end insufficient response in the developed countries even to patent emergency cases, like that of the countries south of Sahara, which with their rapidly increasing population have been experiencing temporary crop failures, as well as the long time reduction of arable land, as the desert is advancing by some thirty miles per year. Bangladesh is in the same emergency situation, having been hit by a sequency of natural catastrophes and by a cruel and destructive war.

And neither has there been much willingness on the part of developed countries to enter into firm food aid commitments for other underdeveloped countries with widespread undernutrition among their masses in the rural and urban slums. To this category belongs vast India but also many other, large as well as small underdeveloped countries.

According to present estimates as many as 10 million people may starve to death this year, and at least half a billion are hovering on the brink of starvation. It is against the background of the expectancy of world catastrophes that the attitudes in developed countries has to be considered in moral terms.

In the United States, where the ideological discussion is always so much fuller and more outspoken than in other Western countries, there has in recent years appeared a rationalization in terms of a pragmatic moral theory, which can be used, and has been used, not to challenge but to justify our being so tardy to provide aid and, in particular, food aid to the poorest countries. This new theory can increasingly be found in books, articles in learned periodicals like the prestigious *Science* as well as popular journals like *Newsweek,* it is referred to in the press and propounded at committee hearings in Congress. Recently it has been endorsed by such a respected authority as the President of the National Academy of Sciences, Dr. Philip Handler.

This new theory has introduced the concept "triage" (from the French "trier": to soft), following out an analogy from the practice in the allied medical tents during the trench warfare slaughters of World War I. With resources limited, a distinction had been made between those likely to die no matter what was done to them, those who would probably recover even if untreated, and those who would survive if cared for. The third group alone received attention. The others were left to live, or to die, on their own.

Based on such an analogy, India is in this literature commonly counted as belonging to the first group, which should be left unaided, but also many other very poor countries. Not giving them food aid is more "ethical" so the argument runs, because those who would be saved will breed, and in the end still more millions will ultimately be starving and dying. In the longer run, aid creates more misery than it alleviates.

The triage theory is not advocating less aid from the rich countries, only that it be distributed more wisely by cutting out from consideration those that are helpless. The new awareness of the poverty in underdeveloped countries, to which I referred in the beginning of this lecture, is recognized, and also that poverty among the masses is continually intensified. Television now brings into our living rooms starving and dying people, many thousands of miles away. The triage theory is said to be expounded in order to help us in a "difficult but necessary and rational psychological adjustment."

As a matter of fact, however, the United States sells most of its surplus grain commercially to countries who can afford to pay for it and even to the poorest, like India. And the United States has actually profited from the rise in food prices; over the last three years commercial food sales have grown from $8 to $21 billion, which has been helpful for its precarious balance of payments. Also most of the food aid has up till now in the alleged national interest been going to satellite governments in Southeast Asia, or closely allied governments elsewhere with only very little to the poorest countries.

The triage theorists do not question this use of the United States' surplus grain. The interest to sell food, and also the severe restrictions on what is made available as food aid and the direction it is given, is taken for granted as having been determined by national policy, which is not criticized. They are merely making the negative point that what little aid is afforded, should not be given to the very poorest countries, but that in regard to them "nature should be left to take its course" as the most humanitarian solution.

The argument is often amplified by the assertion that only such an apparently heartless decision can bring these countries to force their people to bring down the birth rate. This shows ignorance about how any policy of family planning is made even more difficult when development is pointing towards impoverishing the masses.

That this theory of triage is meeting strong opposition in America should not surprise. To decide with god-like finality the death to millions of people goes against all American moral instincts. *The New York Times* in a leading article calls the triage theory "one of the most pessimistic and morally threadbare intellectual positions to be advanced since the demise of the Third Reich."

But in order to overcome "the harsh logic" of the triage theory, the United States would have to come forward with very much more aid, and, indeed, be prepared to initiate and cooperate in planned intergovernmental action in a way pointing towards "a new world order" asked for by the underdeveloped countries, which in turn would necessitate the rational restriction of our lavish utilization of resources. This consequence the paper does state, but again only in general and noncommital terms.

This is the moral dilemma which the triage theory only highlights. And it is a dilemma which faces each of the developed countries, whether they have surplus food to sell or give away or not. It would, indeed, assume that the developed countries began to proceed in the direction of the new rational planning, I have urged above.

I have hitherto focussed on the food crisis in terms of the immediate need for aid, in order to prevent, as far as possible, worsened starvation among the poverty-stricken masses in underdeveloped countries. But the food crisis is not a passing worry. In a somewhat longer time perspective, and taking into account the rapid rise in world population, scarcity of food must be expected even to get worse, if agricultural production cannot be steadily and rather speedily increased.

Simplifying matters to the bone, as repeatedly I have to do in this lecture, and leaving out many important considerations, such a rise in food production can only be accomplished, to the extent absolutely needed to avoid a rising trend of hunger catastrophes, by raising yields substantially in the underdeveloped countries themselves. In developed countries the land resources are already largely brought under fairly intensive cultivation, so that the prospect of additional production is limited, and will have to be bought with rising costs. In underdeveloped countries uncultivated land is usually also scarce and often becoming scarcer by erosion, salination and other forms of soil depletion, if it is not stopped. But apart from this, the yields of cultivated lands are on the average only roughly one third of what they could be.

It has often been wrongly assumed that farming in underdeveloped countries is labor intensive, as an inference from the very large portion of the total labor force sustained in agriculture—in India, which is not selfsupporting in food, about 70 per cent. In fact their farming is extensive. Too few work at all,

276

those who work do it for too short periods during the day, week, month and year, and they work too inefficiently. Part of the explanation is health deficiencies, and in that respect the acute food crisis by increasing undernutrition will only make conditions worse, and actually tend to increase the under-utilization of labor and thus decrease the yields.

Already without any other technology than what is already known and applied by some of the farmers in a district, yields could be increased substantially by raising the labor input and its efficiency. A large part of that labor input should rationally be directed upon cooperative public work, improving the land, building more and better roads, constructing wells, irrigation ditches and storage facilities, and generally ameliorating the environment for life and work in the villages.

Modernized technology can make its contributions by raising the yields still more, though it should be highly labor-intensive as there is so much under-utilized labor, which has no other place to go than to the rapidly growing shanty slums in the cities, where labor is equally underutilized. Totally, the labor force will be increasing annually by more than two per cent for the next 15—20 years, whatever is happening to fertility.

But to transfer new technology of that type to the masses of agriculturalists meets difficulties. Transferring technology to industry, and, in particular, creating modern large-scale industry, has proven quite feasible—at the price, it is true, of perpetuating the enclave economy typical of colonial times. It calls for only minimal changes in the traditional social and political framework in an underdeveloped country and minimal diffusion of skills throughout the labor force. It evades direct confrontation with the institutional and attitudinal obstacles that are holding down economic performance and perpetuate low levels of labor utilization. Trying to raise the yields in agriculture through the application of a modernized, though highly labor-intensive technology, has to confront the entire style of life in rural society, which often has become even more inegalitarian and rigid under the pressure of the population explosion.

Most important is to change "the relation between man and land", creating the possibilities and the incentives for man to work more, work harder and more efficiently and to invest whatever he can lay his hands on to improve the land, in the first instance by his own labors. There are a number of auxiliary reforms—in regard to market organizations, extension service, credits, etc.— but without a land reform, which has been botched in most underdeveloped countries, they have proved ineffective to reach the masses of agriculturalists.

And so we face the inequality problem also within the underdeveloped countries. The fact is, that with few exceptions and largely independent of the constitutions they are operating under, these countries are ruled by tiny upperclass elites of different alignments, in some countries, but not all, having to take some considerations to the "educated" middle class, and sometimes even to organized labor in transport and large-scale industry, which then tends to become a privileged class among the workers.

These governing elites in practically all underdeveloped countries have in general terms explained themselves in favor of greater equality and, in particular, of raising the living levels of the poor masses. But in most of these countries the actual trend has been towards greater inequality. The fruits of whatever development there has been has gone to the upper strata, while the lower strata have not seen much improvement and have often even actually experienced worsening living and working conditions. This trend has recently been pushed forward by the combined effects of the population increase and the oil and food crisis.

Statistics of income distribution, which in some of these countries, for instance India or Brazil, are not entirely unreliable, give important information about this development and illustrate the deprivations the poorest strata have to live with. But a change of the trend towards a more egalitarian society cannot be effectuated by a redistribution of money incomes from the rich to the poor. What the poor masses need is not a little money, the distribution of which in countries with so much poverty and with colossal tax avoidance and tax evasion among the few rich would only spur inflation, that, in turn, regularly works to the disadvantage of the poor.

What they do need is fundamental changes in the conditions under which they are living and working. The important thing is that these changes regularly imply both greater equality and increased productivity at the same time. The two purposes are inextricably joined, much more, in fact, than in developed countries. To these imperatively needed radical changes belong, first, land reform, but also a fundamental redirection of education and health work. And the "soft state" must be made efficient, and corruption, which is now almost everywhere increasing, must be exterminated on all levels.

The reason for stressing the necessity of these radical reforms in this lecture is, that they are all needed for effectuating the fundamental changes of society, which are a prerequisite for efforts to raise labor utilization and permit effective application of modernized technology in agriculture and thereby to increase yields. Beside the international equality problem, there is a national one.

It could perhaps be expected, that in developed countries, there should be an eagerness to point to these problems and to press governments of underdeveloped countries to initiate reforms. They are all in line with old-established Western ideals. For a number of reasons, however, the opposite is true. Any government negotiations with underdeveloped countries, including those concerning aid, have to be conducted with their ruling elites. The same is true of all business relations. Thus developed countries generally come to strenghten and support the groups who prevent the needed fundamental reforms, or subvert them to actually be favoring the not-so-poor, thereby preserving the inegalitarian social and economic structure. During the cold war, particularly the United States' aid and trade became purposely directed upon supporting reactionary regimes.

When developed countries are so tardy to increase their aid to underdeveloped countries even in their present calamitous situation, this must cause a creeping feeling of guilt on their side. This, in turn, must tend to make them less prepared to discuss these countries' lack of will to carry out the social and economic reform they need in order to avoid a steady deterioration of their

278

situation, not least in regard to food production. An exception is, when, as in the case of Bangladesh, the ineptitude of the government could be pointed to as an excuse for giving so little aid.

Quite generally, those who feel warmest for the underdeveloped countries in their present difficulties are mostly the ones who are least willing to discuss faults and failures in their policies. This excusing attitude is made the more possible as the economists, more in earlier years but largely even now, continue to work with development models excluding the institutional and political factors.

It has become a convention adhered to by almost everybody speaking about mankind's future, to stress that all problems are now becoming global, and that they can only be solved by close collaboration between all governments.

The new economic world order, pressed for by the underdeveloped countries and as a general proposition accepted by well-wishing persons in developed countries, sometime even when they represent governments, is becoming another conventional formula.

As I have stressed, we are, however, far from giving any reality to these high ideals in the fields covered in this lecture and I have tried to explain why and how.

Even outside, and beside the oil crisis, the food crisis and the population explosion, there are other imminent pending dangers mounting in the world. The protracted armaments negotiations have not stopped the armament race between the superpowers and the increasing militarization of the national economies in developed as well as underdeveloped countries. The costs for armaments are calculated to exceed total production in all the underdeveloped countries taken together. These huge expenditures most certainly belong to the unnecessary and exceedingly harmful use of resources I talked about that in a rational world should be cut down drastically. As the publications of SIPRI, the independent peace research institute in Stockholm, has amply demonstrated for such a change the prospects have rather deteriorated from year to year.

Peace has not come to Southeast Asia or to the Middle East. Competent observers are expecting that full-scale wars may again break out, in both cases carrying the risk of superpower confrontation. The adverticed detente has implied the abstention from grossly abusive language as between the super-powers, which is all to the good, and some exports from the United States on favorable terms. But very little else in the relations between them has been changed much, and the future of this detente is not assured.

Neither am I hopeful about an early success in most countries to overcome stagflation. Under these circumstances the hopes of creating a more stable monetary system are further from fulfillment than even a few years ago, even if some more or less satisfactory partial recycling of the oil revenues could be organized. The efforts to continue the work on breaking down trade barriers between the developed countries have gone into an impass, when the most we can hope for is the partial prevention of a return to the extreme and self-defeating protectionism of the Thirties.

The continued militarization of the economies in all countries and the foreseable failure to create more normal economic and financial relations in the world are certainly not promising for any progress in governmental co-operation for fighting the threatening impoverishment of most underdeveloped countries which I have been speaking about in this lecture.

But there are worries beyond and above all these problems. I am asking myself what has happened to people's moral valuations.

Wars are fought with increasing disrespect for international law, established for protection of the civilian population. The illegal, immoral and ruthlessly cruel American warfare in Southeast Asia has for the time being marked the culmination of that steeply rising trend from World War I and on. There are terror activities by organized groups, endorsed by some governments and meeting no effective protest by other governments.

Torture has become a regular police practice in an increasing number of countries. In almost all countries there is an increase of violence and crime. The spreading use of drugs, which was not a serious problem a few decades ago, has, as we know, in various ways been a direct cause of increased violence and crimes, and represents by itself an increase of antisocial lawlessness.

A heightened awareness of these developments is pressed upon everybody because of the tremendously more effective communications. By watching television, the broad strata of the American public saw the horrors created by their own government in Vietnam. Too many did not protest, and many more are now trying to live on and forget.

To what extent is the result of all this that we are becoming less morally sensitive? Has it blunted our feelings of human compassion and thus made us more prone to opportunistic indifference? If so, this is also part of the explanation a people's coldbloodedness when facing the problems of sufferings and deaths in the poorest countries, hit by the effects of the oil crisis, the food crisis and the population explosion.

Quite apart from such an enlargement of our perception of those world problems, which I have tried to analyze in this lecture, these problems are in themselves immensely complicated. As an institutional economist, compelled to conceive of development as a movement of a whole political, social and economic system and having tried to deal with the problems in a world setting, I have had to express judgments on a very wide variety of human conditions. Although I have put labor into basing these judgments upon a more intensive realistic study than I can account for in this lecture, most of them remain tentative and anyhow far from being certain, exact and precise.

This is not my fault but is due, first, to the fact that many of the conditions I have been speaking of are difficult already to define appropriately, and the further fact that the coefficients of interrelations between all changes of conditions within the system are very seldom known with quantitative precision. The analyst is left to use whatever knowledge he can acquire, even if it is not in the precise form that economists have been trying to attain. When dealing with wider issues they often achieve it by limiting the scope of inquiry. This, of course, only makes the analysis less relevant, adequate and realistic, particularly in the present world tumult.

Even though my world view must be gloomy, I am hopeful about the development of our science. We can by immanent criticism in logical terms challenge our own thinking and cleanse it from opportunistic conformism. And we can widen our perspective. Everything can be studied. We are free to expand and perfect our knowledge about the world, only restricted by the number of scientists working and, of course, the degree of their diligence, brightness and their openness to fresh approaches.